"There are books that tell half-truths, like
where all that is not traditionally seen as l
And then there are books that tell whole t
pain, grief, and confusion into wisdom, compassion, and love, with
the courage to ask deeper questions and to answer honestly.
Victoria's writing is an example of the power there is in sharing
our stories. As we read another's reflection on their life, we receive
an opportunity to better see ourselves."

— **Rochelle Schieck,** author of Qoya: A Compass for Navigating an
Embodied Life that is Wise, Wild and Free

"When a woman tells her story, she gives others permission to do
the same. Falling Awake – A Heroine's Journey by Victoria Smisek
allows us to look into the past as we reach for a more authentic
future. Victoria takes us on the road trip of a lifetime. By the end
of the book, you'll be inspired to share your story, too."

— **Betsy Blankenbaker Murphy,** author of
Autobiography of an Orgasm

"This memoir, both skilfully and intelligently written, seductively
draws its reader into a sometimes gritty adventure of a life thus
far... filled with poignancy, humour, and self-reflection in just the
right balance that kept me hooked from beginning to end. It was
hard to stop reading once I had started... a must-read for anyone
also interested in self-discovery and life."

— **Sarah Burt ND,** author of Getting healthy in 7 simple steps

"THIS book gave ME permission to explore my inner landscape. Victoria's words will take YOU on a road of self-discovery...what a BLOOMING gift! Read it...share it...read it again...and AGAIN..."

— **Karen Weber**, UK

"Every one of us will see a glimpse of ourselves, past or present, in Victoria's story."

— **Betsy Price**, author of Overgrown

"Original, moving and humorous. This is a must-read for anyone interested in personal growth and the effect of our childhood on our life journey. I found it fresh and fascinating."

— **Kathy King**, UK

"This book was a page-turner for me. While reading Victoria's journey, I couldn't help but reflect on my own and how the various strands of all our lives are so interconnected. The Heroine's Journey will invite you on your own journey of reflexivity, a journey of hope and transformation."

— **Cecelia Shefflin**, Republic of Ireland

Falling Awake

A HEROINE'S JOURNEY

A HEROINE'S JOURNEY

Victoria Smisek

978-1-913590-21-5 Paperback
978-1-913590-22-2 Ebook

The Unbound Press
www.theunboundpress.com

Hey unbound one!

Welcome to this magical book brought to you by The Unbound Press.

At The Unbound Press we believe that when women write freely from the fullest expression of who they are, it can't help but activate a feeling of deep connection and transformation in others. When we come together, we become more and we're changing the world, one book at a time!

This book has been carefully crafted by both the author and publisher with the intention of inspiring you to move ever more deeply into who you truly are.

We hope that this book helps you to connect with your Unbound Self and that you feel called to pass it on to others who want to live a more fully expressed life.

With much love,
Nicola Humber

Founder of The Unbound Press
www.theunboundpress.com

"Until you make the
unconscious conscious,
it will direct your life
and you will
call it fate."
– Carl Jung

TRUTH

Truth is a sketchy thing. Working for over twenty years as a psychotherapist has taught me that and anyone with a sibling will know that too. One event can have many truths. We all see everything through *our* lens, *our* perspective, and that gives us *our* truth, and it will be vastly or subtly different from the next person's. It is even believed that every experience we have is sought out to back up that perspective, that belief system that is formed in each of us in our early years; we are constantly looking to re-enforce *our* version of *the* truth.

So there is no such thing as THE Truth.

There are people featured in the following pages who would doubtless challenge my truth. They would have their own lens, their own perspective, their own version of events, and I respect that, but this is my story, not theirs.

Not only is this just my version of the truth, it's also not the whole truth. Just as when a client spends the first half of a session slagging off a spouse, partner, or family member and then spends the second half of the session trying to retract it because of the guilt that has suddenly kicked in for 'painting a bad picture' of someone (especially someone who's not there to defend themselves). It's OK, I get it. I get that there is always a bigger picture, that there are always many sides to someone, and many sides to any relationship.

So I want to acknowledge that many of the relationships I have talked about here had other sides to them too and it has not been my intention to 'paint a bad picture' of anyone, only to explore (just as I would with a client) the side of things that have shaped me, my learning, my growth, my development. Isn't it usually the tragic, difficult, hideous shit that enables us to do that?

So is this The Truth, The Whole Truth and Nothing but The Truth?

Well, no, absolutely not, (in the words of Natasha Bedingfield)...the rest is still unwritten.

CONTENTS

Introduction

i

ACT ONE – PRIMAL

3

ACT TWO – EVOLVING

85

ACT THREE – ASCENDING

231

Epilogue

321

Music

335

Acknowledgments

339

INTRODUCTION

Apparently, my mum had me for her, because it had become clear to her in the 2 years prior, that she'd had my sister for my dad and my oma (my Czech grandmother, we called her Omi). She says she couldn't get a look in; my omi completely took over. So when I was born, she made sure that didn't happen again. I would be hers. And so the family split began.

What perfect fertile ground for the years to come; years of me having a difficult relationship with my dad, my sister always being at odds with my mum, and my sister and I becoming classic polarised siblings.

So the story goes when I was around three years old, for a whole year all I would eat was boiled eggs with toasted soldiers and Cadbury's chocolate fingers. Breakfast, lunch, and dinner for a whole year. Anything else, I absolutely refused. Eventually, my mum took me to the doctor: "she'll eat something else when she wants to" was both the diagnosis and the treatment plan (it was the early 70s).

But clearly, there was something going on for me, something psychological, right? I've often wondered what it was...were the eggs some kind of unconscious symbolic reference to fertility? Like I was trying to find my way back to the womb, where I was safe and secure before I was fired out of my mother's vagina like ammunition for her side of the conflict that was just beginning.

While I was born into a metaphorical war zone, my dad was born into a literal one that was just beginning in Czechoslovakia. My lineage is fraught with war, conflict, hiding, escaping, resistance, and fear.

So I wonder...how much of that have I inherited? How much of that trauma permeated into my cells, into my heart centre, into my deep unconscious, when I was that fertilised egg, that embryo that became this person. This person who has so often felt trapped, felt the need to escape, felt the need to hide who she really is, and who has felt lost and displaced and always felt the need to be strong to survive.

How much do we unconsciously inherit? How much is karmic retribution from past lives? How much is simply because I was born into an unhealthy relationship between two people?

I don't know, none of us really do, I guess.

But what I do know is what I have experienced along the way, what I have learnt along the way, the insights I continue to have by looking at myself and being interested in my experience – all of it: the loss, the love, the trauma, the adventure, the joy, the pain, the sacred, the mundane, the beauty, the ugliness...this experience we call 'our life'.

The title of this book draws reference from the work of two people; Jon Kabat-Zinn, who developed the MBSR programme (mindfulness-based stress reduction) and is widely considered to be responsible for bringing mindfulness into the mainstream. He talks about the practice of mindfulness not being about relaxing or falling asleep but about *falling awake*.

I started to fall awake in my twenties and then something

happened, and I promptly fell back to sleep. When I started to wake up again, some years later, my world looked quite different and it took me a while to come around and remember who I was. A very long while.

It's like dozing off again when you've had enough sleep already, and then when you wake up you're dazed and confused, you don't really know where you are, what day or time it is, and you've probably had some really weird dreams. It takes a while to get your bearings. Sometimes it takes us a lifetime to get our bearings.

'A Heroine's Journey' comes from the work of Joseph Campbell who popularised 'The Hero's Journey' – the notion that we all have the potential to live the life of a hero.

We are living in changing times and so never mind 'The Hero's Journey', what about 'The Heroine's Journey'? More and more women are finding their voices, speaking out and stepping up. It's even been said that the world will be changed by the western woman.

But whether you are a Hero or a Heroine (or a non-binary equivalent), at some point in our lives we may get *The Call*. The call that reminds us to live the life we dream of, the call that reminds us we all have a higher power. If we have fallen awake enough, we might just hear that call, and then the adventure begins. We go on a journey of transformation, and we all know that's no walk in the park. Transformation is tough. Transformation is about doing 'the work'. It's about looking at ourselves, *all* parts of ourselves. It's about taking risks, breaking patterns, going against the grain. It's about courage and fear, uncertainty and authenticity, and being true to ourselves no matter what, all in the name of being our own heroine and reaching our highest potential. At some point, the heroine, assuming they haven't fallen asleep again, returns with the 'treasure' – aka the wisdom, the learning, the insights, the story.

So this is my story, my learning, my wisdom, my insights, so far at least – I'm finding it's an on-going process. But in sharing this with you, my hope is that you may be able to relate to some of my experiences, and therefore whilst reading, you may find yourself – consciously or unconsciously – processing the experiences of this thing you call...your life.

"Hearing someone else's story is how
we make sense of our own.
Telling our story is what alchemizes our
pain into someone else's medicine."

– Emily McDowell

ACT ONE
PRIMAL

"They fuck you up, your mum and dad.
They may not mean to, but they do.
They fill you with the faults they had
and add some extra just for you."
– Philip Larkin

ACT ONE
Primal

Scene One – Voiceless

I am 11 years old and crying myself to sleep every night.

It's OK, I'm not being abused, I'm just so desperately unhappy. I want my old life back. The life that was just taken away from me by the people who were supposed to keep me happy, whose job it was to ensure I had a safe, secure base from which I could navigate my way through the ups and downs of childhood – a tricky task at the best of times.

A decision has just been made on my behalf and I don't know it yet, but this decision will turn out to have repercussions for the rest of my life.

To be fair, they did ask me, my parents, before they made this decision on my behalf:

"Do you want to go with your sister and live with your dad or do you want to stay here with your mum?"

I'M ELEVEN YEARS OLD!!!!

"I don't care" is my three-syllable reply.

Three syllables that will change the course of my life.

And it's a big fat lie. I do care. I care very much. I care that I was quite happy just the way things were. I care that moving to my dad's means moving away from all my friends; not far away but I'm 11 and 3 miles may as well be 300. I care that I am about to start senior school and that's one scary transition enough to be dealing with. I care that I was rather attached to my bedroom and all the things in it: my Fonzie poster on the wall and my duvet set with the pink and white flowers that Omi gave me.

So that's it then. It is decided for me; it would be best not to be separated from my sister and to go and live with my dad.

I don't even like my fucking sister!!

This is not what is best for me. This is an utter disaster.

Every pulsating cell in me is screaming NO! But I have to go along with it, right? I am a child, what choice do I have?

Where is my voice? Why can't I say "No, I don't want this to happen, please."

Why is that so scary to me?

Well, it's because I have already had a decade of suppressing my feelings, shutting them down tight to fester away in a box of muted secrets.

So, instead of speaking my truth, these feelings join all the others in that box that I am very familiar with. It's already quite cosy in there, but there's always room for more. Until there isn't, of course, but I won't find that out until later, much later.

Every time my parents scream at each other, every time I hear plates being smashed in the kitchen in an explosion of crimson anger, every time my mum badmouths my dad to us, every time my dad says something derogatory about my mum and sniggers like he's just cracked the joke of the year, every time there is an elastic band of twisted tension in the house, every time my dad is late to pick us up after they divorced, every time that gives my mum an opportunity to infer something about him not caring for us, every time my mum and my sister argue, every time I am confused about why the hell my parents can't even be in the same goddam room together, every time I am asked the question by friends "why aren't your parents together?" and I don't know the bloody answer...

Every time those feelings go into the box.

I am living my life in a bubble. It's what I have learnt.

Nothing comes out and I let nothing in. I have no voice.

———————

A few weeks later, another defining moment takes place.

I am sitting on my bedroom floor in my dad's flat, or should I say my new home. We are about to have an exchange, an exchange that will determine my future for decades to come. At 11 years old my relationship patterns with men are cemented. It's a done deal. A karmic agreement between him and me realised.

The stage is set. Let the re-enactments begin...

Him: "Why are you crying?"

I'm just crying.

Him: "Come on, tell me, what's wrong?"

I'm still crying, saying nothing, I have no voice.

Him: "Do you want to tell me what's wrong?"

I'm still crying, saying nothing, I want you to know but I can't say it, I have no voice.

Him: "Well, if you won't tell me what it is, then I'll have to guess."

Yes! Guess! Please guess so then you will know what it is, and I won't have had to say it.

Him: "So...is it school?"

Shaking my head, still crying.

Him: "Are you sick? Do you have a tummy ache?"

Shaking my head, no! Oh come on, just guess. Please.

Him: "Is it your friends?"

Jesus! Come on, please.

Him: "Well if it's not any of that, it can only be one thing then..."

Yes! Here we go, one more minute and it will all be over, he'll say it, I'll nod my head and then he will fix it, he will know how unhappy I am, and he will let me go.

Him: "...that you're unhappy living here."

I nod. Yes!! A feeling of relief, tears slowly drying up, now we can get on with the arrangements, I'm almost free.

Him: "Well, why don't you just give it a bit longer. Let's give it some more time; I'm sure you'll settle in eventually."

I am crushed. I am broken. I am trapped. A part of me has just died.

Me: "OK."

I make a pact with myself. Clearly, me being unhappy isn't enough to change this situation, but what if my mum was unhappy? Right now I know she's OK though, she has a new boyfriend, Derek, and they seem pretty serious and she seems happy because of him. But what if something happens between them? What if she doesn't have him anymore? Then I imagine she might be very unhappy, and then I will need to go back and live with her, so she isn't alone. Dad will still have my sister and Mum will have me. This pact gives me comfort and I fantasise about when the day will come that I can go back to the sanctuary of Fonzie and pink and white bedding and feel free once again.

———————

A couple of months later, my dad is driving me home after returning from a school trip. He pulls the car over to the side of the road.

Him: "I've something to tell you."

Oh, God. Something terrible has happened while I've been away.

Me: "What?"

Him: "Derek has died."

I am frozen inside. My brain won't take it in. I feel nothing.

And somewhere a panicked voice inside me reels:

Did I make this happen??

It turns out Derek has been killed in an accident at work. He was a roofer and fell off some scaffolding after the drill he'd been using gave him an electric shock. His 8-year-old son, who'd been off sick from school, had gone to work with him that day. He'd seen the whole thing happen.

Perhaps it's the shock that he's dead. Or perhaps it's the fear that I might have been wishing so hard that I somehow made him disappear. Or perhaps I realise that the pact to return to mum if she were alone was only ever a fantasy, a coping mechanism, holding onto a thread of hope, a way of convincing myself I had a choice. I didn't think I'd actually be called upon to follow through, to test if she wants me back, to tell my dad I want to leave.

So I don't.

I don't have the courage.

For me, this is the biggest tragedy of it all.

Scene Two – Bike

I am 6 years old and outside my house riding my bicycle. I love my bike. It's painted orange, has a white squidgy saddle, and big chunky white tyres. When I ride my bike, it makes me feel free, it gets me out of the house where all the explosions happen. I can be in my own world when I'm out on my bike.

I am riding up and down the hill. My house is at the bottom of the hill, mostly I have to push my bike up and then ride down. I am just near the top when another bike, a much bigger bike, a grown-up bike, starts coming down the hill.

I am shocked. There are two girls, much older than me, on the same bike. One is riding it, the other is standing up on the back, holding onto her shoulders. They are a cheering and whooping circus act as they come flying around the corner near where I am standing with my little orange bike with the white squidgy saddle and white chunky tyres.

My head goes fuzzy. I *know* something bad is going to happen.

My eyes follow them down past my house and just beyond where there is a crossroads. Everyone knows you're supposed to stop at the crossroads and check for cars. But they aren't going to stop, they're going way too fast and they're almost there now.

There's a car.

My brain doesn't register what colour the car is. But it does register the girl standing on the back of the bike being flung up into the air like my floppy rag doll when the car of no colour crashes into them. It does register their cheering turning into screaming, the scream of trauma, the scream of car brakes. Then the deafening sound of shock, from the girls, from the driver of the car, from the vibrations inside my own head.

What should I do? Run back home? Tell someone what I've just seen? No, much better to do what already comes naturally to me in my short life so far: pretend it hasn't happened. So I carry on walking up the hill with my little orange bike with the white squidgy saddle and white chunky tyres.

But now I can't pretend it hasn't happened because I can hear my mum's bloodcurdling scream coming from outside our house. She has heard the crash and assumed the worst: that it is me lying on the tarmac of the crossroads that you're supposed to stop at to check for cars, that it is my little orange bike with the white squidgy saddle and white chunky tyres that lays buckled and broken next to the car of no colour, that it is my fragile body that lays contorted and bleeding in the road.

I have to turn and go back home, go to my mum so she can see it isn't me, give her living breathing evidence that I am OK. But then I will have to pretend to be surprised at the horror that lays 50 metres from our front door. Because if I let on that I know what has happened, that I have actually *seen* what has happened, then how will I explain the fact that I am still out riding on my bike like it's still 2 minutes ago?

This does not fit with my pretending at all. How can I keep telling myself nothing has happened if all around me the evidence shouts otherwise? How can my brain process the fuss that my mum is now making over the sight of me as she spots me up the hill, if I am simply coming home after I've been out riding my bike?

I reach my house and go straight to my bedroom where I know my dolls will be just as I left them. Downstairs I think someone is calling an ambulance, but I don't know what happens after that. I don't know if these two girls live or die, if I am the last person to see them alive.

And I don't want to know. Because then I can go back to pretending. I can pretend that nothing of note happened whilst I was outside riding around on my little orange bike with the white squidgy saddle and white chunky tyres.

This will be my first memory.

Scene Three – Scared

I am 7 years old and I can't breathe. I am propped up with three pillows in mum's and dad's bed. I don't take up much room; I'm very skinny and very small in my little white nightie. I'm right on the edge of the side where dad sleeps. Or should I say where he used to sleep. I suppose it's just mum's bed now.

My dad has not long moved out. His navy-blue suitcase with the wobbly handle had been in the hallway for a few weeks, I didn't know why it was there, it always used to live on the top of the wardrobe. Every day I have been checking to see if it was still there and to see what it meant. Last week, when I came home from school, it had gone. It means he doesn't live with us anymore. It's just me and my sister and my mum.

The house change has all finished now too. For ages, builders were here making our one big house into two small ones. Where there was one big old wooden front door, there are now two white plastic ones, ours is the one on the right because we only live upstairs now. The bedroom my sister and I shared is now the kitchen and we have a new bedroom in the attic, it's much bigger so we don't need bunk beds anymore. Other people, a man and a woman I don't know, are now living downstairs, sleeping in the room I used to watch TV in.

Everything is different.

But right now my dad is sitting on the edge of the bed singing 'Old Louisiana' to me with his guitar, except he's changed the words to

'Old Wheezy-Ana'.

Even though he's singing, I sense he is worried about me. I think maybe mum has called him and told him I'm really poorly and so he came over to see me, to administer music as medicine.

I have spent a lot of my childhood like this, in bed, frightened and exhausted, whilst my friends play on at school. The doctor says I will have to wait until I'm 10 before I can get an asthma inhaler, so right now I have a long way to go. I hope I can last that long.

My lungs are fighting to do what should just come naturally, but for me, each in-breath is another excruciating effort, each out-breath an intention that never really comes.

Was I born this way or am I reacting to something? And if so, what?

Years later someone will tell me that childhood asthma is related to feeling smothered. Do I feel smothered? I know there has always been an atmosphere in this big house that is now two small houses, an atmosphere that hides in every room and hangs heavy in the air like my mums' pea and ham soup. There is little room to breathe.

I am stifled. I am scared. Scared that I can't breathe. Scared that they hate each other too much.

Scene Four – Ball

I am 8 years old and my ball is in the lead. My sister's is a bit behind, and my dad's is in last place.

The three of us are standing on the small bridge made of wood that curves up in the middle. We are all cheering on our own inflated rubber balls, each one a different colour so we can be sure to know whose has won when they finally get to the end of the stream which is right in town. Mine is white with a blue and red pattern that looks like sandcastles, my sister's is yellow with the same blue and red sandcastles, and my dad's is white with green and red stripes. Because I'm the youngest, I was allowed to choose first. Mine's the best.

We just bought the balls from the newsagent, they cost 99 pence each which was perfect because dad had just over £3 on him, and that leaves 12 pence in his pocket. My sister and I are both hungry. He buys us a bag of mini cheesy cheddars to share. He doesn't have anything; he says he ate before he picked us up.

My dad never has much money and my mum is always screaming at him to give her money for us. But if he hasn't got any, he can't give her any, right? She screams that she is going to take him to court. I guess that's a place where you can get money from.

It takes nearly two hours for the balls to get to the end of the stream. We follow them all the way, who is in the lead keeps on changing. In the end, my sister's ball wins, mine is next, and my dad's got stuck in some branches half an hour ago.

If we want to do this again, he'll have to find another 99p. Maybe that will be after mum has taken him to court so he can get some money.

Scene Five – Belonging

I am 10 years old and we're in London. Dad and my sister are quite a way in front of me. I don't want to be here with them. I want to go home. I feel like I don't fit with them, like I don't belong, like there's no room for me up there with them holding hands together. They're always together, I don't know what they're talking about but she's 12 so maybe she's got more to say or maybe he just likes her more.

And my dad is always winding me up. He seems to take great pleasure in teasing me. If he does something and I don't like it, he'll do it even more. Like when we sleep over at his place and he bursts into my room in the morning and draws back the curtains really quickly and sings "rise and shine!!!" at the top of his voice. It starts my day off really badly and I hate it. This is all it takes for him to do it again and again.

And like the time a couple of years ago when we were on the pier and I was scared of walking to the end because you could see the water between the planks of wood. He knew I was scared and for some reason his response to this was to pick me up under both arms and lift me over the railings, holding me above the deep dark choppy sea, me screaming and crying for him to put me down.

To him, it was a joke. To me, it was terrifying.

I drag behind now, I'm always dragging behind wherever we go, I just want to be on my own. We're going to St. Paul's Cathedral to do some brass rubbings. It sounds really boring. My dad keeps turning around and telling me to keep up. I don't want to keep up. The more he tells me, the further behind I drag. If I slow down enough, I might just get swallowed up by all these feet and legs brushing past me.

Actually...that feels a bit scary, I don't think I do want to get lost really. My navy moccasin shoes shift up a couple of gears until I am close behind them.

He turns his head, "Go away and find your own mummy and daddy, little girl," he jokes.

I told you I don't belong.

Scene Six – Blood

I am 12 years old, I have just woken up and feel wet between my legs. I put my hand down and bring it up so I can see it. Blood. I look down. So much blood. All over the sheets, all over my legs, all over my innocence. I reach on the bedside table for my tatty old handkerchief, scrunched up between my clock radio and inhaler, and stuff it down there. As if that is going to do much.

So this is it. My periods have begun. Apparently, I am a woman now. A 12-year-old woman!

What do I do? Who do I tell? Well, ideally, I'd go to my mum, but she's not here. My dad? Really? I don't want to tell him. I don't want to tell anyone. I wish it wasn't happening.

I pull some knickers on over the hanky and go downstairs to my sister's room.

Me: "I think I've just started my periods. Have you got anything?"

Her: "Oh. OK. Hang on a minute."

She seems less surprised than me that we are both waking up to this news.

Her: "That's all I've got, sorry."

She hands me two sanitary towels from one of her dressing table drawers. They're big and chunky, I wonder how I'm going to sneak them back to my room without dad seeing.

Me: "Thanks."

I manage to cross the landing and get to the bathroom unnoticed. I clean myself up, switch the blood-smeared hanky with the sanitary towel and carry on about my day as if nothing has happened.

Later, my dad hands me a leaflet. It is an information leaflet about menstruation that I assume he has picked up from the library or pharmacy or doctors.

Did my sister tell him what had happened? Or did he just see my sheets? Either way, at least I can now ask for some money to go and buy 'the necessaries'.

He tries to talk to me about it, he's doing his best, but this is the last thing I want.

I can hide my feelings.

It's just a pity I couldn't hide the evidence all over my bed.

———————

A few months later I am in a friend's loo desperately trying to insert a tampon. How does this even work? I read and re-read the instructions, hoist one leg up onto the toilet seat to resemble the hopelessly vague diagram. I discover the pain of a half-inserted tampon. I take it out, try again with another one. Is it me? Maybe it'll be easier when I'm actually on my period!

"How's it going in there? Having trouble?" my friend laughs through the door.

My friends are my new family. Most of the girls at school come from two-parent families but I find myself gravitating toward other girls whose parents aren't together or who have a dysfunctional family system in some way.

We always find our tribe sooner or later.

One friend's mother will become a lesbian by the time we leave school (quite shocking in the 80s). Another friend's dad isn't her real dad; she's never met her real dad. Another's mum had a boyfriend who she has another child with, but the boyfriend doesn't live with her, he lives with his new girlfriend. Another friend will come home from school one day to find her father unconscious in the garden, an empty bottle of whisky in one hand, an empty bottle of pills in the other.

All of this gives me a sense of normal family life. If everything is abnormal then everything is normal, right?

And I am starting to hang around with a group of boys. They are a bit older than me, they're Mods, and they wear big green parkas and ride around on Vespas. They listen to The Who and watch 'Quadrophenia'. They've got attitude and I like that they go against the grain. At school one day, I chicken scratch MODS into the back of my wrist with my compass, it's the same compass I have already used to scratch to death my new shoes that my dad bought me for my first term in my new school. I hate them. They're not the ones I wanted. They're not the ones all the other girls have. He got them from a charity shop because it's all he could afford, but I scratched them anyway thinking he would then have to get me some others. He didn't, he was just really cross with me. Right now

I think I've hidden my scratched wrist pretty well under my watch, but my dad still sees it at the dinner table and tells me how stupid I am and what an idiot I've been.

I am put down.

I am misunderstood. A year or so later he will find out that I have been smoking.

Him: "I bet you don't even inhale."

I stand accused.

Me: "Yes, I do actually!"

Ha! That'll show him! Show him how grown up I am.

Him: "Well, you're even more stupid than I thought you were then."

The 'put down' seems to be one of my dad's favourite parenting techniques. Like each Thursday evening when all I want to do is indulge in the sacred teenage ritual that is 'Top of the Pops'. He sits in his armchair of judgement, interrupting my viewing pleasure with frequent sounds of a sucking tutting noise coming from between his tongue and teeth. It is the disparaging sound of deep disapproval. Every now and then "Yobs!" will intercept the sucking tutting noise and escape from the gap between his tongue and teeth, often accompanied by a shake of his head as if he doesn't know what the world is coming to with the likes of Boy George and Adam Ant.

These 'yobs' are my heroes! I love them! They are changing the times and I want to sit and soak them up. And one day John Taylor from Duran Duran is going to be my boyfriend, so you'd better start chilling out a bit!

I am withdrawing further and further into myself, away from my family.

I don't care.

Except I do.

Scene Seven – Married

I am 13 years old and have just got home from school. My dad comes into the cold green lounge with the big high ceiling where I am watching TV from the sofa. He stands by the door, like he's not going to get settled. Like he's just popped in to tell me dinner is ready or something. Like he's not about to say anything important.

Him: "How are you?"

Me: "Fine."

Him: "I've got something to tell you."

He stands a little closer, closes the door behind him.

Oh God, here we go again...!

Me: "What?"

Him: "Angela and I got married last week."

Whaaatttt??? Seriously?? That's not a sentence you should be saying in the PAST tense!!

Me: "Oh...OK."

Him: "It's just for the business really, makes more sense with the legalities if we're married."

Why would you go off and do it in secret?? Like it doesn't affect anyone else?? Like it doesn't matter?? Like I don't matter??

Me: "Oh...OK."

Him: "It won't change anything here."

Me: "Fine."

Whatever.

This is my second internalised meaning of marriage: it doesn't matter, it means nothing, it's no big deal, and it's something you can just go out and do on a Saturday afternoon and not tell anyone about, like going shopping or going out for lunch.

It sits neatly on top of my first internalised meaning of marriage: marriage is a war zone, it is exploding conflict, it is shouting, it is smashing plates in the kitchen, it is tension, it is not being able to stand the sight of the other person.

Actually, it turns out my dad's second marriage mirrored his first one too.

And like in some kind of selection process, I have been moved from one battlefield to another. Again the machine guns fire and insults are thrown like hand grenades, not all the time, just enough to never know when it's coming, like an airstrike. And I take cover in the place I know so well: inside of myself.

No, I don't think this marriage thing will be for me.

Scene Eight – Date

I am 13 years old and going on my first date. I think I might puke from nerves. I'm wearing my favourite pink pedal pushers, white shirt, and white espadrilles, standing at the meeting spot in town, terrified that I'm going to be stood up.

The boy in question is my best friend's mum's boyfriend's son. Let me say that again – my best friend's mum's boyfriend's son. He's 14 and totally gorgeous, blond hair, blue eyes, really good looking.

Why would he be interested in me?

I know everyone tells me I'm pretty, but so what? What does that even mean? That everything is OK then? That I've got nothing to worry about? But I have got stuff to worry about so it doesn't make sense to me and leaves me feeling even more like there must be something wrong with me.

Last year sometime, I was in town with some friends one Saturday afternoon, hanging around, bored. We wandered into a department store and found ourselves being asked if we wanted to enter a photographic competition. We went along with it just for a laugh and just for something to do. A month later I got a letter through the post saying I had won in my age category. I was half pleased and half mortifyingly embarrassed. There was a presentation, the enormous gilded framed portrait was awarded to us and I was given a £25 gift voucher to spend in the store. I bought myself a pair of burgundy-coloured suede tucker boots which I absolutely loved; my mum hung the portrait in the lounge, which I absolutely hated.

This wasn't the first 'beauty' contest I had won. No, when I was around two years old my mum sent in a photograph of me to a bonnie baby contest, and I won it (or rather she did). The thing about the photograph, though, was that she had cut my sister out of it before she sent it in.

Seriously? Who does that?

Anyway, back to my date. His dad – my best friend's mum's boyfriend – is loaded. They live in a massive house with a swimming pool and tennis courts and he owns a villa in the South of France. He's also a violently abusive, despicable, frightening man. My best friend had never told me this, I had no clue, but I was to discover it for myself when they invited me to said villa in the South of France where they were all spending the summer. In fact, the whole holiday was a bit of an initiation.

Firstly, my dad lied about my date of birth and told the travel agent I was 12 so he could buy a child's plane ticket for me (which was cheaper). Not only was it my first time flying alone, but it was my first time flying altogether and my travel documents contained false information! According to my ticket, I was 12, but according to my passport, I was 13. My dad had totally dodged around this being any significant issue at all when I expressed my concern and worry. He waved me off at the departure lounge, and like in a scene from Midnight Express, I headed through, terrified that I was going to get caught out, be questioned and arrested, and never even make it to bloody Nice.

How the hell can you do this to me? Put me through this stress just to save a bit of money?

But I made it through without incident (they were different times), and my best friend and her mum met me at the other end.

How exciting, my first holiday away from my family, a week of sun, sea and freedom with my best friend and a boy who I already fancied. There was also a friend of his staying and his younger brother too.

A few days in and we were all sitting in the dining room about to eat dinner. My best friend's mum's boyfriend sat at the head of the table, his mood was dark, and there was even more tension in the air than usual that evening. I'd already gathered that his eldest son (my date-to-be) was the main object of his anger, the trigger to his explosions. There had already been a few minor incidents but tonight things were to come to a head. Something was said by one of them – I'm not sure who or what, it all happened so quickly. But the next thing I knew, my best friend's mum's boyfriend had launched himself out of his chair, sent his plate of spaghetti bolognaise flying, sprung across the room toward his son, and had him up against the wall with his hand around his throat, threatening him through seething gritted teeth.

NO! Please! Don't hurt him! I love him!

My best friend, her mum, the younger brother, the other friend and I, all sat in total silence. No one said anything. No one intervened.

Are they rigid with fear too? Or is it just me? Is this what always happens when they sit down to a spag bol in their holiday villa? Is it really just one of those things?

The son somehow escapes his father's hateful embrace and leaves the room. I stare at the carnage of the broken plate and its entrails in the corner of the room and realise I am more attracted to the son now than I was before dinner was served.

He is wounded, I am wounded. Let me heal you so I can heal myself. Let me love you so I can love myself.

That night, my best friend suggests that we wait until everyone has gone to bed and then sneak out and head into town. The son and his friend are in on it too and the plan is set. I guess we all just needed to get the hell out of there. At midnight, we climb out of our respective ground floor bedroom windows, run out across the back of the garden, dodging the security light, over the white brick wall, and into the street.

We are the great escape!

We spend the next few hours hanging out in the bustling town. Our blindingly obvious under-age status means we can't get into any of the bars or discos, but the boys are able to buy a few bottles of cheap wine from the supermarket. We wander the streets and sit in the park generally acting like the confused traumatised teenagers that we are.

Thirteen years old, shaken up, getting drunk and roaming the streets of a foreign town in the middle of the night, no one knowing where we are or what we're doing!

Is this what holidays abroad are like?

A few hours later, all out of cheap wine and ideas, we sneak back in the same way we had snuck out and slide into bed, as sure as the sun will soon rise that we have got away with it.

Not so.

At breakfast, we are hauled into the dining room to be told in no uncertain terms that, if we try anything like that again, I will be on the next flight home and my best friend and her mum's boyfriend's son's lives won't be worth living.

It is towards the end of the holiday that the son asks me out on a date, perhaps he feels we have bonded over me witnessing what really goes on behind the gates of their villa. So here I am now pacing up and down, waiting for his number 17 bus to pull up, hoping he'll be on it when it does. He is.

I don't know if he's nervous or not because I'm so nervous I can't think straight or say anything. I haven't got a clue what's going on around me, everything is a whirly blur. I think I'm playing it cool but, on the inside, I am a sick and dizzy pink and white mess.

We have no plans for the date and have no idea what we can do. I am in no way capable of bringing anything to the table and will go along with anything he wants. So, when he suggests the cinema just across the road, I agree, thinking that's perfect because we won't have to look at each other or make conversation.

We go and see 'Pink Floyd: The Wall'. I pretend I enjoy it but don't actually understand any of it.

When it's over we both catch our respective buses home.

There isn't a second date. I guess he doesn't like me much after all.

Scene Nine – Spliff

I am 14 years old and there is a new girl in my class. Even though she is in my class, she is a whole year older than the rest of us because she has come from South Africa and the school years are different there or something. She is very cool. She wears make-up to school, proper make-up, really professional looking, not just a bit of dodgy blue eyeliner like the rest of us, and her skirt is the shortest in the whole school. All of this, the way she speaks, her confidence, the fact that she's different...I am in awe of her. But the best thing? We are friends.

Our friendship is cemented by the fact that we live on the same bus route. Finally, something positive about living two bus rides away from school and all the rest of my friends. She and I bond over shared fags (she always has cigarettes on her) at the back of the top deck each morning and afternoon. And as if this wasn't all enough excitement, after school one day she tells me she is going around to her boyfriend's flat and do I want to come too. Errr...yes, please!

Her boyfriend greets us at the door with the most enormous spliff I've ever seen, ready rolled and waiting for us. He looks like a young Bob Geldof who's just fallen out of bed. We stand in the doorway in our micro mini-skirted school uniforms.

Her boyfriend is 28 years old.

Yep, this 28-year-old man passes his enormous spliff to his 15-year-old girlfriend who in turn passes it to me, her 14-year-old friend, at 4 o'clock on a Wednesday.

Nothing questionable about that.

Is there??

Although I've been smoking cigarettes for a year already (most of my friends smoke Benson and Hedges but in an attempt to not follow the crowd, I decide John Player Blue is my favourite brand, anyway blue is my favourite colour), this is my first time smoking hash. But I don't tell my 15-year-old friend or her 28-year-old boyfriend that.

And when I get home and raid the fridge, I tell my dad I have hay fever to explain my red, itchy, squinty eyes. To be fair, I have. Smoking weed is definitely a trigger for my pollen allergy, so quite a handy disguise.

For once, I don't think he suspects anything.

These visits to my friend's boyfriend's flat become a regular after-school activity. While other classmates are doing netball practice, I'm working my way through a giant spliff with some 28-year-old guy who lives in a bedsit in town.

———————

When I started secondary school, I was in all of the top sets for every subject. By the time I get to choose my options, 2 years later, I have virtually dropped off the scale. I don't try. I never do any homework. The only thing I like about school is PE – athletics in particular. I will go on to excel in athletics, winning town champion events and even being voted sports captain of my house at school. This gives me a sense of identity and achievement.

The only other thing I like about school is my friends, particularly the other rebellious, non-conforming, messed-up ones.

Who needs a dysfunctional family when you have dysfunctional friends!

My sister, meanwhile, has been voted in as head girl at the grammar school she got into. I didn't get in, but I don't care. If she is the good one, then I must be the bad one. If she is the studious one, then I must be the rebellious one. I can't compete with her academic prowess, so I become someone so far removed from that, that there is no place for comparison (at least that's the plan my subconscious has for me).

We could not be more different.

It's a shame really, I'm a clever girl. But clever is everything I don't want to be associated with. Clever is boring, clever is being a creep, clever is staying at home with your head in a book, clever is not going out and having fun. Clever is my sister.

And clever is hard and, if I'm really honest, I don't really think I'm clever enough. No, if I can't be clever enough, then better to be not clever at all, better to be the rebel. But then being a rebel is hard as well. I am getting quite worn down by it, the effort it takes to keep being cool, to keep pretending I don't care when really I do. But I can't relent now, I've come too far. I have trapped myself in this role. But who else would I be anyway?

Better to be someone than no one.

Better to be something than nothing.

Scene Ten – Escape

I am 15 years old, it's a Tuesday evening and, as always on a Tuesday evening, I am over at my mum's for tea.

Today's the day. Come on you can do it. Just find your voice. Tell her. Don't let another Tuesday go by without having done it.

Deep breath...

I'm terrified. It's not just because I know there is going to be a huge fall out from what I want to say, especially from my dad, I know he's going to take it badly, but I'm also really afraid that the answer's going to be 'No', that she doesn't really want me here. I guess I've been here before, trying to tell one of my parents how I really feel, and that did not end well.

I'm scared that it will be the same. Much safer just to say nothing, I've learnt, and deal with the feelings. But I just don't think I can anymore. It's getting unbearable for me.

It's no longer about wanting my childhood security back – too late for that now, that's a ship that has long since sailed into the distance of unmet needs. No, my agenda now is really about knowing that I will have a lot more freedom at my mum's. I know she'll let me stay out late, I'll be able to do much more of what I want when I want, like start going to pubs with fake ID. All I'm interested in right now is being out with my mates. My dad is so overprotective, he insists on picking me up from parties or youth club way too early.

It is mortifying and it is killing me.

Come on, you can do it.

Just tell her.

You've died inside before, you can do it again.

Me: "I don't want to go back tonight. I want to stay here."

Her: "Do you mean you don't want to go back just tonight, or you don't want to go back?"

Me: "I don't want to go back at all."

Fuck. It's out. Four years of holding that in and now it's out and I don't know what's going to happen next.

Her: "Of course you can stay here. I never wanted you to leave in the first place."

WELL, WHY THE FUCK DIDN'T YOU TELL ME BEFORE!!!

I've spent my entire adolescence feeling trapped by Dad and unwanted by you. Seriously! This could have all been so different. I could have been so different. I could have felt worthy and loved and wanted and free.

But it's OK, she's calling my dad to tell him I don't want to go back to him. And I realise this is the thing I have been avoiding for all these years: hurting my dad's feelings. He'd been so proud when we'd gone to live with him. His girls.

I knew it would devastate him and I was right.

It is a whole month before he will speak to me again.

I must be a bad person.

Scene Eleven – Shit

I am 15 years old and have a boyfriend. A proper boyfriend.

Is it OK that he has just pinned me up against a doorway?

It's all happened so quickly. One minute we were walking down the road quite happily, our friends a few steps in front, the next he's flipped out over something or other.

I was lulled into a false sense of safety and now I'm scared and confused.

I am trapped once again, just for a brief moment and then it's over, and we're back to 'normal'. Just a brief reminder that you're only ever one shop doorway away from being hoodwinked.

But there's something about him I like, I am drawn in like a magnet. He's dark and moody and silent and that's a good match for my silence. In fact, he barely speaks at all, to anyone, including me. I don't know what's going on behind those abandoned eyes, just like no one knows what's going on for me – least of all me. There is a resonance between us, an unspoken understanding; I have no voice, you have no voice.

His shit matches my shit.

Yet I know it's wrong, that moment in the doorway. But do I raise the alarm? Do I call out to our friends? Do I end the relationship? No. I don't know how. I do what is familiar. I do what I do know how to do: I pretend it isn't happening and I stay with him.

I am so desperate to climb into your darkness, your silence.

Tell me what's going on for you.

Tell me all about your shit.

I can help you, I'm here to fix you.

Please let me be the one to fix you.

The relationship doesn't last long, but I don't need to worry, there will be another one along soon, one that even looks the same.

There's always another one. Same shit, different face.

But it will be a few years until I meet him, until I'm ready for that experience, until I call in the re-enactment.

For a while at least, I am free again.

Scene Twelve – Sex, sex, sex

I am 16 years old and I'm not sure if I've just had sex or not. But I shall assume that I have, just so I can say I'm not a virgin anymore (even though I think I probably still am) because most of my friends have had sex already. God, one girl at school has even had a baby and another friend is pregnant. Not that I would want that, but it's about time I had sex (even if I still haven't), I'm 16 after all.

He's 16 too and just about to go and join the army. We've been seeing each other for all of a few weeks, but it feels that his imminent departure is excuse enough for us to conjure up a tragic love scene in which the couple who are about to be separated by land, sea, and potential war, profess their undying love for each other. Having sex will surely seal our love for one another.

Except we're not in love. I don't even think I really like him that much. I don't know what I see in him, but I know I'm chuffed to bits when he leaves me with his bright yellow bomber jacket as a farewell don't-forget-about-me-and-our-undying-love gift.

We don't talk about whether we've just had sex or not. Was it his (not) first time too? We're both too embarrassed, I don't want to shame him into having to admit that it's not actually possible to put a 2-inch, pinkie-finger-sized, soft penis into a vagina, and I don't want to shame myself into looking like I think it might be.

So we focus on the tragedy of our separation and the fact that he's going to leave for the army and become a soldier, perhaps in an attempt to find some sense of camaraderie and purpose in place of his unhappy family life – his mother left him and his brother some years ago. He is going to fight, he is going to channel his anger, he is going to become a real man, he is going to escape.

I, on the other hand, am going to find another boyfriend.

And I do.

I am still 16 years old and I still don't know whether I've just had sex or not!

WTF! How difficult can this be??

It's a simple Yes or No, right? A line that gets crossed. You go from being a virgin to having sex and not being a virgin. There's no middle ground. There are no conversations that go: "Are you a virgin?" "I don't know"!

But I think this time it's a little closer at least. I think we're almost there as I straddle him on my single bed upstairs in my room at home. But now he's feigning a headache or something and says he has to stop trying. I'm embarrassed, I suspect he is too.

But I really fancy this guy, all the girls do, which is why I can't quite believe he would want to be with me when he could have his pick (I will later find out that he is having his pick at the same time, I just don't know it yet). He's tall with brown hair, short at the back, floppy long fringe hanging over one eye. He always wears a full-length black leather jacket (a vast improvement from the bright yellow bomber which now sits sorrowfully neglected in my wardrobe and will soon be cast away in a charity bag for collection), a black polo neck sweater and black trousers. Oh, such style. He and his best friend turn heads when they walk into the ice disco on a Saturday night. They don't skate, they are way too cool for that, they just hang out in the bar – which is where I make sure I am, especially since we are 'a couple' (or so I think), and especially after we've had sex (even though I suspect we haven't).

The 'relationship' doesn't last long. I'm not sure what happened, we don't even acknowledge it, preferring to both give the impression that we are too cool to care, when all the while inside, I, for one, am confused and embarrassed.

It must be me. I'm not good enough.

And he is a closed book. I find out later that he suffers from epilepsy and that one time he stood me up because he had cuts on his face from when he'd had a fit and fallen out of bed, hitting his face on a plate on the bedside table. He made some excuse at the time, didn't tell me how it really happened. I guess he is full of shame and silence about his dirty secret.

Oh, you could have told me. I would have looked after you. I'm looking for someone to fix so I can fix myself, don't you know.

So it is third time lucky! No question about it now. I am definitely, unquestionably, without a shadow of a doubt NOT a virgin anymore. I am still 16 (it's been a busy year) so that's OK then. I certainly don't want to be a 17-year-old virgin. God. Imagine that? Mortifying.

After all this, it feels a bit anti-climactic. Perhaps the two false starts have lessened the impact somewhat.

But this time it's a proper relationship, defined by going on the pill, because that's what you do when you're 16 and have a boyfriend. We're hanging out all the time, mostly in the back of his black Ford Fiesta (he's 17 and just passed his test), fumbling around in the dark, parked up in some car park. Our great love affair lasts all of 6 months before he finishes with me, then we get back together, then I snog someone else and it's all over.

I just want to be loved. Anyone will do.

Scene Thirteen – Orgasm, orgasm, orgasm

I am 17 years old and I've just had my first orgasm. I am lying on a hotel bed with my work uniform on from the waist up. My grey pencil skirt and knickers sit in judgement on the chair in the corner of the room.

I haven't had sex. We don't have sex, my boss and I, he just makes me have multiple orgasms. Not makes me in an against-my-will kind of way but makes me in an if-you-do-this-then-this-is-what-happens-cause-and-effect-mechanical kind of way.

He's 34.

And he has a girlfriend.

Do I feel anything about either of those facts?

We work in the hotel, and when he and I have both finished our shifts, he takes his master key and sneaks us into a vacant room where he teaches me how to orgasm, like some extra-curricular school activity that I've signed up for. I learn a lot. I am top of the class. And I think I'm strangely grateful; I'm not sure how many of my peers are having orgasms at 17, a lot of women go their whole lives without ever having any apparently, so maybe I'm lucky that

35

he's chosen me as his student.

But, OK I know, there's something not right about it. It feels seedy, like it shouldn't be happening, but I can't quite figure out why.

I should be flattered, right?

I *am* worthy after all.

Please let me be worthy.

I continue to have lots of casual relationships and one-night stands throughout my teenage and young adult years.

I am a confused leg-spreading dichotomy of needing to be loved and not wanting to get trapped.

I say 'Yes' when I really mean 'No'.

I seek affirmation from boys (and men), through my body, through sex.

Lots of sex = lots of affirmation; I am wanted, I am loved, I am worthy.

But I won't get trapped again.

Until I do.

Scene Fourteen – Guilt

I am 17 years old and my dad is at the front door. My mum goes down to let him in. This is extremely unusual because my parents still can't stand each other, even after 10 years of separation and divorce. He never comes to the front door and she never goes down to see him.

They are speaking.

I am anxious.

I think I can hear my dad crying. I think I can hear my mum being kind to him.

I don't know which unsettles me more.

But I do know why this is happening; I just don't want to acknowledge it. I would prefer to rewind the clock to 2 hours ago, before the phone had rung and my mum had answered it. I would prefer not to know that my dad was on the other end of that phone and that after they had spoken my mum came into my room and said to me:

Her: "That was your dad on the phone...I've got some bad news."

I really don't want to know, whatever it is. Don't tell me. Please don't tell me.

Me: "What?"

Her: "I'm afraid Omi has died."

NOOOOO!!! That I didn't want to hear. It's not true. Why are you telling me this?

Me: "OK."

Her: "We think she had a heart attack. Dad found her body this morning, it was in a terrible state. Seems she'd been dead a couple of days before anyone knew."

NOOOOO!!! Not that. That's horrible. Why are you telling me this? Don't say those things.

Me: "OK."

Her: "Dad's coming over soon. To see you."

NOOOOO!!! Please not. I don't want him to. I don't want him and his grief here. I don't want to be with his emotion, his upset, his loss, my loss. I don't want this to be happening.

Me: "OK."

Now they are in the kitchen and she's making him a coffee. He's still crying. She's still being kind. I'm still being anxious. I want him to leave. This is too much in one day: first the news of Omi, and now I have to cope with my parents being in the same space as each other. I can't process it.

I'm staying in my room as long as possible, to avoid him, to avoid the feelings, to avoid the truth. And when I can't avoid it any longer, I visit the kitchen only briefly. I don't speak. I have no voice.

After he has gone, I play my cassette of Simon and Garfunkel's 'Bridge Over Troubled Water', just that song, over and over again.

I am sadness.

I am grief.

I am...GUILT.

The woman who lived for her granddaughters, who loved us with all her big, kind-hearted love, who looked after us when we were young, who spoilt us with treats and sweets and vanilla-infused icing sugar, who sung us lullabies in German at bedtime, who let us sleep in her soft comfy bed with the feather duvet when we went for sleepovers, who made picnics for us to eat at the clifftop in the long hot summers, who saved up money to give us £1000 each for our 16th birthdays, who cooked delicious dishes tasting of love for us every Tuesday night...had died alone and lonely, not having seen either of us for ages – my sister had moved to London a year ago, and I had simply preferred to spend all my time with my friends.

I AM SO SORRY.

I didn't know you were going to die. I thought you were here for a long time yet.

If I had known, I would have come to tea last Tuesday, and the one before that, and the one before that, and the one before that...

"...like a bridge over troubled waters, I will ease your mind...."

If I play it enough times, the feelings might just come out.

Scene Fifteen – Seeds

I am 18 and want to go to a kibbutz. I don't really know what a kibbutz is, but I want to go to one anyway. I have a cousin who went to a kibbutz and it means you're away from home, in a different country, living with new people, in a different culture, speaking a different language, doing different things. It's all different! A whole different world, and for that reason, I want to go.

I want to get the fuck out of here.

I send off for some information through the post. When it arrives, I lose myself in fantasies of being there, in Israel, picking fruit and living the dream! I want to be one of those people in the pictures. They did it, I can too. I want to be there. I don't want to be here.

Or Summer Camp USA. Now that looks like fun. The brochures are full of sexy-looking tanned teens swinging from ropes in trees, singing around campfires, flinging themselves around playing ball games, and helping American school kids to enjoy life. Hey, I can do that! I can enjoy life!

But it feels too big. It feels like a pipedream.

No, you can't do it, silly girl. It's just a fantasy.

Just like when I am in a nightclub one night, and a guy tells me he is a photographer and is scouting for models to go and work in Manhattan. Manhattan! Wow! That sounds incredible. Me? A model, in Manhattan! Where the fuck is Manhattan??

He gives me a business card. I get home and look at the atlas. Oh, there's Manhattan! Who knew?!

But my friend (who he didn't ask) thinks he's probably just some pervert and I can only imagine how my dad would feel about the idea, and...and...my self-esteem screams loud in my ear.

It's a fantasy, I tell you! Come on, you? You couldn't really do that! You're not pretty enough. You're not good enough.

So, because it's easier, I also tell myself he's a raving pervert and the whole reason that I'm definitely NOT going to Manhattan (where?!) is just because of THAT! And it's got absolutely nothing to do with the fact that I'm too scared and don't believe in myself.

Nothing at all!

But what if I did believe in myself? What if I did have more courage? I could at least investigate it, check this guy and his credentials out a bit, give it a try perhaps? I am 18, a perfect time to set out in the world.

But no. I go through the sliding door marked NO.

I choose NO. I choose fear. I choose staying small.

But as some kind of consolation prize to myself, I do go on holiday to Israel with a friend and what a time we have! I can do what I like when I like. Nobody knows what I'm up to or where I am. I don't have to answer to anyone.

We spend most of the week hooked up and having sex with two Welsh guys who work in our hotel. We sneak them into our room at the end of their shifts; they would have been sacked if they'd got caught, for sure. And we meet loads of other people who are travelling and working abroad. They are so cool.

I want to be her, and her, and her.

I want to be *that* girl.

I don't want to be *this* girl.

Something inside me is stirring. A tiny little seed is being sown. An idea that doesn't feel 'too big' or 'too scary'. Something that doesn't just need to be a fantasy. Something that can now be a reality.

I've got it!

I have my escape route!

Scene Sixteen – Freedom

I am 19 years old and my bags are packed. My friend (the one I went to Israel with) and I have left our jobs in the hotel we both worked in and we are Corfu bound! We have booked a 2-week holiday during which we intend to find jobs and an apartment for the season.

I am young Shirley Valentine, full of excitement and adventure.

This feels so good, so right, and I feel ALIVE.

Within a week we both have jobs and an apartment for the summer. I am working in 'Mistrale Fast Food Bar'. I have landed on my feet and they itch no more. My boss is lovely; he takes me into Corfu Town to get me a work permit. Unlike most of the other young English people working here, I am a legal alien!

I love everything about my new life: I love walking around barefoot, I love knowing that the sun will be shining every day, I love the new friends I am making, I love the laughs that I'm having, I love going out at night, getting drunk and having fun, and I love that I'm not at home anymore, away from the drudgery, the routine, my family.

I am a butterfly emerged from its cocoon, metamorphosis itself!

Home feels like a million miles away and I know I don't want to go back, I can't go back. Nope, this is the life for me, travelling, nothing pinning me down, new experiences, new places, new people, a new me perhaps.

I belong yet I am autonomous. It feels like true freedom.

The weeks roll on, one sunset merging into another, this is the life.

Today, which has started out like any other day, I am walking – barefoot – to work. 'Mistrale' is halfway down the long beach strip of bars and restaurants. It's quite a long walk but I always know I'm almost there when I can see the white plastic chairs and tables outside on the street. I like to see how many people are sitting there, so I know how busy it is. I like to know what I'm walking into, whether I need to hit the sticky lino running, or whether I can kick back, sit and drink a coke, and chat to my workmates.

As I approach, I can make out just a few people: a couple at one table, a single man at another. Not too busy then.

As I approach closer still, I feel that I recognise this single man – something about his posture and his body language is familiar, but I can't quite make him out.

Until I can.

DAD!!! WHAT THE FUCK!!!

Are you shitting me??!! Is that really my dad sitting there, tucking into a burger and chips, as if he's some normal guy on some normal holiday??

WHY IS HE HERE???

I am the OPPOSITE of FREE.

Him: "Hi."

Always the practical joker!

Me: "H...H...Hello."

Him: "How are you?"

Like this is normal???!!! Are you for real???!!! WHY are you here???!!!

Me: "W...What are you doing here?"

Him: "I just thought I'd come and see you, see how you're getting on."

Well, I WAS getting on just fine. I was HAPPY. I was FREE.

Me: "Why didn't you tell me you were coming?"

Him: "I wanted to surprise you."

You don't trust me!!! You're checking up on me!!!

Me: "You've certainly done that! How long are you staying?"

Him: "Two weeks. I'm booked in next door."

Whaaat??? TWO weeks??? WHY???

Me: "Great."

———————

'Next door' is an 18-30s hotel. My dad is neither 18 nor 30 nor anywhere in between. He is older. Much older. So typical of my dad. So embarrassing.

He shouldn't be here. He should have been able to manage his feelings of worrying about me. He should have talked to someone about it, tried to distract himself, let it go. He should have been able to sit with himself and not have had to react. He should have called me up on the phone and talked to me until he was reassured

44

that I was OK.

He should have been able to let me go.

But here he is and so I'm going to have to deal with it. And I won't let this spoil my new life. I will carry on enjoying myself and he can fit in around me! I am 19. I am an adult. Maybe it will be OK. Maybe we can even have a nice time.

And actually, we do. We have some fun and I think some bonding is taking place. He has a good holiday, I get over my shock, he leaves knowing that I am OK.

I guess he just had to see it for himself.

I go back to being free once again. For a while, at least.

The months roll by in a hedonistic haze of retsina, moonshine, and kebabs. But all too soon there's a change in the air, the sweet smells of honeysuckle and pine needles fade, the flocks of tourists thin, and the autumnal thunderstorms loom, heralding The End! The sundial is ticking and there'll soon be nothing left for us Brits working here. So, like squeezing the last luscious drops of juice from the oranges that grow outside our apartment, we desperately squeeze what fun we can out of the time that remains.

By mid-October, the inevitable is here. We were two of the first to arrive and we are now two of the last to leave. But not straight home, please no, we're not ready for that yet.

So we are taking the 'long way home' via Egypt and then back to the place where this idea was first conceived – back to Israel (yep, that's definitely the long way home). The place that, just 1 year ago, I found a cure for my itchy feet, my need to get away, to escape. The place where I looked on in total envy at all of the 'travellers'.

Now I am one of them. I am that girl, the one I wanted to be. And I know that going back to that place will feel different this time, I know that Corfu has changed me, it has shaped who I now am.

It has given me a sense of self.

It has given me a sense of freedom.

But that's the thing about freedom: it can slip through your fingers if you're not careful with it, if you don't hold onto it with all your might, don't honour it, don't treasure it, don't protect it, if you allow the patterns of the past to re-emerge.

It seems we're not actually done until we're done.

As I am about to find out.

Scene Seventeen – Knife

I am 19 years old and standing in my mum's kitchen. The carving knife sits innocently on the draining board acting like nothing has just happened, like it's been there since my mum washed it up after her dinner.

But that's not true. Once again, I am pretending that something hasn't just happened. Something bad. Something really bad. Ahh, sweet denial, my old familiar friend, come wrap me up in your all-encompassing arms, slide over here and cover my mind, envelop my heart, soothe my terror, like a dark cloak as heavy as forever, that covers me from head to toe so not a millimetre of light can get in, not a millimetre of truth.

But the truth always sneaks in there somewhere. Denial promises

46

so much but delivers so little, in the end at least.

My new boyfriend and I have just been out on our 'leaving do' because in the morning we're going to Australia. Finally, just about as far away as you can get. I've been wanting to go there for ages, so when I met him just a couple of months ago and he told me he was going to Australia for a year and did I want to come with him? Well, fuck yeah, I wanna come with you! Even though I've already started kind of making plans to go there with my friend who I'd been in Corfu with, this is a much better offer. She'll understand – except she doesn't, but never mind, that's her problem, right? I'm in love and I'm going to Australia! And New Zealand, Hawaii, LA and New York too, around the world tickets for a year. I don't think she and I would have managed that between us.

We've just been to a club and a bar before that; a handful of our friends were there to see us off, wish us well. Now we're back at my mum's place, it's pretty late, I assume she is asleep. We're standing in the kitchen, we've both had quite a lot to drink and I suspect he's been smoking hash too, a lethal combination for him, not a cocktail I want to be on the receiving end of.

I say something and out of nowhere there it is. That look in his eyes, those eyes of a thousand burning flames, those eyes that say, "come on inside, it's a long way down into the firepit, go on, I dare you." And right now, rage pierces beyond those flames and I am staring into a soulless void.

With the quickest sleight of hand, he's picked up the knife from the draining board in a flash, neither of us has time to blink. The knife is up against my throat, and his other hand grips my neck.

Terror paralyses me.

But hang on, now the knife is back on the draining board as quickly as it had left it and his other hand is back at his side.

"It's OK," my brain says to my heart. "Nothing just happened, nothing at all."

But it *has* just happened. I *know* it has. *Don't* I?

In this one precious moment, I know I have a choice. I can raise the alarm, back out of the whole damn thing, cancel my trip, tell everyone it's all off and why. I can remind myself that this isn't the first time I've experienced his sudden flashes of rage, that I know he can just flip when somebody says a particular something, does a particular something, looks at him in a particular way.

I can keep myself safe.

Or...I can pretend (seemingly like he's just done) that it hasn't happened.

I choose the silent suffocating screams of denial.

It's intoxicating in its seductive familiarity.

He is also my ticket out of here.

So we don't talk about it. We don't acknowledge what has just happened. We carry on like normal, have a glass of water, head off to bed, like I'm not just about to fly to the other side of the world, where I don't know another single human being other than the man who has just held a knife against my throat. We climb the stairs silently up to the attic room.

He is my captor.

I am trapped.

It is perfect.

Our year of travelling passes relatively without incident.

If you can call him tossing the sofa back with me sitting on it, jarring the life out of me, without incident. If you can call him starting a fight in a bar with someone who looked at me, without incident. If you can call him smashing a glass ashtray in the kitchen into a thousand crystallised pieces, without incident. I know I prefer to.

I am living in Bondi Beach!

I am living the dream!

I am living in fear.

The subtle stench of threat hangs in the air, the constant possessiveness, the constant control, the smouldering charcoal anger that brims under the surface each time he is triggered by who knows what, who knows who, who knows when.

Like the eggshells that crack beneath my feet no matter how lightly I tiptoe over them, I am breaking.

My self-esteem, my sense of worth, are like the tide going out.

Three hundred and something days later, when we arrive home, I am a shadow of myself. I have stress pains in the base of my skull, I feel dizzy.

I smile. I pretend.

I've pretended before, I can do it again.

I tell no one.

Until I do. Until I have to.

Scene Eighteen – Broken

I am 21 years old and shaking from head to toe. My friend is handing me the neat vodka she has just poured me. I take it and tentatively bring it in my trembling hand to my lips.

I sip. I swallow. It helps. Repeat.

Adrenalin calms a little but the wild beast of remembering still runs riot in my head.

Her: "What the fuck happened?"

Me: "I don't know really."

Her: "Start from the beginning."

Me: "I said something. I'm not sure what. And he just flipped."

I sip. I swallow. It helps.

Her: "Go on."

Me: "The next thing I know he's trying to grab me and I'm running for the door, but he gets me before I can make it. He ripped my shirt. And he dragged me into the bedroom."

I sip. I swallow. It helps.

Her: "Fuck. Then what?"

Then he pinned me down on the floor so I couldn't move, and he looked like he wanted to kill me. Then he raised his fist to smash my face in – but I'm not telling you that.

Me: "Then I don't know. It all happened so quickly. But he's smashed the flat up, I think."

Her: "Has he hit you?"

No! He would never hit me. He loves me.

Me: "No, he hit the wall instead. I think he's hurt himself. Then he just sat and started crying. That's when I ran out and called you."

Her: "Shit, has he done this before?"

I sip. I swallow. It helps.

Not exactly but...YES. He's a bad man. He's a broken man. But I can fix him. I want to fix him. Don't get in my way; I'm going to fix him.

Me: "No, not like this, he's just got a bit of a temper. He freaks out sometimes. It's OK."

Her: "It's NOT OK! You can't go back. You know that, right?"

I can go back. I shouldn't go back. I want to go back. Don't let me go back.

Me: "I know."

I sip. I swallow. It helps.

The next morning I go back.

I go back because, when he calls in the morning, he says he's been thinking about me all night. I go back because I owe him the chance to explain himself. I go back so he can apologise and show me how sorry he is.

Mostly I go back because it's easier than not going back.

Our flat, along with my sanity, is in a million pieces. There is a hole in the bedroom wall where he put his fist. There could have been a hole in my face. Somehow, I appreciate his self-control.

Together we salvage what we can from the contents of our flat and the contents of our relationship. We gather up the glass fragments of hope.

But a fear the shape and size of a frightened child has curled itself up deep inside my belly.

Fear is my great pretender.

She tells me it's all OK.

She tells me he will change.

Scene Nineteen – Gatekeeper

I am 22 years old and have fallen to my knees. Every piece of clothing I own is in a pile in the middle of the bedroom floor. The enormous mountain of material parallels the mountain of helplessness I feel inside. I am broken.

He stands in calm fury next to the mountain.

He created the mountain.

And (just like my dad 11 years ago) he is the gatekeeper to my freedom.

I honestly thought he would let me go. How stupid am I to think I could tell him that I was leaving him, and he would simply set me free. "I'm leaving you." "Oh. OK. That's fine, here let me get the door for you, do you need a hand?" As if! What the hell was I thinking?

It had taken me so long to find the strength to pack my bags – a whole year after going back to him that night. A year in which we carried on as if nothing had happened, again.

A year in which we moved out of our flat and into his friend's house so we could save up money to go travel somewhere again. We had Canada in mind.

A year in which he hurled a frozen leg of lamb at me across the kitchen in another momentary lapse of reason, hitting me on the shoulder. I stood still. Like taking a bullet.

A year in which I discovered he had drained our travel fund account to buy and sell hash. How could I not have known?

And a year in which the frightened child inside my belly slowly began to unfurl herself, until she could stand tall and begin to embody me. Together we would set me free.

Today seemed like a good day to walk away. It's a Sunday, he would go to the pub at lunchtime with his friends, I would stay at home and pack. I would then wait for him to come home and I'd tell him I was leaving because that's the decent thing to do, right? That's what brave, grown-up people do.

But what I hadn't anticipated was that he wouldn't let me go. How naïve. But that's what I do because that's what I do – I ask to be set free by my gatekeeper, and I assume that they will unlock the door and let me pass.

Instead of letting me go, he has emptied my bags. My bags in which, along with my clothes, I had dared to pack the fragments of my strength, my self-esteem, my future hopes, and my frightened little girl. Now she lies amongst my clothes like a rejected rag doll in an unfathomable heap in the middle of our room. Everything I had spent hours painstakingly packing, blown apart and destroyed in less than a minute.

Now, he stands at our bedroom door, his arms outstretched, blocking my planned point of escape.

He is strong.

I am weak.

"No. You're not going anywhere. I'm not letting you. I can't."

His words fill the whole doorframe.

My legs go from under me.

I fall to the floor and curl up in a ball.

He leaves the room.

I crawl into our bed.

———————

When I get up out of that bed, 10 days later, it will be when he has just left for work for the day. It will be when I re-pack my bags and every last ounce of me – past, present, and future. It will be when I don't even leave a note this time. It will be when I get in my car and drive to my mum's and don't look back.

Whatever you do: Don't. Look. Back.

Later, when he gets home from work and finds me gone, I will get a phone call.

"I always knew you would leave me one day. I just had to try to hold on to you for as long as possible."

WHY???

I never see him again.

I have escaped.

And I know one thing for sure, every cell of my body shouts at me: You will NEVER let this happen again!

Scene Twenty – Trapped

I am 22 years old and have a morbid fascination with books about imprisonment. I am lost in a world of capture, conflict, torture, solitude, suffering, and eventual release. I read John McCarthy and Jill Morrel's 'Some Other Rainbow', Terry Waite's 'Taken on Trust', and Brian Keenan's 'An Evil Cradling'. I'm not really the typical demographic for these books, I mean, why would a young girl be interested in middle-aged men being taken hostage in the Middle East? But I am. They do something to me. They speak to me in a way that Jackie Collins or Danielle Steele never can.

They reach a part of my soul that is desperately trying to be heard:

"I know how it is to be trapped, to be suffering."

And I think I am unconsciously trying to find stories of entrapment that are far greater than mine so that I negate my own story, so that I can put it in perspective:

"Oh, that? That's nothing compared to this. You don't even need to think about that."

I am a rubber band ball of internalised conflict.

It doesn't matter/it DOES matter.

I don't care/I DO care.

I don't need anyone/I NEED YOU.

And somewhere...a voice..."their story is my story is your story."

Two girls from England have been arrested for drug smuggling in Thailand. They have been sent to the notorious Bangkok Hilton prison. I am obsessed with news updates of their story, their impending fate. I feel their fear, their panic, their despair, their helplessness, their loss.

They are a little younger than me.

That could have been me.

That could have been my prison.

I hope their gatekeeper sets them free.

Scene Twenty-One – Control

I am 23 years old and he is 18. *He* is my new boyfriend. *He* is very cute. *He* is sweet and caring. *He* is unassuming and shy and, most importantly, *he* is *completely passive.*

He will do anything for me.

He is *just* what I need.

I am in *total* control.

We met at the hotel where we both work: he works behind the bar, I am in reception. We flirt a lot. I seduce him.

My self-worth rises with each affirmation – I am wanted, I am loved, I am worthy.

And what a bonus, his parents have a villa in Mallorca!

Before too long, I have persuaded him to ask his mum to lend us said villa for the summer, so we can go to Mallorca, stay for a while, find jobs. Yes! I need to get away again and this is my ticket.

Another guy, another ticket, another repeating pattern.

Why couldn't I just go on my own?

Surprisingly, his mum isn't so keen on the idea of losing her just-out-of-college son to an older woman, a 'bad influence'.

Good God, my self-esteem and I are dining out on our long-overdue reunion!

His mum reluctantly agrees to loan us the villa for 3 weeks. That'll do, I'll take that! Once again, my notice is given at work and my bags are packed.

I'm back in the sunshine, I'm back in flip-flops, things are looking up – for me, but not for him. By the time our 3 weeks are up, I'm fully committed to staying, he's homesick and wants to leave. And I realise that's exactly what I want too, for me to stay and for him to go. So that's what happens. Like I say, he will do anything for me.

Oh, I didn't mean to use you, really I didn't. I just needed help to get back to myself. To feel strong again. So thank you so much for all you have done to help me with that, but now I need to be free and you deserve more.

Now I don't need to hold back anymore, now I can stop pretending that I wasn't sure either so as to conceal the gap between us. No more pretending. I'm just going to be myself...whoever the fuck that is.

I find an apartment. I find not one but two jobs: a few days a week I pull pints of Guinness in an Irish Pub, and on the other days I meet tourists from the airport and sit with them on the bus that drops them off at their various hotels around the island. I make friends, I party hard. For the next few months, I am happy, really happy.

So maybe I should have just left it that way, carried on being with myself, by myself. Maybe I should have resisted him. But, oh, who could resist! They're practically queuing up for him at the bar where he plays guitar and sings in a tribute band every night. Like an excited teenager looking for my next love, I happily join the line.

He looks like Jesus.

He is talented.

He is popular.

He is kind.

He wants me.

Really?

And so it is, for the next 2 years, I pretend that I'm not intimidated by his looks, his talent, his popularity, his kindness. I pretend that I feel worthy of his attention.

So why wasn't this an affirmation? Why didn't I internalise this as "this incredible man wants me...I must be incredible too." Why was it more like "this incredible man wants me...WHY???"

I guess my self-esteem and sense of self hadn't recovered after all. I hadn't nurtured them enough, cultivated them, hung out with them long enough, just the three of us – me, myself and I. I made it all about him, naively believing that if I hung out with him long enough, I could become like him.

I wanted to be *like* him more than I wanted to be *with* him.

Now, after 2 years of us living together in Mallorca, he wants to go back home to Ireland to study. He wants to return to university and then he wants to teach science to school kids. He wants to settle down, he wants a different life, he's ready to be a grown-up.

And me? What do I want?

Oh, don't worry about me. I'm quite happy to just follow you into your new life, so I don't need to look at myself, so I can just keep looking at you. So I'll just tag along if you don't mind?

Turns out he does mind. Turns out he doesn't want someone just tagging along, following him around, vicariously living their life through him. Honestly, some people!

We do try for a little while, I go and stay with him in Dublin, and he asks me one day if I can see myself as the wife of a science teacher. Wife?? I allow myself to entertain the idea but it's like I'm imagining it happening to someone else, I can't connect with it at all. One day I go with him to have all his gorgeous, long, dark hair cut off. He doesn't look like Jesus anymore.

So, between his kindness and my inability to know anything about how I feel, he gently and gradually encourages me to look at myself whilst simultaneously gently and gradually extracting himself from our relationship. He suggests I might be suited to teaching English as a foreign language. I've never heard of TEFL, but it sounds cool, you can travel with it.

I express mild interest. He virtually signs me up for the next course back in England!

Scene Twenty-Two – Confused

I am 26 years old and my dad has been diagnosed with cancer. This is bad timing. Really bad timing – I've just bought myself a one-way ticket to Thailand. My friend and I are planning on travelling from there to Australia, where we're going to find work and stay for a while, potentially a long while, potentially for good. Not that

I'm telling anyone that last bit.

But now this... these words that I don't want to hear. These words that I can't hear but now I can never unhear them.

"I've got cancer."

I literally feel myself disassociate. That familiar sense of a constricting void in my throat, my neck. Not only does it render me voiceless, it also serves to sever my head from the rest of my body, from my heart most importantly, so I can't feel. I can only think.

And what I think is this:

Is he going to be OK? Is he going to die? No, of course he's not going to die, he's just sick, they'll fix him, and he'll be OK, and I can still go travelling and search for myself. God, I really need to do this, I just feel it pulling me, please don't take it away from me. Of course I can't go! How selfish. I must cancel everything and stay here and be with him and watch him get sick. I don't want to watch him get sick. I don't want to see this happening. I can still go and come back if I need to...or...or Fuck, I don't know what to do!

My decapitated head protects me from feeling. It's better that way, or so I think.

"You should still go, and we'll just keep in touch," my dad offers as a telepathic response to my unspoken thoughts.

Is he just in denial too? Does he not want to face the reality of what the doctors have told him? Is he pretending as well? Does he need to pretend in order to survive? Or is he pretending in order to protect me?

"OK," I say.

But it's already spoilt and no amount of anyone's pretending can disguise that.

My bags are heavy this time; my guilty conscience weighs a ton.

My internal conflict, my confusion, my fear, my intrusive thoughts, my frightened little girl, are all coming with me. There's barely room in my backpack for my clothes.

How can I leave and feel free when I am trapped once again?

Oh! I know! I'll pretend.

So I do. I set off with my friend into the big wide world on my next adventure, not knowing if or when I will have to return.

Scene Twenty-Three – Soul

I am 26 years old, it is New Year's Eve 1995, and I'm on a beach near the Krabi coast in Thailand drinking whisky and ducking from stray fireworks. Tomorrow, I will sit and reflect with my journal, as is my compulsory new year's practice. But tonight, tonight is for having fun, tonight is for laughing, tonight is for friends, tonight is for whisky, tonight is for forgetting.

1995 has been quite a year for me. Since things ended with Jesus and TEFL came into my life, I feel like I've come into my own a bit more (hurray!), I've met some likeminded wanderlusting souls, had a lot of fun, earnt some good money, and spent 4 months enjoying myself in Tenerife, shacked up with yet another guy (well, I needed somewhere to stay, and I don't think he minded having a roomy).

I'm beginning to find a sense of direction, a sense of purpose.

Turns out I'm quite a good teacher even if my imposter syndrome sits in silent condemnation at the back of the classroom in each of my lessons. But it's feeding my desire to travel more, to explore the world, and to hopefully meet myself somewhere along the way.

'95 has been a busy year for relationships too, each one a repetition of me either quickly losing interest if he was just simply plain nice to me (Mr Tenerife), or me getting caught up in the challenge of persuading him to be with me if he was ambivalent.

Oh yes, there have been lots of ambivalent ones – "I want you but...I can't commit", "I want you but...I have a girlfriend", "I want you but...I need to be free."

Each one a perfect match for my own ambivalence – "Please, love me...I can't get trapped" – and, simultaneously, a chance to re-enforce my core belief of "I'm not good enough."

Having pushed all of that under the surface, though (as I would thoroughly recommend doing), it's been the Summer of Love! There have been lots of long hot days spent on the beach, there have been lots of parties, I've drank a lot, I've been stoned a lot, and I've had a fair amount of no-strings-attached sex – of course, the perfect solution to my internal conflict!

I've been aware of a growing sense of independence and a growing sense of self. Through the people I've been meeting, I've begun to have interesting conversations, begun to look deeper into things, into myself, into my spirituality. I've read 'Conversations with God' and 'The Celestine Prophecy', and both have had a profound impact on me. I've tuned into the frequency of 'coincidences', to the law of attraction, to energetic vibration.

I've begun to get curious and, like suddenly finding my holy grail, I can't get enough.

I've lit a match and held it at the entrance of my soul, and she's shot off like a bloody firework, cascading into a million multicoloured stars out into the universe and beyond.

So, by the time I met Alexia in the language school where we were both working, and we started talking over the photocopier one day about a shared love of travelling, I knew I had met a kindred spirit. We quickly hatched a plan to get some money together and bugger off.

But how do I map these two things together now – the trajectory I am on for my journey of self-discovery, to get far away and put distance from all that has ever defined me, while at home my dad is dying from cancer? How can I follow my excited pumping heart out into the world *and* be with the monstrous fear of what's happening to my dad?

These two things are just not a good fit.

So, I roll up the monstrous fear inside my mosquito net and squish it down into the crevices of my backpack and focus on my trip of a lifetime, ignoring the voices in my head.

———————

I am sitting next to a guy on a minibus travelling across the Thai/Malay border. I feel incredibly self-conscious. The energy between us is hard to ignore and when my leg brushes against his, electric currents shoot through my body.

Whoa! Did he feel that too?

I sense he is as self-conscious as I am. We both do a good job of playing it cool.

We soon all start chatting – me, Alexia, him, and his friend.

They're from Sweden. Sun-bleached hair, mahogany tanned, wearing tie-dye trousers and toe rings, the classic traveller vibe. They're also heading to Indonesia. Well now, what a lovely 'coincidence'!

The next day in Malaysia, as Alexia and I are walking through town, we spot them sitting at a roadside cafe. They spot us too.

Them: "Hey."

Us: "Hi."

Them: "How's it going?"

Us: "Great. We just booked our ferry tickets for tomorrow."

Them: "We too!"

Us: "Cool. We'll be going together then."

Them: "What are you doing now? You wanna hang out? Go to the tower? Be tourists for a day?"

Us: "Sure, why not."

He and I are still self-conscious and still playing it cool.

Up in the sightseeing tower, we're messing around, acting like kids, and taking silly pictures with the disposable cameras that we bought with the five-dollar gift tokens we were given with our entry tickets.

This is exactly what I need. They are the perfect distraction for me.

Are he and I flirting? It's hard to tell.

Is his friend flirting with my friend? Oh, without a doubt!

They invite us to meet them for drinks later at the 'Bob Marley Reggae Bar'. There are more stupid jokes, more laughs and more flirting – overtly (his friend and Alexia) and covertly (him and I). These are all more welcome distractions from the shit I don't want to think about.

We've all had a few whiskies and head to our separate hostels at the end of the night, looking forward to meeting up the next morning on the boat to Medan.

We are slightly less self-conscious but still playing it cool.

———

Three weeks later, he and I are on one of our daily walks around Lake Toba in Sumatra. Water buffalo plough the surrounding paddy fields; the lush Indonesian countryside is all around. It's just the two of us. We've come to like it that way. These walks are a chance for us to connect. We walk and we talk. He opens up to me about stuff he's never told anyone, like how he doesn't really know who he is or what he wants, how self-conscious he feels all the time. I listen; I think I help him to understand himself better. I think I've had some experience in the not-knowing-who-I-am department.

I love our walks and my feelings have really grown for him over the past few weeks. We've bonded over spending a week with orangutans in the jungle, climbing an active volcano, surviving near-death experiences whilst rubber tubing down the river rapids, taking several shit-your-pants bus rides, drinking uncountable bottles of whisky, playing cards and singing songs until the early hours, laughing a lot – a hell of a lot.

He and I have shared a couple of drunken kisses too, but nothing more. Strangely for me, I haven't wanted it to go further, not because I don't fancy him but because I don't want to follow my usual pattern of always shagging someone I'm remotely interested in. I'd already done that in Thailand with a super-skinny Kiwi guy I met, we had a great connection too, but it somehow feels different with this Swedish Viking. I like him, I like the way things are between us and our combined energy, and I like how I feel when I'm around him. I don't want to spoil that.

The nature of travelling is that you keep moving on, however, and tomorrow we will head our separate ways. The Vikings have been on the road for 6 months and have come to the end of their budget and the end of their trip. They are homeward bound. Fortunately, Alexia and I are not. We're moving on to Nias, another Indonesian island. I'm still heading south, I'm still determined to get as far as I can.

I've had regular contact with my sister in the 6 weeks I've been away and have spoken to dad a few times too. The last time he asked me when I was coming home.

Fuck, I hate this fucking situation!

But I don't want to think about that now. Now I want to make the most of the last hours hanging out with The Viking. We only have one more night to spend together. There's been a lot of bed swapping going on, due to his friend and Alexia hooking up together (it was inevitable), and something tells me that will happen again tonight.

We spend the night curled up together, nothing more, nothing less. It's perfect.

The water taxi arrives to take Alexia and me to our next destination. We're both hungover, sleep-deprived and emotional as we climb on board, waving madly to our two Swedish travel companions. As the boat begins to pull away, they both turn around and drop their pants! The last thing we see is their gleaming white bums fading into the picturesque distance.

There's a bad vibe in the air.

The overnight boat ride here was the most terrifying transportation to date. The wind whipped up a storm; our vessel didn't look seaworthy when it was tied to the dock let alone when it was set loose into the churning Indian Ocean under a pitch-black sky. But at some point during the night, between a life-risking squat over the edge of the boat for a desperate wee, and swaying like pendulums, spooned up on the floor of the hull with the 30 or so other passengers, I transcended terror and found myself in some kind of strangely peaceful, resigned acceptance – tonight I will die. Well, that would be one way of avoiding it all.

There are times in life when you know you're in the right place at the right time, things unfold with ease, joyful synchronicities show up in your path, there is a positive energy, inside and out.

There is increasing evidence that now is not one of those times.

A few nights ago I was chased down the beach by security guards after me and an American guy we've met here had snuck into a hotel swimming pool and gone skinny-dipping. The lure of the 'Hotel Round the Corner' (so coined by us following the locals' misinterpretation of the Eagles classic 'Hotel California') was too great to resist. Its fancy outdoor pool overlooking the ocean was beckoning us in for a cool dip, we planned to go after dark, when we could climb over the railings unnoticed.

Let's just say, being chased down the beach in the middle of the night by angry security guards is one thing, being chased down the beach by angry security guards when you're stark bollock naked, is another. We didn't have time to dress before they were shining torches in our direction and heading our way. We just managed to clamber out of the pool, grab our little pile of clothes, and run like hell.

The four guards quickly caught up with us, but my American friend held them off long enough for me to climb into my yellow fisherman pants and blue vest top. It seemed they saw the opportunity to earn a dollar and just wanted to fine us for trespassing, but I really didn't feel safe. We didn't have any money on us and the outcome could have gone either way. Thankfully, my American friend managed to convince them to let it go – he was my hero. I climbed into bed feeling like I'd had a very lucky escape.

The next day, Alexia came back from a beach walk, unusually flustered and saying she had been hassled by security guards telling her she owed them money. She didn't know anything about my previous night's escapade, having left before I'd got up, but not before climbing into my yellow fisherman pants and blue vest top.

Then last night I had a pretty bad allergic reaction to a chocolate bar that obviously had nuts in – I have a serious nut allergy and

I'm normally so careful. As I stood on the veranda of our beachside hut, drinking gallons of water and trying to stay calm, I threw up all over the feet of my skinny-dipping accomplice who had been kindly rubbing my back and reassuring me it would be OK. Even with chocolate-coloured chunks of my regurgitated veggie noodles between his toes, he continued to kindly rub my back and reassure me it would be OK. Meanwhile, I was having visions of being carted off to the nearest hospital in the back of a chicken truck. Is there even a hospital on this island?

Bottom line is I feel vulnerable and I'm beginning to feel like I am in the wrong place at the wrong time. Because, deep down, I know I am avoiding, I am pretending, and the universe can see right through me.

But still, I don't face it. Even when my last phone call with my sister suggested that Dad had deteriorated so much that it might be time for me to think about coming back.

No. Still I need to bleed every last drop.

So Alexia and I spend 4 days on a boat getting to Jakarta and then we make a decision to take a flight to Bali. We had vowed to only travel by land or sea on this trip, but the luxury of time is no longer my travel companion, and if this is the quickest way I can get as far as possible, then so be it.

But, unsurprisingly, the bad vibes have travelled with us. We've only been in Bali for 24 hours when I get back to our hotel after a night out and there are two messages waiting for me...

Alexia has been robbed, and I need to call my sister.

My time is up.

Two months after I was last here, I'm back in Bangkok. But this time I'm not the wide-eyed excited traveller setting out on the adventure of a lifetime with her friend. This time I am a scared, resistant, emotional wreck, and I am alone. But as I wander down the Koh San Road, I hear someone call my name:

Him: "Vikki?"

Me: "Oh My God!! What the hell?"

Seriously, what the hell??

Him: "Why are you here? Where's Alexia? I thought you were going to Bali? Are you OK?"

OK? Who? Me? Oh yes, I'm fine, totally and absofuckinglutely fine!

Me: "Not really. I've got to go home, my dad, you know. Alexia is carrying on to Australia, we made it to Bali together then I said goodbye to her there. I couldn't re-arrange my flight for another 2 days so I'm here until then."

Him: "Oh shit, man, I'm so sorry."

Me: "Yeah, me too."

Oh God, me fucking too.

Him: "Hey come on, let's go for a drink. I'm here for a few days, we can hang out, it'll be OK."

Me: "Yes, please."

Oh, thank you, universe.

Who is it? Only the guy who protected me from angry security guards when we were running naked down the beach together. Only the guy who rubbed my back and kept me calm whilst I was puking up all over his feet during my nut reaction. Now he shows up here to take care of me in my hour of need.

I think that's what you call a guardian angel.

But little did I know the biggest shock was yet to come.

Another day, another trip down the Koh San Road. My Guardian Angel and I amalgamate into the crowds of travellers who bulge out of every café, market stall, and street food stand. It's a backpackers' haven of magical chaos. But wait...through the crowd, there, heading in our direction, I can make out two familiar figures, two tall, skinny, tanned, sun-bleached-haired guys in tie-dye trousers.

Oh my fucking God, it's The Viking!

I am already unravelling. I don't think I can take much more!

Him: "Oh My God!"

He looks as stunned as I am. But he has a huge smile on his face.

Me: " I can't believe it! I thought you were back in Sweden."

Still gorgeous, still the connection.

Him: "We're just on our way. We take the bus to the airport in an hour."

Me: "I can't believe it!"

Really. I can't believe it!

Him: "I know. This is crazy."

He glances towards Guardian Angel. Do I detect a hint of jealousy? I introduce them all. I hope he doesn't think we're together-together.

Him: "Are you OK?"

Me: "Not really. Where are you going now? Maybe we can grab a beer somewhere before you leave? I'll tell you all about it."

Things like this don't happen for no reason and if he and I have 1 hour left in the same city in the world, then I want us to spend it together.

This time it's even harder to say goodbye.

We hug.

"I'll write," he says. "Me too," I say.

But what I really want is for the world to stop turning. For him to scoop me up and transport me to another time-space reality, and to protect me from all that is to come.

Oh, rescue me, please!

But I also know these synchronicities are telling me something: I'm on the right track. I found my way to the right place at the right time.

I'm doing the right thing.

My dad needs me, and I need to go home.

Scene Twenty-Four – Going, going, gone

I am 27 years old and watching my dad die. Or maybe I'm waiting for him to die. Can I even think that? I arrived home in February, it's now May. Why isn't it over yet? Every day I throw up what little food I'm eating. Every night I smoke a joint in bed, listening to Pink Floyd. It's the only way I can sleep.

The food throwing-up thing is something I started to do in Bali. Rejecting the farewell pizza that Alexia and I shared on the last night of our trip together meant rejecting the circumstances under which I was eating it.

Since I've been home, watching my ejected food chunder into the toilet bowl has become a more frequent event, along with restricting what I eat. Sometimes I only eat one bowl of cereal a day, and I still throw that up. The milk that was cold and fresh on the way down is positively warm and sour on the way up, and it sets my throat alight. But at least the taste of acid overrides the taste of impending death.

I am a mess.

To add to this hideous situation, like some weird fucked-up replay, I am living back in the flat that I shared with that boyfriend, the one who made my life hell, the one who it took me 2 years to escape from, The Psycho – you remember, right? I know I do.

But I'm trying my best to forget. Trying to forget that I am sleeping back in the bedroom where he attacked me, looking at the wall that he put a fist-shaped hole in, cooking in the kitchen with the flying frozen leg of lamb, sitting in the lounge of a million shattered pieces.

You see, when The Psycho and I moved out, my dad moved in. He and my step-mum were separated at the time – one of the many times in their 'can't live together; can't live apart', fractious and volatile relationship. Once he started dying though, he moved into her home so she could care for him.

For some reason, he kept the flat on – was that for him or for me? Did he secretly hope he was going to get better and be able to live alone again, or was it all part of his departure plan, knowing I would have to come back and need somewhere to live whilst I watched him die?

Either way, it seems like a better option than living with my mum while I go through this, she's not exactly oozing compassion and sympathy toward him, or to me for that matter.

Maybe, somehow, now I can reclaim this space. Re-write the story, change the associations I have with this nice little one-bedroom flat just on the outskirts of town. Except I'm finding there is no escaping, it is still the address of the living nightmare, it's just that the nightmare is different now.

And as if I'm not already going through enough, I've also got something going on down below! I have blisters breaking out all over my fanny. I have incredibly sharp nerve pain down the backs of my legs. I can barely sit down, and it hurts when I wipe myself after doing a wee. I am swollen, sore, and I don't know what the fuck it is. I can't even begin to think how to deal with this too. The overwhelm, coupled with the massive shame and stigma of having obviously caught an STD of some kind, mean I push my sore fanny into my box (so to speak) along with all the other unspeakable things that fester and blister there.

I go to work.

I smile.

I pretend I'm OK.

I pretend that witnessing your dad wasting away, until he's a barely recognisable yellowish skeleton of the man he once was, is a normal everyday occurrence. I pretend that pushing him out in a wheelchair with an oxygen tube up his nose and a blanket over his legs, is the way that he and I have always done coffee. I pretend that him wanting to take me to the jewellers to choose myself a ring to remember him by, is just a regular thing to do on a Wednesday morning.

Inside I am screaming.

But it seems he's pretending it's all quite normal too. He's not acknowledging that he's dying, we're not talking about it. Unless you call him making a joke the other day about apologising for still being here and bringing me back from my trip under false pretences, talking about it?

The cancer-ridden elephant fills every corner of every room.

I have no one showing me the way, you see. I have no role model to help me express my feelings in a healthy way – "this is how you deal with difficult stuff when it shows up; we acknowledge it, we face it, we talk about it." No way! We deny, we avoid, we leave the unspeakable unspoken.

I have also learnt, since I've been back, that my dad had known about his diagnosis for some months before I did. He only told me because I'd booked my flight to Thailand; I'd unknowingly forced his hand.

When the fuck would you have told me then?

I've also learnt that the operation he had around five years ago to remove a grapefruit-sized growth on his spinal cord, was the beginning of his cancer. I knew nothing of this at the time, believing, as I was told, that it was no big deal, and it was all fine now.

Did you keep these things from me to protect me?

Or to protect yourself?

Is there even a difference?

My mum barely has two words to say about my dad's impending death. It seems there are no feelings there, other than her age-old anger with him for being a lousy husband and father that still rears its engorged head when triggered.

HE'S DYING FOR FUCK'S SAKE!!!

YOU LOVED HIM ONCE!

CAN YOU NOT JUST LET IT GO?

IF NOT FOR YOU, IF NOT FOR HIM, THEN FOR ME!!

And my sister? Well, she has her own family now, a husband and a 1-year-old son. I know she's there for me, but she has her own sanctum of support.

I have no one.

Sure, I have my friends – and they're good friends – but I need their support in other ways. I need them to distract me, to keep me smiling, to meet up with me outside of the parameters of my living-hell compound.

Yes, right now, I need my friends to be the colluders of my avoidance.

No one knows I'm both restricting and throwing up my food.

No one hears my internal scream.

I barely hear it myself.

The Viking and I are still writing to each other. I love receiving his letters, I love writing to him. If I try really hard, I can read between the lines. It's subtle but I think it's there – the odd flirtatious comment, the suggestive remarks – he hints at coming over...

Yes! Come please. I'd love to see you again but know that I am a fucked-up mess right now.

I reciprocate with an equivalent amount of subtlety and holding back. I don't trust myself with anything more right now.

I dream about him sometimes. We're travelling together, having fun, barefoot in warm sand... Does he dream about me too? He is my link to another time. I miss everything about that trip.

But it's getting close now, I think. It's almost 'The End', my dad's finale. He is so weak, his body is shutting down, he is slowly but surely checking out.

Surely, please, surely.

I've just been to see him; no one thinks he will last the night. I've just seen my dad alive (barely) for the last time.

I am resigned and accepting.

I am faintly relieved.

It's over.

———————————

It's 10 a.m. and the phone is ringing. This is it. This will be my step-mum telling me he's gone. I will soon be able to breathe again. I will soon be free.

Me: "Hello?"

Him: "Hi darling, how are you doing?"

NOOOOOOO! You're supposed to be dead! This was supposed to be over! No more. Please, no more.

Me: "I'm fine."

Him: "What are you doing today? Do you want to pop over?"

Me: "OK."

Somehow, he finds the strength to carry on for another few weeks. Somehow, so do I. Then finally, in the early hours of this Sunday morning, after a day spent on the beach with his family... me, my sister, his son-in-law, and his grandson, he quietly slips away.

My dad has taken his last breath and I can breathe once again.

He is gone.

Who will I be now?

Now that there is no one and nothing holding me back. Can I get back to where I was? Get back to *who* I was? Can I go away again, this time with a clear conscience?

I suppose, for the first time in my life, I am properly free.

Where shall I go? Where did I leave myself? Where was I again?

Alexia is back from Australia and she and I talk about going to India. I just need some money. I will work for the summer, save up, and we will head off in September, October at the latest.

I write to The Viking, I tell him all about my dad dying, it feels good to be telling him, for some reason he is the person I want to 'talk' to about how it all happened. I ask him about India as I know he's been there – where to go, where to stay. I hint that he might like to come too, I am feeling a little braver. But when he writes back he tells me he has no money and needs to keep working.

Doesn't he realise I am hinting?

Meanwhile, I need to find somewhere to live and leave this flat behind once and for all. A friend at work tells me her ex-brother-in-law has a spare room, it's just around the corner from work and he's not asking much rent.

Excellent!

I ring the doorbell.

Him: "Hello!"

Oh! He's quite cute. Wasn't expecting that.

Me: "Hi, I'm Vikki, I've come to see the room."

Him: "Oh...yeah sure...come on in."

He seems a bit taken aback too.

Me: "Thanks."

Him: "So, this is the lounge... and upstairs is the room... here... and the bathroom... and then I'll show you the kitchen downstairs."

*Oh, it's all so lovely. I love this room. The whole house is really nice. He's really nice. Oh God, no! That's the last thing I need. Nope, that's **not** gonna happen. I can still move in and that **doesn't** have to happen.*

Me: "It's all lovely. I'll take it."

Him: "Great"

He seems as happy as I am with our new arrangement.

Me: "But it'll probably be just for a few months while I save up some money to go away again."

Him: "That's fine, however long you like."

I spot the guitar on the armchair and the song sheet to Ralph McTell's 'Streets of London' on the table. Dad used to sing that song.

Me: "Do you play?"

Him: "Yep, I do, and sing a bit too."

Just like my dad. I think he would have really liked this guy.

A week later, I am moving in. As I unpack my few belongings into my new room, the sounds of guitar and singing float gently up the staircase. Part of me is transported back to another time...

I am 11 years old and sitting in the games room of a hotel. It's Saturday night and my dad has a gig in the bar. My sister and I are playing pool, eating salt and vinegar crisps, and drinking glasses of lemonade through straws. I can hear my dad singing in the next room.

"...So how can you tell me you're lonely, and say for you that the sun don't shine..."

During his break, he introduces us to a friend, "These are my girls, they've come to live with me." His smile fills the whole room.

"...well let me take you by the hand and lead you through the streets of London, I'll show you something, to make you change your mind..."

It's hard to grieve the loss of my dad when it feels like he's still here.

As I continue to unpack my things, what I don't realise is that I am about to stage the biggest replay yet. One that will change the course of my life completely for decades to come.

ACT TWO
EVOLVING

"Go on adventuring,
changing, opening your mind,
and eyes, refusing to be
stamped and stereotyped."
– Virginia Woolf

ACT TWO
Evolving

Scene One – Rebirth

"Birth and death are not two different states,
but they are different aspects of the same state."

– Mahatma Ghandi

I've just had a baby.

Yeah, yeah, that's right, with the guy that nothing was gonna happen with, my landlord, but you knew that, right? You probably knew it before I did.

Thing is, I've been completely disassociated, and don't tell anyone but, I've been pretending again. Pretending that I'm fine! I'm cool! Shit, I've been pretending so well I've even convinced myself this time. Good job, girl!

I pretended that I didn't have a care in the world when I set about flirting with my landlord. He was pretty smitten, it didn't take much, and it didn't take long. Somewhere within the 2 months it took for me to stop paying rent, we took a trip to Ireland for a week and I came back pregnant.

A little bean incubating inside me, something to keep my frightened little girl company. She's just lost her dad, she's watched him vanish, like in a puff of smoke – Puff, no more! There one

85

minute, gone the next! "And for my next trick, ladies and gentlemen...drum roll please...I shall make myself disappear without a trace!"

And she hasn't got the first clue how to deal with that.

So she and I both fell back into what we do know, because that's what we all do – in the absence of knowing what to do, we will always unconsciously default back to our habitual patterns.

I hid in the false confidence of my sexuality.

I became sexy Vik.

I became cool Vik.

I became good-time Vik.

I became funny Vik.

But inside, Vik wasn't laughing. Because there was nothing funny going on at all.

At least I have stopped throwing my food up and getting stoned, so things are looking up. I even managed to take myself (in secret, of course) to the GUM clinic to get checked out. I suspect I have herpes and I suspect I know who gave it to me: the super-skinny Kiwi in Thailand, he was the only guy I slept with the whole trip (thank God I didn't shag The Viking). But the clinic tells me they can't test for anything unless I currently have symptoms – which I don't – and that I should come back when they re-appear – which I also don't. I've been a bit pre-occupied with ushering my grief through the nearest exit sign, germinating a baby, and maintaining my usual impeccably high standard of rebuffing the slightest sense of awareness. Oh, and the shame, yes, let's not forget about the punitive oozing shame.

Now this. This beautiful incredible little thing that I have just squeezed out of me. I hope he hasn't been too infused by my pretence while he's been cooking in my tummy for the past 9 months. Marinating in my fucked-up amniotic cocktail of stress, denial, fear, and suppressed grief.

I'll do my best to love it out of you, to cradle you clean.

And I'm sorry for what might come, because in my heart I know this relationship isn't right. I know sooner or later I will have to leave him. Not you – I'll never leave you. But I know I can't stay with him, I can't be myself, whoever the fuck that is, but somehow, I know it isn't this and I know the suppression will feast on me limb by limb if I don't free myself. But not yet baby, don't worry, not yet. Let's try, let's see how it goes for a while at least.

You've chosen this, right? You've chosen this life experience? These parents? This is your karma. It's not all on me. Please, it can't all be on me.

It's been 12 months and 2 weeks since my dad died. I've been pregnant for three-quarters of that time.

My dad has died and my son has been born in 1 year.

What happens when we become a parent for the first time?

What happens when we lose a parent for the first time?

What happens when we lose a parent *and* become a parent at the same time?

What happens when a daughter loses her father and gives birth to a son at the same time?

These things change you to the core. I suspect it helps a lot if you are connected to your core at the time, if you have a fractional sense of who you are. If not, then good luck with that!

Sure, you have a baby with someone you hardly know, while you are still trying to figure out who you are and process the trauma of watching your dad die.

I think I might be in shock.

As my dad exited stage left, his understudy entered stage right.

"In tonight's performance, and for the rest of the run, ladies and gentlemen, due to his untimely and unfortunate death, the role of father will be played by the understudy."

In birthing a son with Understudy, I have doubled the number of males in my family. I never knew either of my grandfathers and my dad was an only child. So, before his untimely and unfortunate death, my dad had been the only male member of my family I had known. There have never been any other male role models to show me the way, to show me what it is to be a man, a husband, a father, a son. To demonstrate how a man relates to a woman, how a husband relates to his wife, how a father relates to his child, how a son relates to his parents. It's all been on my dad and, through no fault of his own, it turns out he wasn't perhaps the best man for the job.

Which means I'm not sure if how Understudy is relating to me is OK. He's kind and caring and sensitive on the one hand...but there are always two hands, right? And in his other one he covertly holds cards of judgement, disrespect, and criticism. The expert croupier, he deals them out unexpectedly and swiftly, like paper darts flying through the air.

He treats me like a naughty child.

He is my critical parent.

The resemblance between Understudy and father is, at times, uncanny. Perfect casting.

Oh, I'm doing this for you, dad, to make you proud. Look what I can do...I can find a nice guy, someone like you, and settle down and have a baby, see? Look how normal I am, I can do normal, I can be this girl, the daughter that you wanted me to be. I know this will make you happy. I'm not too late, am I?

So I carry on playing house...mummy, daddy, baby.

What else should I do?

I had a brief moment to get back to my tour of self-investigation, but I didn't take it because I couldn't see the road. My vision was blurred through my loss and grief-steamed glasses and instead of reversing back to where I'd left myself, I slipped into first gear, put my foot to the floor, and drove straight into a brick wall.

And I know that I will have to scale that wall at some point to get over the other side, but not right now, I don't have the strength. It takes a lot to scale a wall, especially with a baby perched on your hip and a backpack bulging with bereavement.

No, this will take some time and I can't even think about it right now, what with the constant cycle of feeding, changing, not sleeping.

Oh, the not sleeping. Why won't you sleep, baby?

Why are you always crying?

What's wrong?

What are you trying to tell me?

Are you crying for both of us?

Scene Two – Baby

"Problems do not go away. They must be worked through or else they remain, forever a barrier to the growth and development of the spirit."

– M. Scott Peck

I am squeezing milk out of my lactating breasts into the sink in the bathroom at the hospital. I have done this in tears. I have done this with an overwhelming sense of wrongness and loss. The loss of the ability to feed my second baby. I am unable to nurture him, to give him life. He lies in a hospital cot with tubes up his nose; he weighs 2lbs less than he did when he was born 10 weeks ago. He is a sorry sight, his miniature body. Lifting him is like picking up a bag of crisps.

For 10 weeks I've been desperately trying to feed him, getting him to latch on, trying every which way of holding him, every which pillow combination on my lap to support his tiny head and get just that right angle which would mean we would have a successful feed. I've been to breastfeeding support groups, I've been to cranial osteopaths, I've been to allergy specialists. I've cried, I've felt inadequate, defeated and beyond despair.

I've still had a 2-year-old to look after. A 2-year-old who's still not sleeping properly.

A non-sleeper and now a non-feeder.

What are my boys trying to tell me?

I am a sleep-deprived zombie of stress. I am barely holding it together. Understudy and I take it in turns to sleep at the hospital each night. We alternate between each having a night at home with boy number one and a night at the hospital with boy number two. My life consists of playgroups, shopping, cooking, washing, and now squeezing my tits over the hospital sink.

They've told me I can't feed him; they think he's allergic to my milk. Even though I stopped eating everything he might be allergic to, apparently it doesn't matter, he's hypersensitive and the only way to feed him is with special milk through a tube.

They may as well have said he's allergic to me.

Hypersensitive? What the fuck was he marinating in?

And due to our new routine, Understudy and I are barely functioning as a couple. We're supporting each other practically but not emotionally. Have we ever done? Who are 'we' anyway?

The truth is there is no *us* beyond *them*.

We are just co-parents existing together – he gets up early and goes to work, I get up early and am a mum, he gets home and is a dad. And he's a good dad, and I'm a good mum, but there is no us. There never was, of course, which is why now when the going's got tough – the time when a couple really needs to fall back on the solidity of their relationship with each other to get them through – there is no relationship to fall back on. Turns out that 8 weeks of flirting and having sex wasn't really enough to build a strong foundation for a lasting and healthy relationship to see us through the swamp of gruelling family life.

So I become more mum, he becomes more dad, the separation grows and each day another brick is added to the wall.

Our baby stays in hospital for one month, by the time he comes home, my milk has long gone.

But it's not over yet. He has also developed eczema so severely he has to be wet-wrapped from head to toe in minuscule bandages that need changing three times a day. As the clock strikes midnight on millennium eve, and the rest of the world parties on, I am at home reapplying soggy bandages and slippery ointment.

There are more hospital referrals and more investigations to be done. Apparently, a liver biopsy is required, a bone marrow sample too. Really? We're not sure about that at all, it doesn't add up. But what can we do? The unimaginable 'what if' rings so loud in our ears that it decides for us.

I hold him down on the hospital table while somebody drills into his tiny little leg, and while somebody takes the biggest needle I've ever seen and prods it into his defenceless body.

His scream reverberates around my blood like a million electric shocks. I am complicit in his trauma. I am robotically calm, I attempt to soothe him with my words, my anaesthetised touch.

On the inside, I am screaming too.

No! Get off him!! Leave him alone! He doesn't need this!! It's not right. My poor darling boy.

As we had suspected, they find nothing, so they eventually leave us alone and he gradually starts to get stronger, and by some miracle, after the biopsy, his eczema disappears overnight. I am convinced he has shocked himself out of it.

Although he's eating now, it only takes a cough or a sneeze or a laugh for him to churn up the entire contents of his stomach and expel them out through his smiley little mouth. This can happen anytime and anywhere. Neither the washing machine nor I can keep up with this joyful little 10lb vomiting machine.

It is a continual cycle of dressing, feeding, changing, washing, drying, dressing, feeding, changing, washing, drying, dressing, feeding...you get the picture.

I still have a 2-year-old to look after.

I still have a dead father to grieve.

I guess that will have to wait.

Scene Three – Truth

"Only the wounded healer can truly heal."

– Irvin D. Yalom

"This course will change your life!" The head of the counselling training school that I've just signed up to proclaims in his welcome speech.

Well, let's fucking hope so!

All I know right now is that I need *something*. I'm not sure if just being a mum is too much for me or not enough for me. Could it even be both?

Unconsciously, I think I know I need to look at myself, know myself better, and have the courage to face up to what I might find. I need something that will flush out my truth, so it erupts to the surface like an underwater bomb and demands to be seen and heard for what it is. Then maybe I can gather up those pieces of truth, stitch them together into a cloak and wear it. This super hero cloak will then enable me to do what I need to do.

We are given our first assignment: "Write the significant events of your life in 5-year segments."

OK, 0–5, that's easy – I don't remember shit.

Then 5–10, 10–15, 15–20, 20–25, 25–30, well, you know all that now. It's an interesting process. I remember things I thought I'd forgotten, I slowly begin to look at my life, my childhood, my relationships...and as the contents of my life begin to take shape and form, I too begin to take shape and form.

I feel like I belong here, with this diverse bunch of fellow navel-gazing soul-searchers. You would never put us together in a million years, yet here we are, our tribe of seven, getting emotionally undressed in front of each other and swimming in each other's blood, sweat and tears every Wednesday. I safely float in a paradox of being myself and discovering who I am.

As well as our assignment, we are required to journal daily, something I have gotten out of the habit of doing since boy number one and boy number two came along, but something I am glad to have permission to get back into. So much has changed for me in such a short time, maybe journaling will help me to process some of it.

Another thing that's changed is The Viking and I don't write anymore. We were still sending each other letters right up until I wrote and told him I was pregnant. I didn't get a reply. I then sent him a photo of me with boy number one when he was a baby, but again, no reply.

I guess he's moved on, I guess I have too.

I miss his letters, occasionally, I still dream about him.

He is still my link to a parallel universe.

Understudy is a curious mix: vaguely supportive and vaguely patronising of my counselling course. It feels like he doesn't take it seriously, doesn't take me seriously. It's like he's letting me 'get it out of my system' and 'allowing' me to do it. I need to be more independent. I want to find a part-time job, I'm sure I can make the childcare work for those times and that way I can pay for my own training. I need to break away from this bloody parent-child dynamic.

I've virtually been financially independent since I was 14 and got a job in a newsagents, just before I went back to live with my mum. (I eventually got fired because I was caught stealing the damaged packets of cigarettes from the back room, which I would share out amongst my friends at school.) Since then, if I wanted to buy anything, I bought it myself. So these past few years have been edgy for me: not earning my own money, feeling like I need to ask if I want something, and being given a weekly allowance for the food shopping like daddy giving a little girl her pocket money.

I am walking around town, job hunting. As I approach the bottom of the hill, I can't help but notice the drop-dead gorgeous guy that steps out of the Levi's shop. He is standing outside chatting to someone, it seems like he works in the shop. Now if only they were looking for staff!

I walk past, feeling self-conscious, half convincing myself he will notice me too and half already convinced that he won't. I spend another hour or two unsuccessfully scouring the town for potential jobs.

Then, as I make my way back to the car, up the hill with the Levi's shop where the drop-dead gorgeous guy works... I can't believe it! A large white piece of card has appeared, taped to the inside of the window: STAFF WANTED. APPLY WITHIN.

Thank you, universe. Oh, how I've missed you!

For some reason, I feel the need to lie about my age when they ask me to bring my CV in the next day. I quickly sussed that the average age of the girls working here must be 17 and both of the managers (drop-dead gorgeous guy being one of them) are only in their mid-20s.

At 32, I am ancient.

I tell them I'm 27.

Interesting. Of all the ages I could pick, I pick that one, the age I was when my dad died, and the course of my life changed. Whilst the rest of my body moved on, my heart stayed 27.

I get the job and when I later tell them how old I really am, I am teased about it endlessly.

I should've just stayed 27.

The drop-dead gorgeous boss is fast becoming the object of my affections, I am obsessing and fantasising over him endlessly. But I suspect he has something going on with at least a couple of the young girls here, and – although it appears I have forgotten – I am practically married and a mother of two young boys.

What the hell am I thinking??

The relationship between me and Understudy is hanging by a thread. The only thing that keeps us together is the shared love of our boys. There has been no physical contact between us for a long time. I honestly can't bear the idea of it and keep rigidly to my side of the bed.

This is what we have become.

I remember when I found out I was pregnant with boy number one, I was really scared, I knew the relationship wasn't right, but I also wanted this baby. I remember crouching down on the upstairs landing, eavesdropping on a conversation between Understudy and Alexia (who was back from Australia and staying with us for the weekend). He was telling her about how all the issues in the relationship lay with me, he didn't know how to get through to me, apparently.

Well, stop treating me like you've rescued me from the gutter and show me some respect! That might be a start!

Thoughts crashed in my head like a motorway pile-up. But somewhere amongst the honking horns, crunching metal and screeching tyres, I saw the junction ahead and knew I had to make a choice: terminate this pregnancy and terminate the relationship, or keep the baby but terminate the relationship, or keep the baby and keep the relationship, or...

And in that moment, sitting huddled on the landing, I knew the road I would take.

I would have this baby and stay in the relationship for now and then I would get out of it later.

I chose that because that's what I had learnt, that was my experience of relationships so far, demonstrated nicely by both of my parents: you get in when you want to and then you get out when you want to.

I had no clue how to have a healthy conversation about the situation we had *both* created, just like when my dad was dying, you just brush it under the carpet and deal with it later. Or not.

Just like when Understudy accuses me – with such disdain – of passing on the unconfirmed STD that I am still in denial about. Such disgust and judgment, he practically spits the words at me, "And what's this? What have you given me? What bastard were you sleeping around with before?" while he presents exhibit A – a few red spots on a penis. I mumble something about not knowing anything about it. I'm not proud of this but I wasn't exactly feeling the conditions that would lead to a healthy, adult, responsible conversation about it.

Nope. I have no clue how to deal with the difficult stuff, and it seems Understudy doesn't either.

It's not surprising then that here we are: me fantasising about other men, him treating me like the shit on his shoe.

I would say we are broken but we were never whole in the first place.

So the next logical step I take? To not just fantasise about other men, but to have an affair.

Yeah, great idea. Of course that's going to help!

Scene Four – Journal

"We are what we pretend to be, so we must
be careful what we pretend to be."

– Kurt Vonnegut

You think it's with the drop-dead gorgeous boss, don't you? Well, it's not. (Well, it will be but that comes a bit later.)

I am at a music festival with a friend. It's mid-afternoon of the second day and we're hanging out in our tent, drinking beer and chatting. I'm vaguely aware of some guys kicking a ball around nearby.

My babies are at home with their father. I'm not sure if this makes me a terrible mother or not. I am ignoring the heart-scraping separation pangs and my inner critic telling me I should be at home. My internalised judgement about being a neglectful mother encases the guilt I feel at leaving them behind for 2 whole days.

So I drink, I watch the bands play, and I do my best to pretend I am someone else.

Now one of the guys has come over to retrieve his ball which has landed just next to our tent.

Him: "Hi, sorry about that."

Oh, he's Scottish, quite fit actually, bit young, but quite fit.

Me: "That's OK, no problem at all."

Him: "Are you having a good time?"

Me: "Yeah, great thanks, you?"

Him: "Yeah, what's your name?"

Me: "Vikki."

Him: "Hi Vikki, nice to meet you."

With a casual kick of the ball, he jogs back to his game.

Hmmm, did something just happen?

Later that night there is no doubt that something has happened. We spot each other through the crowd at the main stage listening to The Strokes. At the end of the night, after consuming many beers and smoking a few joints, me and Fit Festival Guy are spooning together, fully clothed, inside his sleeping bag.

Do I feel guilty? Have I crossed a line?

Yes and yes. But it's OK! Don't worry, I can just push those feelings down. I can assure myself I'm not causing anyone any harm and if this is what I want, if this is what makes me happy in this moment, then why shouldn't I be able to do it? No one needs to know, it's just a weekend thing.

Guess what? It isn't just a weekend thing! Seems we're quite keen on each other. Well, that's putting it mildly, obsession rampages through my every waking moment. We text each other whenever we can, he knows my situation and seems quite happy to go along with it. A couple of weeks later, I fabricate some story about going to visit a friend so I can go and stay with him in London. The sex is as enjoyable as it is inevitable.

I am living a parallel life.

If I didn't know who I was before, then I certainly don't now. I pretend that I am an exuberant teenage girl buzzing around a new relationship, not a messed-up mother of two, lost at sea.

All of this – my infidelities and innermost processes – is being logged in my college journal. The journal that I don't protect under lock and key, the journal that I leave in my bag on the stairs, the journal that I unconsciously want to be found so that all of this can EXPLODE OUT into the open air.

I need this ever-growing Goddam brick wall to blow up into a thousand pieces. It's got too high to scale, instead, maybe I can clamber my way through the debris of dust and devastation and out to the other side.

I need something to GET ME OUT.

By leaving my journal in my bag, I have detonated the bomb.

It's only a matter of time before the explosion comes.

Scene Five – Madness

"That ugly part of your story you're living through right now is gonna be one of the most powerful parts of your testimony."

– Billy Graham

I am standing in the aisle at Waitrose. My head whirls, my heart is about to rocket out of my chest. My breath is barely a suggestion. Every fibre of my being is tense and rigid, consumed with panic that I am being ignored. I thought he had feelings for me. I thought he would at least stand by me if this happened. I thought he'd at least show me some support as a friend, we're in this together kinda thing. But no, he is ghosting me, and I can't fucking bear it.

Why can't I just say "Fuck him"? He's showing his true colours, I should be glad to be rid of him. But it's not even that I want to be with him, it's the fact that he's ignoring me that has sent me into some kind of hysteria. It's like I don't exist, like I'm nothing, and it feels so fucking familiar.

When else have I been ignored? Well, by my dad for a whole month when I was 15, he treated me like I didn't exist. Could it be linked to that? Did I panic then? Or is the panic I'm experiencing now really for that? Like a delayed reaction that has lain dormant until a certain set of conditions conspired together to create the perfect re-enactment – only now can they come to life.

The deep crusted fear that – it's true – I really am not enough.

I know the reason he's ignoring me is because Understudy called him up after reading my journal and looking at my phone. He called him up and warned him off, threatened him with goodness knows what. I didn't hear this from Fit Festival Guy; I haven't heard a word from Fit Festival Guy since our last conversation before the bomb went off. I found this out from Understudy, who told me it with such authority and aggression, asserting his status in this deadly love triangle.

My self-esteem is a dot on the horizon as I blindly chase my panic down the supermarket aisles.

———————————

What the fuck am I doing standing outside the offices in London where Fit Festival Guy works?! My panic has transformed itself into incensed rage and I have become a woman possessed!

I WILL FORCE YOU TO ACKNOWLEDGE MY EXISTENCE!!

I walk around the block and take several deep breaths before my rageful madness propels me through the revolving door.

"Hi, I'm here to see (Fit Festival Guy)."

"Do you have an appointment?"

"No, but if you tell him Vikki is here, he'll know what it's about."

WTF am I thinking?? Stop!! Stop now before you have lost every ounce of dignity!

Too late! I look out across the open-plan office and see him walking toward me with a look of horror on his face, like he's seen a ghost!

Him: "What. Are. You. Doing. Here?"

Me: "Well you won't reply to my messages, what choice did I have?"

Lots of choices. Lots. Like, let it go. Like, talk to someone. Like, do anything to stay SANE!

Him: "I can't talk here. Go to the coffee shop on the corner and I'll meet you there in half an hour."

I go to the coffee shop on the corner. I wait. Half an hour comes and goes. I wait some more. He's not coming, is he.

Thankfully, my dot of self-esteem picks up my shattered ego and damaged inner child, and together we head for the train station.

It's time to go home and start picking through the rubble.

Scene Six – Buggy

"We're all just walking each other home."

– Ram Dass

"Look what the cat's dragged in, boys," Understudy sneers as I walk through the door.

It's 11 a.m. on a Sunday and I've been out all night. Drop Dead Gorgeous Boss has just dropped me home. To be fair, Understudy knew I wouldn't be home. I didn't just stay out all night unexpectedly, I told him I was at a friend's – I suspect he doesn't believe that for a minute.

We are living separate lives.

We are separating.

I am looking for somewhere else for the boys and me to live. Understudy would prefer it if I went to live in a bedsit in the shadiest part of town, on my own, and the boys stay with him. That's not gonna happen, but this will still be their home and they will have a new one with me too.

To be honest though, I do feel like something the cat has dragged in. I am every dirty inch the shameful mother he says I am, and I feel like a teenage girl berated by her father for staying out all night. Except he's not my father, he's the father of my children who look on innocently and welcome me home with open arms. At least they're not judging me, it's just him and just me, that's plenty enough to stoke the disgraced flames of my ever-decreasing sense of worth.

Drop Dead Gorgeous Boss and I have started a very casual thing. Mostly we're friends and I seem to be able to talk to him about what's going on in my life, just the practical stuff like looking for a house, getting furniture, moving out etc. He's quite supportive, maybe he understands, his parents divorced when he was young and the court 'awarded' him to his dad and his brother to his mum. It's fair to say he still has some issues from that nice little family split, and it's fair to say that I am attracted to him because of it. Same old pattern!

I've learnt in my training that 95% of our attraction to someone is unconscious. Only 5% is about liking what we see, common interests, physical attraction. The rest is about recreating what is familiar to us, acting out patterns from our childhood, looking for someone whose shit will be a good match for our shit. It seems we're all just shit-matching machines trying to find our way back home.

Drop Dead Gorgeous Boss and I don't talk about what's happening between us. I don't think either of us really knows. Anyway, I have other things on my mind, I am about to do the hardest thing I have ever had to do so far in my 4 years of being a mother.

I am walking up the road, pushing boy number one in his red and blue buggy. Boy number two is indoors with Understudy. I have to tell him. I know I have to tell him, I've been putting it off for as long as possible. But I don't know how. How do you tell a 4-year-old that you're uprooting him from his home, from his father, from every secure thing that he's known in his little life so far?

My guilt is insatiable.

I am about to change this little boy's life forever, just as my parents did to me. I wonder if anyone sat me down when I was 7 and told me my dad was leaving? No, I think not. So, as much as I want to avoid this, I know I have to tell him. He's only 4 years old but he has a right to know.

I literally can't face him and so I realise this is my moment, whilst I'm behind him, walking up the hill, him sitting in the buggy facing away from me. I know I'm avoiding but it's all I've got.

I'm sorry baby, I wish I was stronger. I wish I was less fucked up. I wish I could sit you down and look you in the eye while I say this, reassure you with my physical presence, but I can't. This is the best I can do and I'm so sorry about it all, but... it's time. It's taken me 4 years (just as it did with leaving my dad and going back to my mum's), 4 years of getting so far lost that I needed to find my way back, 4 years of gathering strength and trying to find out who I am. And I'm still lost, and I still don't know who I am, but I do know that I'm not being the best mum that I can be. If I can't be the best version of myself in this relationship – and there is no doubt in me that I can't – then how can I be the best mum that I can be? And I so want to be a better mum. And right now I am so suppressed that I can't even breathe. I need to set myself free and then I promise you things will be better. I will be better. I will be happier and therefore I trust you will be happier too.

I don't say any of this out loud.

All I can manage is:

"So, tomorrow, you and me and your brother are going to move to another house. You'll still be coming to this house, but you'll have another house too. So one house where you live with me and one house where you live with daddy."

The red and blue buggy is silent except for the squeaks of its wheels as we make our way up the hill, and then:

"OK," he says.

Scene Seven – Learning

"Forget the perfect offering. There is a crack in everything,
that is how the light gets in."

– Leonard Cohen.

I am a single mum. Just as my mum was a single mum and just as my dad was a single dad and just as my Omi was a single mum.

But one pattern I am determined not to repeat is having a hateful relationship with the father of my children. I won't let them grow up in a plate-smashing environment of resentment and bitterness as my sister and I did. It might take some time – that's quite apparent right now – but I will do all I can to work on a healthy co-parenting relationship with Understudy, so that my boys don't go through what I went through, so that they don't turn out like me.

I am learning a lot about patterns on my course. We are taught to ask our clients questions:

"Does that feel familiar at all?"

"What – or who – does that remind you of?"

"Where does that take you back to?"

It seems like we are full of patterns and we don't even know it. We repeat things over and over until we can (if we're lucky) see it for what it is, until we can escape our past, our parents' shit, their parents' shit, their parents' parents' shit…

I have been escaping my whole life.

Only to find myself trapped again.

I am beginning to learn why I do this – to find the familiar, to attempt to still get the unmet needs met.

I am also beginning to learn that there is one little word that I need to change. If I always say "only to *find* myself trapped again" that will never change anything. The 'find' in that belief renders me powerless, a victim to my circumstance: "oh, here I am again, why does this always happen to me? How did this happen again?" A crucial part of the process, I am learning, is to change the 'find' to 'get'. That's all: a simple little word replacement re-frames everything – "only to *get* myself trapped again."

It's a game-changer.

If *I* can see how *I get myself* trapped, then I can start to change it.

For as long as it's something that happens to me, I'm fucked.

I am also learning that everything is about relationship and everything is about loss. Every issue a client presents with will be about loss of some kind, without exception.

Always, whenever there is change there is loss.

The loss of a loved one.

The loss of a marriage.

The loss of a job.

The loss of health.

The loss of identity.

The loss of hope.

And for everything there is a relationship, to other people, things, ourselves, and the different parts of ourselves. Therapy is all about that relationship to ourselves. Everyone else will come and go, every other relationship is transitory, the one with ourselves is permanent. From the moment we're born to the moment we die, it's the only one we have. It's the only one that really counts so isn't it a good idea to make it as good as it can be? Make it the best, healthiest, most fulfilling, loving relationship we have in our lives?

Speaking of my patterns, unbelievably within a couple of months of moving into this new house with the boys, although I have left my job and stopped shagging my boss, I have started shagging my new landlord.

REALLY?? What is WRONG with you??

He's not a live-in landlord. I'm renting through an agency. Turns out there is a family of squirrels living in the attic and one night one manages somehow to find its way into the wall cavity and into my bedroom. If you've ever had a squirrel freaking out in your room at night, frantically throwing itself at the windows, making the most godawful screeching sound, you'll know how terrifying that is. My landlord comes around the next day with the pest control team and the squirrel is 'dealt with' (I don't want to know how). He then fixes the gaps in the fascias, normality is resumed, and somehow, he is my hero. It seems that's all it takes these days.

The fact that he's in the army adds to that sense of seeing him as my protector, a big strong man that can keep me (and my children) safe and fight off any predators (or squirrels).

He represents father.

The warrior.

The provider.

Just as Understudy had when I first met him. Another landlord, another crossing of a boundary. Another entertaining anecdotal drama to distract from the pain of the broken little girl inside.

Squaddie Landlord starts to come around more often, fixing this, fixing that. The appropriate response would have been a thank you, a cup of tea and digestive biscuit, perhaps. But no, I decide to fuck him whilst my boys are at school, in the bed that he used to share with his ex-wife, in the house that he is renting to me.

And I'm training to be a counsellor??!!

Get a fucking grip, girl!!

———————————

Fortunately for me, and any clients I might be let loose on, part of my training is to have 40 hours of personal therapy (I actually end up staying for 3 years, I suspect my therapist feels this is a drop in the ocean, I suspect she's right).

I begin to see that I am not one hundred percent responsible for breaking up my family. The sack of guilt that I drag behind me is weighing me down, I carry it everywhere I go, we are attached, and I can't see any way of losing it.

It must be all my fault, right? I knew what I was doing when I got into it. I chose to have two kids with someone that I didn't have the right relationship with. I wasn't into it. I had an affair. I left. I took his kids away from him, away from their home.

But I start to realise something really important. This sack isn't just full of MY shit, Understudy has slipped HIS shit in it too! Seemingly, when I wasn't looking, so that he doesn't have to carry anything.

My therapist helps me to see that the affair has become a convenient scapegoat for the reason we broke up. Because an affair isn't the *problem* in a relationship, it's the *symptom* of another problem, but this now conveniently seems to prevent Understudy from taking any responsibility for his part in things.

Like the fact that he was *equally* responsible for us getting pregnant in the first place. Like he *chose* to have sex with his young lodger who was in between travels and going through a major bereavement. Like he was already a single dad who had been left by his ex-wife – perhaps he could have been a bit more cautious if he'd wanted to protect himself from the same fate happening again. Like he *too* was responsible for our relationship getting to the point where we were living separate lives, of creating an environment where we couldn't talk about the stuff that we should have been talking about.

Oh yes, it's amazing what a bit of re-framing can do.

Now all I have to do is practice believing it.

I also begin to see my patterns of crossing boundaries with men, sleeping with bosses, landlords, brothers – oh yes, brothers, I forgot to mention that, didn't I? After I thought Drop Dead Gorgeous Boss wasn't interested in me, I decided it would be a good idea to sleep with his younger brother.

Genius!

I think I became a symbol of their mother, loving (or at least shagging) them both, repairing the family split for all of us. Add to that my patterns of allowing men to break my (non-existent) boundaries – my first ever boyfriend, the psycho that I spent 2 years with, and the relentless repetition of saying 'Yes' to sex when really, deep down, I was silently screaming 'No'.

However, my ongoing inclination toward inappropriate sex aside, I am starting to regain my independence and I am starting to feel free once again. My life is beginning to change a little, I have an exciting new career developing as a counsellor, a growing new sense of myself as a mother, I've regained a new sense of my independence, and I'm developing a willingness to break free from a shit load of old patterns. I'm also starting to have fun again thanks to my new neighbour and friend.

Nelly is loud and proud. He is as colourful as he is gay. He is as hilarious as he is unique, and he has a disco glitter ball hanging from a tree in his garden. He will break out into show tunes mid-conversation and will dare to say what everyone else only dares to think. Nelly likes to push the boundaries, perhaps this is why we hit it off immediately, and over the next 10 years, he will become one of my best friends.

He is just what I need, a gay best friend. A guy that I can get close to, open up to, get drunk and stoned with, have a serious conversation with, have a laugh with – all without any chance of us shagging!

He is perfect and he brings sunshine, music and laughter into the lives of me and my boys.

Life is taking on a sense of new beginnings: Squaddie Landlord is selling his house and so we have to move. It's a good thing, moving away from this house feels like a chance to move away from the destructive old behaviour I've been acting out with him even though we stopped the sex a while ago anyway, both knowing it wasn't healthy and certainly wasn't going anywhere.

And guess what? I'm even starting to grieve my dad. Just a little bit during a grief and loss workshop at college. I started to feel a few feelings, get in touch with the sadness. It will be almost another 20 years before that happens properly though.

Scene Eight – Grown Up

"Be happy in anticipation of what's coming."

– Abraham Hicks

I'm just buying my first house. The boys and I have moved five times in five years from one rental to another; it's time to take some control. My mortgage repayments will be through the roof, I am a part-time working single mum, and if I stop and think about it, start doing the maths, I know I'll get the fear and back out. So I don't think about it, I do what I am doing more and more these days, I tune into how I *feel* about it, I trust my intuition and I surrender into my mantra of trusting in the process. It seems to be working so far.

Trusting in the process is something I am learning through my training and through my work with clients, and through believing that everything happens exactly as it is meant to in exactly the way it is meant to, and that it might not always be easy or fun or even bearable, but it will always be for our greater good and because we have (albeit unconsciously) asked for it in some way.

I am learning about the law of attraction, how everything is vibration, we are vibration and every thought and feeling we have is vibration, and if we practice those thoughts and feelings enough (even if we don't want to), then that vibration becomes so big, gathers so much energy, so much mass, that it has no choice but to manifest.

How cool. I love that!

I am starting to re-ignite my spiritual flame that I lit 10 years ago. I am opening myself up to ideas and concepts that I can't always explain, but that just resonate with me. But I will stay in my spiritual closet for some years to come, only poking my head out when I know I am in the same company.

What is that about?

Still developing and growing, best keep quiet about it until I'm sure so I don't make a fool of myself along the way, isn't that how it goes?

I have a new job too, an actual paid counselling job. I'm working in a university, counselling students with issues ranging from relationship breakups to suicidal intent. There is lots of suicidal intent, and self-harming, and eating disorders, and anxiety and depression, and OCD, and the whole spectrum of mental health issues. I am increasingly aware of the disparity between seeing all these students walking around campus, seemingly happy, and having inside information on just how many of them are so hopelessly broken to the point of wanting to kill themselves.

It's a thing in the psychotherapy world that whatever demographic of client you 'choose' to work with, will be a projection of your own issues. A way of vicariously healing that part of ourselves through the client group we counsel. What does this say about my inner young adult? My 19 to 22-year-old? Well, it doesn't take 5 years of training and 4 years of therapy for me to work that one out!

As well as working 3 days a week at the uni, I am also working in private practice from home (just to ensure I vicariously work through all those other life stages of my shit too). I have also been to university for the past 2 years to get a BA degree in counselling and psychotherapy.

I love my work.

I am good at my work.

People seem to open up to me really easily and together we set about healing what needs to be healed.

It seems that everything is about freedom. Everyone just wants to be free from whatever particular suffering they are trapped in. Psychotherapy is all about seeing the choices we have in setting ourselves free, it just takes some time to get there, as I know only too well.

I am the wounded healer.

Aren't we all?

So, get me...quite the grown-up – a mortgage, a career, a degree, and a new relationship about to (literally) come knocking on my shiny new front door.

Scene Nine – Denial

"Let everything happen to you, beauty and terror,
just keep going, no feeling is final."

– Rainer Maria Rilke

I would say I am surprised to see him when I open the door but, truth be told, I've already seen him walk past my window and up my front steps. My heart pounds as I stand up to answer the doorbell.

Him: "Oh...er...hi...er..."

My God, he's more nervous than I am.

Me: "Oh, hello."

Feigned surprise.

Him: "Um...er...I was just...er...wondering if...er...you...um..."

Oh for God's sake, spit it out, I'm in danger of becoming less keen by the second!

Him: "...if you would...er...like to go out for a drink sometime?"

There we go...

Me: "Yeah, I'd love to, that'd be great. Do you wanna come in for a cup of tea?"

I need to do something to rescue him, it looks like he might topple over with the stress of it all, he's clinging onto my railings for dear life!

Him: "Oh, OK...er...cool."

He manages to let go and step inside without falling over – bless him, that obviously took so much courage. In my ego battle between judgement and flattery, flattery wins out.

Him: "Are the boys here?"

Me: "No, they're at their dad's. Yours?"

Him: "At their mum's."

Hmmm...

My boy number one is in the same class at school as his boy number two. My boy number two and his boy number three are also in the same year at the same school. We are playground single parents. As is his ex-wife. I chat to her sometimes, she seems nice, but little do I know how much this will change once she has found out that he and I are dating.

I soon realised when I moved in that the garden of my new house backs onto the garden of the quite fanciable dad I see in the playground at pick-up time. We got talking in the playground and arranged a few convenient lift shares for our boys after football practice.

Now we're out on a date, just to the local pub; clearly there's a strong mutual attraction and I really like him. I like him because he's normal, he's a similar age to me, and he's a dad – a good dad. I like him because there aren't any boundary issues. He's not my landlord. He's not my boss. I haven't already slept with his brother. He hasn't got a wife or girlfriend. I like that he seems to be just a regular guy. He is literally the boy next door.

It's been 6 years since Understudy and I broke up; I think it's time I had a proper relationship. Understudy has moved on and he and I have a good relationship now, plus he has a new partner.

Yes, it's time.

———————

I am sitting on one of my kitchen stools. Back Garden Neighbour is standing next to me. We have been dating for 6 months. It's late in the evening and we've just got back from the cinema. We're having a row about him not defending me against his mad ex-wife. She hates me. She hates my boys. She uses their boys to turn them against my boys and me. Where they all used to be friends, her boys are now manipulated into not talking to mine. Daggers stab through her eyes every time we cross paths at the school. She literally turns her head away from my boys if she sees them. She is evil. She is consumed with rage toward me because I started dating her EX husband who she had been divorced from for TWO years already.

And him? He does nothing about it. He buries his head in the sand. Allows it all to just happen. Doesn't say a word to her, just carries on as if nothing is wrong, telling me he doesn't want to make things worse.

Oh, I'm sorry to be a nuisance! But how much worse do you think this can get for me??

I have palpitations every time I get within 500 metres of the school, every time I see her in her car, coming and going from his place doing a drop-off or pick-up. For some reason, I am terrified of her. I can't face her to defend myself and I am incensed about the way she is treating my children, the way they are suffering as a result of her madness, her insane jealousy. They don't know why their friends don't like them anymore, why they don't want to play with them anymore. Boy number one is massively affected by this and I hate her for that as much as she hates me.

Back Garden Neighbour thinks I'm overreacting. My therapist thinks she reminds me of someone in my past.

Really? Isn't it enough that I just hate her because of the way she's treating us?? The woman clearly has some kind of personality disorder, my boys and I are the target of her malevolence, and I am supposed to just chill out about it?

To be fair, I secretly think my therapist might be right. I am aware of my perhaps disproportionate reaction. I am aware that I have an extreme flight or fight physical response when I see her. It feels like trauma and although in my head I can't really link it, somewhere deep in my psyche I think she is triggering events from my childhood.

Before my mum's boyfriend, Derek, was killed, he had a mad ex-wife, and I mean mad. She was insanely crazy with jealousy too. She hated that my mum had come along and taken her husband away – I think they were still together when my mum came into the picture, so fair enough, but she did some pretty horrific things to act it out.

I remember one night a disturbance outside our house. She was outside screaming like a banshee, swinging a large carving knife around, having just slashed all the tyres on his car. The police were called and eventually she left.

She also reported my mum to the social services, allegedly telling them that my mum was an unfit mother to my sister and me. We had visits from a social worker to assess the situation.

Another time, my sister and I were on holiday with mum and Derek at some holiday park. His son (a few years younger than me) came with us too. It was odd, we'd never all been together like this before, I think it was the first time we'd even met his son. It's like we were playing happy families with a dad and a brother that we didn't even know. A few days into the holiday, his mad ex-wife turned up, causing a massive scene and demanding that their son came home with her. I think the holiday park security had to be called and everything. That was an already weird holiday totally ruined. And, of course, not talked about. None of it was ever talked about. We were ushered into another room or nudged out of earshot in some way, some excuse and smokescreen was fabricated in an attempt to act as a decoy from the drama that was going on around us.

I was about 10 years old (same age boy number one is now). This all went on for some months, perhaps a year. I didn't realise at the time but of course it was traumatic for me. So sure, I can see the similarities now, the mad wicked stepmother (not to mention other horrific experiences with our actual stepmother that would soon follow in our childhood).

And you know another interesting connection? Derek's mad ex-wife and Back Garden Neighbour's mad ex-wife both have the same name.

So, yeah, maybe, just maybe, the universe is trying to tell me something and she does remind me of someone.

But you should still stick up for me! Defend me! Tell her that no one treats me like that! Protect me! Cos I'm just a kid, right...

But he doesn't, and in this moment, sitting on my kitchen stool, a sinking feeling creeps in and I know in my heart of hearts that this isn't going to work anymore. We're done. I feel it in my whole body.

But I WILL NOT LET THIS GO!

I am SO invested in this relationship.

These past 6 months have been so amazing. We are so right for each other. We both feel it and I have such high hopes for us, such fantasies about our future together. How we and all five of our boys and his dog will live together in one big house like the Brady Bunch, and it will be filled with noise and laughter and testosterone and love. I have spent so much time and energy fuelling that fantasy, I CANNOT let it go.

I am a dog with a bone, determined and relentless.

I am in total denial.

I will make you love me, take care of me, make myself the most important person in your world. We WILL be a big happy family.

This will not fail.

I will not fail.

So I push down that feeling in my heart of hearts. That feeling that is my instinct, my intuition. That feeling that is there to act on my behalf. That feeling that only has my best interests at heart. That feeling that is the love for myself. Yes, I push it all down, ignore it all, take no notice of it whatsoever because my sabotaging self is in charge right now. My destructive self who would rather continue in this traumatic, unhealthy, drama triangle than save herself and step away. Or rather, my destructive self who is *stuck* in a *pattern* of traumatic and unhealthy relationships. She just can't get out yet because she can't yet see it, there will need to be more destruction before she realises.

Much, much more.

So we continue on like this for another 2 years. Me feeling unloved, not important enough. Him trying to manage everything on his overflowing plate: a single dad to three boys, a full-time stressful job, a house that he is refurbishing, a mad ex-wife screaming maniacally in the background, and a girlfriend who is continually demanding that he does more to make this relationship work. It's hardly surprising he can't cope. It's hardly surprising he only has half an hour for me here and there.

It's hardly surprising too, then, that I feel unworthy. I try everything I can think of, every trick and therapeutic intervention in my book, to try to make this work. I am so lost in my determination that I cannot see the very obvious fact that it is just not working.

I am about to find out the full cost of that enormous oversight, the devastating consequences of my denial-fuelled determination.

Things are about to never be the same again for me.

Scene Ten – Bang

"How do you know the experience you are having is the one that you need? Because it's the one that you're having."

– Unknown

Someone has just hit me over the head with a baseball bat. A thousand sticks of dynamite have exploded in my skull.

Back Garden Neighbour is with me, looking (mildly) concerned. Thirty seconds ago we were having sex on my sofa, squeezing in a 'quick one' before he had to go back home for his boys to be dropped off and before mine were dropped off back to me.

OK, let's just finish this quickly. Are you going to come or not? It needs to be quick.

I move his hand down there, that's the only way this is gonna happen in a hurry!

Ooh...yes, here it comes...oh no, gone. OK, find it again quickly...oh come on, not there, there it is, OK, yep got it now, just a bit more...boys are due back...fuck, Understudy's van could pull up any minute...come on, come on...there...yes, left a bit...and I've got a student arriving soon...got to get some dinner on for him and the boys...just something from the freezer, I think I've got some chicken nuggets, that'll do...oh God, if I can just bloody come then I can get on with everything...here we go...Yes! Great! That's done, thank God!

OH WOAH!!! FUUUUUUCK!!!

That's when the baseball bat came in.

124

I am staggering to my feet, pulling up my knickers – everything else was still on anyway – my peach-coloured cotton skirt was up around my waist, it falls to where it should be as I precariously try to stand on legs that aren't there.

I feel very very strange.

Him: "Are you OK?"

Me: "Uhhh..."

I can't speak properly. Why won't my words come out? My brain can't connect somehow...thoughts...words...something is not right.

"...headache," I manage.

Him: "OK, you don't look too good. Maybe you should go and lie down for a bit. Take a paracetamol."

Lie down? Are you mad? I can't lie down! The boys are due back, the student is arriving, the chicken nuggets need to be on... But, fuck, something is wrong. I know something is wrong.

Him: "I 'spect you've got a migraine or something, here take this and go upstairs and lie down for a while."

I can barely co-ordinate my hand to my mouth to take the water and paracetamol. I've never had a migraine but I'm sure as hell that's not what this is.

Something is wrong. I know something is wrong.

Back Garden Neighbour helps me upstairs, lays me on the bed and tells me he will go down and start getting the dinner on, he still has a while before he needs to go home and thankfully it seems that Understudy is running late bringing the boys back. The later the better right now.

I – can't – keep – my – eyes – open – the – light – is – so – bright – I – think – I – might – pass – out.

Even with my eyes closed. It hurts so much.

I fumble around for my eye mask. The instinctive knowing that I won't be able to turn my head saves me from trying.

OK, that's – a little – better, but – the pain – my head – my neck.

Something is wrong. I know something is wrong.

I think I need help.

Fear creeps quietly into the bed beside me.

I'm alone up here in my room. Downstairs I can hear Back Garden Neighbour clanging around in my kitchen. I need him to come back up. I think I need an ambulance.

Something is wrong. I know something is wrong.

I open my mouth to call out to him. Nothing comes out. Fuck. It might be ages before he comes to check on me. It might be too late.

I manage to tell my brain to tell my left leg to slide out from under the duvet towards the floor. With all the focus I can muster, I raise my leg and let it drop to the floor three times.

I really hope he bloody heard that. The kitchen is directly below my bedroom. I listen – straining to hear for any evidence that my signal got through. Nothing. I manage to try again, a little heavier this time. Footsteps coming up the stairs. Thank God.

Me: "I – think – I – need – an – ambulance."

I am barely audible.

Him: "Shit. Are you sure? Really?"

Yes. No. I don't bloody know!

Him: "Right. OK."

Ten minutes later, more footsteps on the stairs, two pairs this time.

Them: "Hi there, what's your name?"

Me: "Vikki."

I am scarcely a whisper.

Them: "OK Vikki, so what's happened here then?"

Loud. So Loud. Why are you being so loud?

Me: "Um – my – head – the pain – the light – hurts."

Them: "OK, let's get you checked out then, see what we can find. Pop your finger on this..."

They are way too bubbly, upbeat. Like a couple of kids' entertainers arrived to cheer me up cos I'm feeling down!

"...and pop your arm into this, can you open your eyes for me?"

Me: "It – hurts."

Them: "OK but we need to just take a look inside..."

I peel back my mask, squint my eyes open half a millimetre.

"...right OK, that all looks fine, and blood pressure is fine and SATS are fine. It all looks OK."

OK? IT'S NOT FUCKING OK!

Something is wrong. I know something is wrong.

Them: "So I expect you've just got some kind of virus, just rest a while, see how you feel, if you need to then just call your out-of-hours GP."

NO!! DON'T GO!!

Something is wrong. I know something is wrong.

COME BACK!! YOU CAN'T JUST LEAVE!!

They leave and Back Garden Neighbour goes downstairs to check on the chicken nuggets.

I'm terrified.

I'm alone.

The pain.

The pain.

Something is wrong, I know something is wrong.

"Call – the – doctor," I manage when he comes back to check on me.

He speaks to the doctor. He passes me the phone as instructed.

Doctor: "Hello, Vikki?"

Me: "Yes," I whisper

Doctor: "So I'm going to ask you some questions and I just want you to answer them."

Me: "OK."

Doctor: "So I hear you've got a lot of pain in your head which came on suddenly, and the light is hurting your eyes, and this happened around 45 minutes ago?"

Me: "Yes."

Doctor: "OK, so I'm going to ask you a very important question now. Do you have pain running down your neck into your shoulders?"

Me: "Yes."

Doctor: "OK, listen very carefully, you need to call the paramedics again and get them to come back and take you into hospital straight away. Let me speak to your boyfriend again and I'll tell him what to do."

I TOLD YOU SOMETHING WAS WRONG!!!

Back Garden Neighbour has called my mum, my mum has called Understudy, Understudy will keep the boys with him until we all know more.

I am being carried down the stairs by the same two paramedics who, half an hour ago, told me I had a virus. They're not so cheery with me now, a distinct change in their attitude, now they are notably hostile.

Well, I'm fucking sorry to be a nuisance!

Back Garden Neighbour is waiting at the bottom of the stairs. He now looks more than a little concerned.

As they lift me through the doorway and down the front steps, a taxi pulls up and a young man with a suitcase gets out – my new Spanish student. Excellent timing!

Oh, hi there, I'm your host mother. I'm just being taken to hospital in this ambulance but there are some well-cooked chicken nuggets in the oven for you. I'm not sure when or if I will be back, so enjoy your stay. And, oh – welcome to England!!

I am strapped down in the back of the ambulance. One paramedic sits behind me, the other next to me. My eye mask is on so I can't see them but, through my pain and delirium, I can still hear them.

Paramedic 1: (in a mocking voice) "Oh, I've got a headache, I think I need to go to the hospital."

Paramedic 2: "I wish I got paid £200 an hour to sit behind a desk and tell someone over the phone what's wrong with them."

Paramedic 1 and 2: laughing.

WHAT THE FUCK??

They're supposed to be making me feel better, safe, reassured, not taking the piss and making me feel like I'm fucking putting them out.

I am paralysed by a head of dynamite and a world of fear.

Something is wrong. I know something is wrong, and I am NOT in good hands.

We have arrived at the hospital and I am casually handed over by the paramedics from hell to the A & E staff, hopefully now I will be taken seriously.

It seems not.

Five hours later and I am still lying on a trolley in a cubicle, waiting to be seen. I can only assume they don't think I'm dying. Eventually, I am wheeled off for a CT scan, but nobody tells me anything about it before or after.

Back in the cubicle, I drift in and out of awareness. Still the excruciating pain. Still the blinding lights. Still the delirium. Still the inability to speak properly.

Back Garden Neighbour sits by my side. Seems he's managed to stop his kids coming back too and apparently the Spanish student is now in the care of Nelly (God help him!).

And now I am being trolleyed into a ward for the night. The only ward where there is a bed for me, the gastro ward.

Now, I'm not a doctor but I'm pretty sure what's going on for me has NOTHING TO DO WITH MY GUTS!!

Back Garden Neighbour goes home.

I spend what's left of the night drifting in and out of a hazy, numbly terrified, otherworldly kind of sleep.

It's morning and the doctor is making his rounds.

Doctor: "Morning Victoria."

Me: "Hi."

Doctor: "How are you feeling?"

Me: "Er...Um...I – don't – know – why – I'm – here, what's – happening?"

Doctor: "Oh, well, you've had a bleed on the brain."

Oh right!! Well nice to finally be fucking told! OMG! Is that serious??!!

He's saying something about another scan, a possible lumbar puncture, spinal tap (I always wondered what that was).

Back Garden Neighbour comes back. And my mum and sister come to visit – my sister has driven from Kent; she's tearful and concerned. My mum has remembered to bring her brave face with her, along with some grapes.

My scan has apparently been sent to another hospital, the top neurological hospital in the country, which happens to be just 30 miles away.

Time fades in and out of my awareness.

The daylight has gone along with all my visitors and I am lying in a bed behind a curtain in a side ward somewhere. On the other side of the curtain is the nurses' station. They are doing their handover.

Nurse 1: "And in bed two is Victoria Smisek. She's going to be transferred to Southampton."

AM I???!!!

Nurse 2: "Oh, it must be serious then."

HELLO???!!! I'M ON THE OTHER SIDE OF THE FUCKING CURTAIN. I CAN HEAR YOU!!

Nurse 1: "Yes. We're just waiting for the ambulance to come now."

Why hasn't anyone told ME??!!

I am being blue-lighted up the motorway to Southampton hospital.

I am scared shitless but something inside me is relieved, finally I am being taken seriously.

When we arrive in the ambulance bay the staff are there to meet us.

"OK, don't try to move, just lie still and especially keep your head completely still, don't move at all, we need to assess you."

THIS IS MORE FUCKING LIKE IT!!

I am in a room with a massive machine. A nurse is injecting something into my groin. And through my delirium...a tsunami of nausea.

I'm gonna puke.

I vomit into the pan that is held under my face, but nothing can catch the shit that has just exploded out of my arse. I reassure myself that it doesn't matter. I don't know why I care, but somehow I do.

Another tsunami...my head, OMG, my fucking head, spinning, spinning, around and around. The static, excruciating pain has now become sharp, darting, dancing pain, swirling into every crevice and corner pain, spinning whirling dervish pain.

The dye has shot up from my main artery from my groin into my head. The machine is reading the dye. It's looking to see where the hole is. The hole where the blood came out of its rightful and safe place and spilled out into my brain. It's looking to see if there are other places where holes might be about to burst open.

Apparently, there aren't.

Just the one hole.

Just the one bleed.

Just the one brain haemorrhage for me.

For now, at least. Apparently, the next 2 weeks are crucial.

I have been wheeled into the high-intensity ward. From now on I will not be able to get up. I will not be able even to sit up. I will need to pee and shit in a bedpan. I will need a bed bath each morning. And I am morphined up to the eyeballs!

It is the middle of the night. On the other side of the curtain, I tune into voices, bumbling, mumbling, murmuring voices, something is being recited...

"...may the Lord in his love and mercy...grace of the Holy Spirit...save you and raise you up..."

OMFG! Is this the ward they bring people to die??

I spend the next week like this, being monitored every 2 hours around the clock, morphine, bedpans, bed baths, immobile and quietly scared to death.

But each day that passes poses me less at risk. Apparently, 90% of people's brain haemorrhages are caused by aneurysms. Of those, 30% will die on impact, 30% will have another within two weeks and die, and the other 30% will survive but may have some residual symptoms. In the remaining 10% of cases, they don't know what causes the bleed, but it will be a one-off and not leave any residual symptoms, and there's no more chance of having another one than there is for the next person. After a week, my second angiogram – the big machine and the dye (this time I manage not to puke and shit myself) – reveals that's my category.

Yep, that's me! A lucky ten percenter!

So why the hell has this happened?

You don't just have a brain haemorrhage for no reason, not when you're a fit and healthy 40-year-old. But the doctors don't know, and I get the distinct impression they don't really care – about the why, I mean. I am notably the most well person on my ward; they have far more pressing cases on which to focus their time, attention, and resources.

But somewhere along the line, stress is mentioned. Stress? Me? But I know all about stress and self-care, I'm a therapist for Christ's sake, I'm aware, I pay attention to what's going on inside me, I couldn't have missed this.

Could I?

After a week, I am moved into a recovery ward. The monitoring is less and not only am I allowed to move around slowly, I am also encouraged to get up and go to the bathroom, walk up and down a little.

But the pain is still immense, although interestingly, it's moved. The bleed – a teaspoon's worth apparently – over the course of the past week, has travelled from the base of my skull, down my spinal-cord and has now lodged itself just above my coccyx. There it sits in a teaspoon-sized pool, wreaking havoc and sending shock waves of pain throughout my entire body.

It's not just the pain, everything in me has slowed down, my thoughts, my speech, my movement. It takes me a full half-hour to make the round trip to the bathroom just across the corridor. It's like I have to concentrate hard on every single step to keep going, to not wobble and fall over. It is mentally and physically exhausting.

But, apparently, the more I move, the sooner my tiny puddle of blood will get re-absorbed into my body. No need for surgery or intervention in my case, just got to wait till it's all been soaked up.

———

So it is, after another week here, I am discharged. Back Garden Neighbour comes to collect me and take me home; it takes me an age to climb into his car, clutching my paper bag full of painkillers, my hospital tag still wrapped around my frail wrist. By the time we get me home, I am shattered. But there is something I need to do before I take to my bed. I am compelled to do a circuit of every room in my house. It's like I have to re-establish a connection with how it was before, to have some evidence of normality, to see everything still as it was, all present and correct, before we had sex on the sofa and my head exploded with dynamite. I shuffle inch by inch, subliminally taking it all in.

Tomorrow, my boys will come home, somehow, we'll manage. They are 10 and 12 now and this must have been bloody scary for them too. Understudy brought them in every other day to see me in the hospital; thank goodness they've had him to help them feel safe. My sister will come and stay for a while, my mum too, and Back Garden Neighbour will be here when he can. So between everyone, I won't have to manage alone. Just as well as, let's face it, I'm not exactly up for much!

For the next 2 months, I am house-ridden. Once, I venture out to the shopping centre with Back Garden Neighbour, I walk like a 90-year-old, the world and his wife are racing past me, it's all too much, overwhelming and exhausting, it takes us nearly all day. Clearly, I am rushing my recovery with crazy ideas like this.

All this time in bed is giving me sores all over my legs and bum. It's not attractive. I can see all my muscle tone starting to fade away. I have lost almost a stone, my clothes are hanging off me, I have no strength at all.

But worst of all is the fear. The first few weeks of being home I am scared to close my eyes and go to sleep in case it happens again. If I cough or sneeze it terrifies me that my head will re-explode. Any sudden movement and I am jolted into panic.

An orgasm is definitely out of the question.

When I do get up to try to do something, I am literally seeing stars. This really freaks me out. I call my doctor, he comes to see me. He reassures me it's all OK, it's the painkillers that are causing the stars, I can take less and see how I get on. He also encourages me to put in a complaint about the paramedics, but I just haven't got it in me right now. I resolve to do it at a later date when I'm feeling stronger.

I never do.

But slowly, slowly, I start to recover. The fear begins to decrease; some strength begins to return to my diminished body. The pain is gradually lessening and eventually, after two and a half months, it finally feels like the little teaspoon of blood that shot out of a vessel in my head, into my brain, and slid down my spine and wedged itself in my sacrum, has finally been sucked back into my body.

Incredible.

And if nothing else, these past 2 months have given me time to reflect, time to question. Just because the doctors couldn't give me answers, doesn't mean I can't find them myself, from within myself.

We always have all our answers, we just need to tap into them.

So why the fuck did this happen?

How the fuck did this happen?

What is my body telling me?

What is the universe telling me?

And – most importantly – OK, what do I need to change?

Over time, the answers begin to emerge. I don't necessarily like those answers, I try to deny them out of some kind of pride or shame, not wanting to accept that I'd messed up in some way and feeling like I should have known better.

But OK, I have to start to admit it, maybe working three different jobs, being a single parent, having an enormous mortgage, spending every spare minute rushing around doing something, always out and about on the go, smoking a bit, drinking a bit, and being in an unhealthy relationship...well maybe, just maybe something had to give.

I know I have been given a warning here.

I know I have to make some changes.

But it's only when I am having coffee with my very good friend, a few months later, that something really hits me, tells me just what I need to hear.

Her: "So how are things with you and (Back Garden Neighbour)?"

Me: "Oh God knows, I feel like I'm just **banging my head against a brick wall.**"

There it is!

In that moment, I know what I have to do. I know in my heart that the biggest stress in my life is this relationship, and I know it's never going to change.

This relationship is literally *doing my head in*. It has to stop. Now.

Thank God I can hear myself.

Thank God I can take the learning from this.

Thank God I can step back and see what's happening.

Thank God I can change what needs to be changed.

And because these changes are about to take my life in a whole new direction, one where everything is different in so many ways, it will only be a matter of time until I am saying:

Thank God I had a brain haemorrhage.

Thank God I nearly died.

Because in that nearly dying...I am finally waking up.

Scene Eleven – Aware

"We're always looking for something outside to make us feel whole.
Mindfulness teaches us that we're already complete."

– Jon Kabat-Zinn

"...and on the next in-breath...send your attention all the way down to the toes of your left foot and just rest there...as best you can...seeing what you notice...sensations of tingling, buzzing, numbness..."

This is what my new life sounds like. My eyes are closed and I am lying on a shabby yoga mat on the blue-carpeted floor in a classroom of a large university building in the north of Wales. I am surrounded by 30 other washed-up bodies covered in an assortment of blankets, cushions under our heads, all looking for something more, or maybe just looking for some peace, and right now all desperately looking for a tingle in our left big toe. Or is it just me? Am I the only one who can't feel anything here?

"...don't go looking for sensations...rather just allow them to come to you...open up to what is already there..." Oh, right, I see, I think...feel into my toes...nope, still nothing!

Oh well, apparently it doesn't matter. Apparently, it's not about whether you actually feel anything or not, it's about noticing what it's like whether you do or you don't, it's all about noticing your experience. My experience? ...Err...confused, frustrated, tired, bored, impatient...that's all good apparently, all good noticing. Right!

This is a whole new world, a whole new language, and although I don't exactly understand it all yet, I know I need to be here.

It's been 2 years since my head exploded. A year since I finally ended things with Back Garden Neighbour. That was easier said than done. We tried the whole staying friends thing, but does that ever really work? We were never friends in the first place. We were lovers, partners, boyfriend and girlfriend, whatever, but not friends. Friends are something else. So inevitably the boundaries end up getting blurred when you're trying to make something fit into something that it isn't. We did the whole still keeping in touch thing, which sooner or later led to meeting up for a drink, which sooner or later led to having a hug, which sooner or later led to having sex. Cos the sex was always so good and the feelings were still there. But that doesn't make it right. That doesn't make it healthy. It does make it bloody hard to say no to, though.

But this is my work, right? This is what I need to do if I want to break my unhealthy patterns, I need to learn to say 'no' when I know it's not right, when my body is telling me one thing and my head another...

"He lived a short distance away from his body" – A James Joyce quote that raises more than a few identifying sniggers in the classroom.

Thankfully, through this mindfulness business, I'm learning to tell the difference between my head and my body.

Actually, we're still in touch – not only my head and my body, but me and Back Garden Neighbour, just a little. I'm determined not to sleep with him again, but I'm not quite ready to let him go yet. But I will be soon. Soon something will happen to make me realise I need to dissolve him from my life altogether, just as we are invited in the mindfulness session to allow the sense of our left knee to dissolve into the background of our awareness as we move our attention up to our left thigh.

Meanwhile, that part of me that is still acting out, that adaptive child part of me, thinks it would be a good idea to fall back on some old coping mechanisms in an attempt to get him out of my system. I mean, clearly that's not the best way forward here, you and I both know that, but familiarity sure has a seductive grip on us...

It was a year ago I discovered mindfulness. I'd heard about an 8-week Mindfulness-Based Stress Reduction course that was being held near me and, under the guise of 'professional development' – and still in enough denial about my own stress levels, despite having had a brain haemorrhage – I signed up.

Now, I'm not sure about stress reduction, by the time I'd arranged for a kid sitter every week, done everything I needed to do to get me out of the house on time, make the half-hour drive over there, rush back to relieve the kid sitter, find the money to pay for it, try to keep up with the daily home practice – I think I just about broke even when it came to my stress levels!

But something resonated. That healthy part of me that had demanded to be heard after my head exploded was nudging me, "yes, this is what you need, keep going with it, you don't need to know why right now, just keep going with it." And mindfulness is becoming a bit of a buzz thing, I am still working at the university and they want to start offering it to students, and because I've already done an 8-week course and have a 'daily' practice (albeit a sketchy one), they want to send me for an all-expenses-paid week to Northern Ireland to attend a teacher training retreat. Oh, um, let me think...hell yes!

It is on that retreat that I have two very significant encounters.

Firstly, I meet my brain haemorrhage.

Yep, it's like it hopped on an earlier flight and is sitting there waiting for me in the hall in full lotus position. I sense something as soon as I arrive – the setting, the atmosphere, I just know this is going to be big, this week, this experience – and on day two during a practice, there it is. As I am invited to bring my awareness into the area around my head, to notice sensations, in my mind's eye I see jaggedy spikey colours of deep red, orange and purple emanating from my skull, I feel my spinal cord swarm with confused blood particles as they try to find their way back home. My eyes fling themselves open at the hurling surge of being embodied by my brain haemorrhage (a bit like Whoopie Goldberg in Ghost). I am unable to stay in my seat, unable to even stay in the room.

One of the tutors is just outside, tending to someone else who is having their own emotional breakdown (or rather, breakthrough) – it seems I am not alone in this retreat bringing things to the surface. I leave the room as discreetly as my emotional crisis will allow, and head to the tutor in the (aptly named) breakout room for support.

I love this tutor.

I've only known her for 2 days, she's probably over twenty years older than me, she has a no-nonsense, say-it-like-it-is teaching style fused with wisdom, compassion and humour. When she speaks, I hear every word. It's fair to say I am in awe of her and am delighted to have this chance for some one-to-one time. Now I can tell her my story, tell her all about my brain haemorrhage, that will get her attention, that will make me special, set me apart from the other 19 trainees here, make her love me back. She indicates for me to wait in the next room, she will be with me shortly. Excellent.

Her: "OK, so just sit, put both feet on the floor, connect to your breath...

I don't want to connect to my bloody breath, I want to tell you my story!!

Her: "...and just focus on the connection between your feet and the floor, the contact between your legs and the chair..."

Fuck my feet on the floor! Let me tell you my story!!!!

Her: "...and find the beginning of the in-breath...follow it all the way to the top...and notice the pause..."

I sob between breaths.

This is NOT what I had in mind for our big bonding moment.

The moment when this incredible woman sees the incredible in me, hears my pain and loves me like her own, and in that moment she will become 'the good mother', the mother who wants me, who has time for me, who loves me beyond all others.

Her: "...and as best you can follow the out-breath towards the end..."

My ego deflates.

My inner child yearns.

But I feel her kindness, her presence. She might not indulge my story, but I sense she is fully with me in this moment.

"Here..." she reaches on the table behind her "...why don't you draw it." She hands me a packet of coloured felt-tip pens and a stack of white A4 paper.

So I do. I go to my room and I draw it. Even though this is not my usual style, not my usual way of expressing myself; I'm a psychotherapist, I'm all about the telling of the story. But because she has suggested it, and because it seems that's all there is on offer, I do it.

And WOW. *That's it!* That's exactly what it looks like! Who knew it even *looked* like *anything*? And seeing it, I connect with it in a whole new way. I relate to it, I *feel* it, I *meet* it, all in a totally different way than if I'd talked about it. Apparently, I am accessing a different part of my brain, where I can relate to my experience differently – mindfulness is all about cultivating this part of the brain.

It took me 2 months to recover from the physical symptoms of my brain haemorrhage, it seems it has taken 2 years to even begin to be ready to start processing the emotional impact.

Only now can I start my full recovery. My path to healing, to change.

But it seems I have to have my swan song first. To tango with my familiar seductive dance partner one last time. This is the second significant encounter I have on this week's retreat.

If you're going to have a swan song, a finale, an encore, make it big, that's what I say! Make it count. Showcase all of your skills and talents for one final performance to remember!

The incongruence is not lost on me. Here, on this mindfulness teacher training retreat, I am acting out the opposite of everything we are learning. Go inward, not outward. Learn to accept things just the way they are, not strive to make them different. Simply observe the ego, not indulge it. Be in comfortable silence with yourself, not flirt tantalisingly with the blatant sexual chemistry between you and that married man on the other side of the room so that it hijacks your every present moment.

By the end of the week, we are like a couple of coiled springs ready to jump into bed with each other at the first opportunity. And so that's just what we do, in a hotel in Belfast before we catch our respective flights home. Even though I feel the loudest NO in my whole body to date, and hear it in my head too, I override it anyway.

Well, you may as well go out in style.

———————————

But the good news is, on the back of the training retreat, I sign up for the Master's degree, and because I am now immersing myself totally in this world of mindfulness, I am starting to actually *feel* how unhealthy these patterns are for me. Each time I sit and meditate, I cultivate more awareness, I get more out of my head and into my body. The once reassuring numbness of disassociation no longer feels reassuring. It jars, its edges sharp and unfriendly. And when I move up closer to those edges, I can tune into the voice of my heart telling me softly..."enough, you don't need this anymore."

After a week spent on a silent meditation retreat during this first year of my course, I know I am learning masses about myself from simply sitting and being with things just the way they are. Noticing the patterns of my mind and not acting out on them, well, it gives a different perspective. It helps me see things for what they really are: just a set of thoughts which arose from a set of conditions, which I practiced like my life depended on it, so they arose some more, and I acted on them because I didn't know I had a choice. And those behaviours had consequences, like leaving me feeling not great about myself, which I shoved down under the surface, which just attached themselves to the set of conditions that were there in the first place...and so it goes and so it goes...

I feel more illuminated after that one week than in all of the years of psychotherapy.

I am developing a whole new relationship with myself, one which isn't all about judging and analysing and problem-solving and doing. (Isn't that so often the first thing we say to someone when they tell us a problem: what are you going to *do* about it?) Well, I'm learning that the solution to problems comes from the being with them not from the doing.

And as the affair that began on the teacher training retreat tips into 2 months of intense, obsessive, hedonistic meet-ups, followed by his wife finding out and him cutting me off without a word (here we go again), this time I am able to process it in a different way. I am able to *respond* from my healthy adult state rather than *react* from my insecure, hurt, abandoned child. I am able to feel just how wrong this is for me and, well, yes, there is a moral code here too. I've always dismissed that before, but even that slips itself into my expanding awareness. I don't want to be *that* girl anymore.

What's it all about anyway?

Some desperate attempt to get attention, to be loved, to heal myself, to feel worthy?

Seriously? Am I still banging on about that?

This isn't love! This isn't the attention I need! This isn't worthy! This isn't healing, this is the opposite of healing!

I AM WORTHY OF SO MUCH MORE!!

Really? Did I actually just think that?

Am I actually starting to believe that?

On top of all this, I have to admit, it's losing its cool. It no longer feels like an entertaining anecdote, it feels quite sad. I am a 42-year-old mother of two teenage boys with a career and more education underway, not some teenage girl starting out in life without a care in the world.

I am loving what I am learning, all the Buddhist stuff is just landing in a place of TRUTH in me. I feel myself naturally inclining away from alcohol, my occasional smoking habit has finally stopped, I am losing interest in eating meat...all from a place of intuition and instinct rather than a cognitive decision or moral judgment. I'm paying more attention to what I put into my body and how I treat it, I am starting to practice yoga again from a new perspective. I used to do a bit of yoga years ago and I was the girl who gathered up all her things and scurried out of the room before savasana, I didn't have time to lie down for 5 minutes for God's sake, what was the point anyway?!

I have also left my job at the university as I realised the commute and the stress of doing a job where you're trying to heal people's broken emotions in an organisation where it's all about money and budgets and figures, was totally depleting me. It felt like a massive risk to leave and trust that I would have enough clients coming in privately to sustain us financially. But by some miracle, without any advertising involved, over a matter of a few months the universe has provided me with another 10 clients a week.

And, perhaps most significantly, for the first time since I started dating at age 15, I am giving myself a break from men and from relationships, and it's about bloody time. I'm always going on about it with clients, "we all need to have time just on our own, to truly be in a relationship with ourselves, relationships with others, no matter how good, can really distract us from that... blah blah blah" so it's about time I put it into practice for myself. For nearly THIRTY YEARS, there's always been someone, some guy or other who I've been seeing, planning on seeing, ruminating about, fantasising about, always SOME BLOODY GUY occupying WAY too many of my waking thoughts.

It has been utterly relentless.

And where has it got me?

Here I am, nearly three decades on, and I'm sneaking around shagging some married man!

Sometimes you just know when you're DONE.

It will be two and a half years before I allow another man into my life, or should I say before a certain man comes back into my life, but first let me tell you about the something that means I finally end all contact with Back Garden Neighbour.

Scene Twelve – Friend

"I've learned that people will forget what you said, people will forget what you did, but people will never forget how you made them feel."

– Maya Angelou

The phone is ringing, I come in from the garden to answer it, it's my mum.

Her: "Oh, hello darling, have you heard about Nelly?"

Me: "No...heard what?"

Her: "Well, I just had a call, they've had to leave the ship and Nelly's been admitted into hospital, in the Caribbean."

Why have you been told? Why am I hearing this from you? Why didn't they call me?

Her: "He said he's tried to message you but couldn't get through, so he asked me to tell you, it's not good news I'm afraid."

So why do you sound so chirpy, why does it feel like you're almost enjoying telling me??

Me: "What's happened?"

Fuck! No. I don't want to hear this. No. No. No.

Her: "Well, you know he had pneumonia before they left for the cruise, and he's just got worse over the last week, so they called the doctor and they thought they should take him ashore and get him treated, and now they've done some tests and...oh, dear, he's got cancer, he's riddled with it I'm afraid."

Riddled with it? I hate that fucking expression! I hate the way you've just said that! Embellished it...like you've sprinkled glitter all over a grenade and launched it at me without warning!

Me: "Shit. What's happening then?"

Her: "Well, they've got to stay there for now, and see how he is over the next few days, we'll know more after that."

Me: "Right, OK, well, thanks."

I have no more words right now.

Cancer? What the fuck?

Nelly has lived with being HIV positive for nearly thirty years, been on medication for that, with all sorts of side-effects, but has stayed ahead of it, just about the only remaining survivor of his peers who all got diagnosed around the same time back in the 80s. That's what I was always expecting. That's the news I was always prepared for, eventually. Something HIV-related. Not this. Not cancer. What the fuck!

How can that be right? How can that be fair!

After a couple of weeks, Nelly is well enough to fly home, but the prognosis is not good. The cancer has spread from his kidneys throughout his body and is even in his brain. (*Riddled.*)

NO!!! This isn't happening. Not again! I don't want to lose someone else I love in this way!

But it doesn't have to be *this way*. I realise I have a choice.

I will *not* avoid Nelly dying like I avoided my dad dying.

I am *not* the messed-up girl in my twenties that I was then.

I *can* cope this time.

I *can* face it.

All of it.

I can watch someone I love die, and I can be present.

So I try, I really do. I don't shy away from his deterioration, I cry, I talk to him about it all, I tell him that I'll miss him – oh fuck, how I'll miss him.

We've seen each other every week for the past 10 years. He's been my friend, my confidant, my babysitter. He's helped me move house three times, he's put up shelves, painted walls, and puffed up cushions whenever he came around. We've swum together, we've shopped together, we've drunk together, we've got stoned together, we've danced in the garden together, we've laughed together...belly-crunching, breath-restricting, bladder-leaking laughing.

But within 6 months of being diagnosed, just 2 weeks after his 50th birthday, my amazing, unique, fabulous friend is gone and there will be a giant disco-glitter-ball-shaped hole in my life forever.

Barbara Streisand's "Somewhere" pipes out of the speakers and I sob uncontrollably from the minute his funeral service begins. My boys are either side of me, he was a big part of their lives too and this is their first experience of losing someone close. We are in the same chapel where my dad's funeral was. It seems the ghosts of my unshed tears from then have been waiting here, hiding behind a pew for 16 years, for my return.

The next day, I reach out to Back Garden Neighbour. He'd known Nelly, they'd got on really well, and right now I need a link.

I need a living connection to my dead friend.

He knows it was Nellie's funeral yesterday, he's also said to me during one of our many 'how to re-frame our relationship' conversations that he would always be there for me if I needed anything. I realise I do need something from him.

My text: "Hi, hope you're OK, wondered if you're free to meet up? I could do with a chat."

His text: "Hi, yeah all good thanks, sure, I'm free this evening, I could meet you up the road, take it from there. Everything OK?"

My text: "OK that'd be great thanks. Not really OK. What time?"

His text: "Ah OK. 7ish?"

My text: "Yep great. See you then."

See! He IS there for me. I knew it.

So often, when we were dating, he'd let me down, prioritise something else, someone else, always something more important. I always felt on the bottom of his pile (perfect for re-enforcing my core belief). Since we've been doing the 'friends' thing or whatever we are, it still happens, but it doesn't matter so much or I can't expect so much from him, at least – we're not a couple anymore. But now it matters. Now I need a hug. Now I need to fall apart. Now I need someone to hold me. Now I need him. He is there for me.

6.45 p.m....

His text: "Hey, really sorry, need to take a raincheck on this evening, something's come up, OK to do it another time?"

I am unimportance and unworthiness covered in skin once again.

But...

Another part of me calmly deletes his number and all messages from my phone.

Clarity and empowerment rise up...I am DONE.

He's NOT there for me. It's NOT my fault. And it's about fucking time I saw that.

So, two significant relationships end in my life at the same time. One through losing my dear friend who didn't have any more fight in him and whose body just couldn't take any more. The other through me finally losing the illusion and just not being able to take any more.

Thanks Nelly darling – your parting gift to me.

Scene Thirteen – Elephant

"We shall not cease from exploration and the end
of all our exploring will be to arrive where we started
and know the place for the first time."

– T.S. Elliot

It seems I have unfinished business with someone – with a few someone's actually but "one at a time, I'm not that kind of girl...form an orderly queue, please, I'll get to you all when I can!"

Out of the blue one morning, I get a message from Drop Dead Gorgeous Boss. He's asking how I am and, a few exchanges later, he's asking me if I want to meet up for a drink and I'm saying yes.

Do I mean yes, or do I mean no? What's the difference again?!

I have said yes (I think) partly out of curiosity and partly because well, it's been a long time since a guy has asked me out for a drink. But it always feels a bit dead end with Drop Dead Gorgeous Boss, like he and I are stuck in some kind of loop of being attracted to each other but not being able or not even wanting to make it work. A few years ago we ran into each other on a night out and I ended up going back with him (when Back Garden Neighbour and I were on one of our many breaks). That was it, just a one-night thing following our 15-year what-are-we-doing-here-on-off a few times thing.

We meet up now at his place and head straight out to a local bar. It's nice to see him but I'm determined the night isn't going to end up the way it seems he wants it to. I don't want to be that girl anymore. I'm *not* that girl anymore. Someone you can just call up out of the blue after years of no contact and end up getting laid. Many years ago, shortly after I'd left Understudy, I was seeing a guy for a while, we'd broken up and then one night (when the boys were at their dads'), months later, he called me at 2 a.m. saying he was in town and was I still giving those amazing blowjobs. And the sad, really sad, thing is I let him come around. That's how desperate I was. Not for sex (or the chance to give an amazing blowjob) but for some kind of affirmation.

For fuck's sake! Did I really take that as a compliment?

I am not desperate anymore.

I'm not. Am I?

It's the end of the night, I'm heading for the bus stop and he is literally pulling me by the arm and dragging me in the direction of his flat. He's being playful about it in a 'Carry On meets Benny Hill' kind of way but I know this performance just disguises his inability to actually, God forbid, talk about how he feels.

Whose resolve will win this tug of war...? His, of course.

It just feels easier. And so I grab my inner Barbara Windsor and follow the path of least resistance up to his front door.

Once inside his flat, we do the deed (always an interesting expression, perhaps quite fitting here), and I tell myself it's what I want too; it's definitely not unpleasant and surely something needs to play itself out here so we can either try to have a proper relationship or have a proper ending once and for all.

Over the next couple of months, things move along quite smoothly. We meet up a couple of times a week, have contact on most other days, but it's still not really happening, something is blocking us. It's always been clear that he has massive trust, intimacy, and commitment issues going back to his childhood. Maybe – just maybe – he's mirroring me?! We are one and the same which is why we're stuck, both afraid to make the leap, both unsure if it's the right thing. And for me, I don't think it is the right thing. There are lots of reasons on paper why I don't want to be in a proper relationship with him but – unconsciously, karmically if you like – we are drawn together.

Another weird thing is that, over the years, I've barely given him a waking thought, and yet SO often he is cast as the male lead in my dreams. Many mornings I will wake up having had a vivid dream about him and then go back to totally forgetting all about him. Is it the same for him? Is that why, when he got back in touch, he messaged me at 8 a.m.?

There's something that needs shifting here and my growing sense is that there is an elephant lurking at the end of his bed.

That's usually the issue in any relationship. It's not what's said that is the problem, it's what *isn't* said that's the problem.

There is something which he and I have never named and until we have named it, I think we're always going to be stuck. Of course *he's* not going to name it, it's got to be me, I'm the one with the awareness (or maybe he is too, I don't know cos we've never talked about it), I'm the one with the psycho theories. I need to take the lead and I have no idea which way it will go, but my gut feeling is it just needs to be said.

I arrange for us to meet up. He senses I have an agenda. We're both edgy. My edginess tells me it would be a really good idea to have a large gin and tonic...and then another.

Me: "So there's something you and I have never talked about in the 15 years that we've known each other."

Him: "Um, OK...is there?"

Me: "Yes, you know there is. And it just feels like it needs naming, cos otherwise...

Steady. He's not a client. Don't go getting all psychobabbly. Don't knowingly cross your legs and slide back into your therapist chair with your G & T.

...well, it just feels like it's there, I guess." I manage to contain myself.

Him: "What is?"

You know! You're just being coy (or terrified) as you sip your beer, I know you know what's coming.

Me: "Well, we've never talked about the fact that I slept with your brother."

And...there it is!

Him: "Yeah, right, no we haven't."

Me: "And that's weird, right, that we haven't ever mentioned it. So should we talk about it now? Cos I'm not sure what this is and where it's going and how we feel about each other and if we want to be in a proper relationship or not, it feels like we're both holding back."

Oh, Christ. The gin. Stop talking now. He's looking bewildered, overwhelmed, like he wishes he'd stayed at home to watch the football he's already mentioned more than once.

Him: "OK, so why did you do it? That was pretty fucking hard for me."

Ooh, some feelings, he's rising to the occasion.

Me: "Well, cos I thought you weren't interested in me and he was, and I know it wasn't my finest hour and I'm not proud, but I did it and I'm sorry."

My gin-fuelled words hang in the air. Especially the last two.

Is that what this was all about?

"I'm sorry I chose your brother over you." Have I been 'mother' in this all along?

Has the fact I ended up acting out some 15-year relationship with you (and not your brother) 'proved' that I didn't really choose him over you, that, even though that's what the courts decided when you were children, I (she) never stopped loving you, wanting to be with you. But you must have been hurt beyond measure, felt abandoned and rejected and therefore couldn't trust me (couldn't trust any woman), couldn't really let me (her) in. And when you add my shit into the mix of feeling rejected and not good enough and trapped and my own family split...well, no wonder we've been bloody stuck in something together. You are me and I am you. I am mother and you are mother, not quite letting me in, leaving me questioning whether I'm really wanted.

I don't say any of this, obviously.

I don't want him thinking I'm a total nutter.

The atmosphere has shifted. The elephant has left the building and has been replaced with a slight awkwardness but at least now it's out. Maybe now the hurt we didn't even know was there can be healed.

We've finished our drinks, we mutter a few things of no importance, it seems there's nothing else to say. He wants to go back and catch the end of the football. He offers to drive me home. We're both quiet in the car, things are different between us, not bad different, there is still a friendliness there, a fondness even.

He says he'll give me a call. I say I will too.

He doesn't. I don't either.

The spell is broken.

So that's that particular piece of unfinished business done but, oh... hang on, seems there's another one just around the corner...NEXT...!

Scene Fourteen – Honeymoon

"Until you heal your past, your life patterns and relationships will continue to be the same, it's just the faces that change."

– Unknown

I'm sitting at home watching TV. It's fairly late in the evening. The phone rings. Who would be calling at this time of day?

On the other end of the phone is the 'he half' of my friends, a couple who moved to New Zealand many years ago. She and I had been friends at school. She and he had been going out together since she was 15 and he 16. We'd stayed friends over the years despite our various travels and despite the fact that when we were 18 and I cheated on a boyfriend, she told him about it. Bitch. But that's all long forgotten...or is it?

It's early morning in New Zealand and he is in a right state at the end of the phone, telling me she's left him, she's shacked up with her boss, and did I know anything about it?

Oh shit. I wish he wasn't asking me that question. Sure, I know she hasn't been faithful over the years but (unlike her) I've always kept out of it, none of my business and all that. Did I know about this particular infidelity? Well, a bit, but she didn't tell me much and I didn't ask.

She and I have always been very different people and recently I'd been questioning our friendship more and more. As I'd moved on in my life, it was clear I was far more in tune with the friends I'd met through my counselling and mindfulness training. Increasingly, it was feeling like my friendship with her was based on an old connection from our school days, a habit rather than a true friendship. We didn't even really get on that well then, come to think of it.

"I think you ought to be asking her that." This was the only way I could find to not blatantly land her in it and not blatantly lie to him. I've always liked him, in fact, he and I have far more in common than she and I, we've always had a laugh together, we've always had a connection, and I suspect she has always been only too aware of that and has held a resentment toward me because of it.

As it seems I perhaps might have with her! OK, I might not have blatantly landed her in it, but I think I've definitely more than nudged her face down in her own proverbial shit.

But I feel for the guy, I really do. And do I feel for her? Knowing how she's had numerous affairs in the 30 years they've been together, knowing how she's lied about a pregnancy and termination that wasn't his? Well, I guess not so much, no. I've held her secrets for a long time and it just doesn't feel healthy anymore. I'm sorry but it just doesn't fit with my new congruent lifestyle!!

So the cat has finally burst out of its bag. He's challenged her, told her what I've said, she's furious with me (ironic), cuts me off, refuses to engage with my messages. I send her an email explaining I was in a very difficult position and I did what I felt was right, what felt healthy to me, and I'm sorry if she didn't like it (am I?). I don't know why I bothered, I could have quite happily just let our so-called friendship go, but I think I wanted some kind of closure after 35 years.

I have to admit though, now I have a sense of relief. I've never felt that she was honest or authentic with me, it felt like she put on an act every time we spoke on the phone. She insisted on knowing all the ins and outs of my life and when I asked her how she was she always replied in the same way: "Oh, fine and dandy!" Apparently, she'd then come off the phone and slag me off. Nice! It feels like there's always been more than a hint of jealousy, of control, of manipulation. Yep, the more I sit with it, the more I realise I am well rid.

As I move out of relationship with her, I move more into relationship with him. But that's just inevitable when three become two, right? With her out of the picture, he and I are free to be friends. We speak more regularly as he comes to terms with their relationship ending, and when he asks me, I confess to more of the stuff I know – well, I've nothing to lose now – but I still don't tell him everything, I don't want to get too ensconced in the shit

162

throwing, it's a filthy business.

And as the months go by, it seems like he and I are flirting a little. I guess it's always been there under the surface, but we were never allowed to indulge it, and of course it would have been inappropriate – and you know me, I am nothing but appropriate when it comes to men! Anyway, it was there and we all three knew it.

He's planning a visit back to the UK next summer to see family and old friends, and that includes me, apparently.

Hmm...could be interesting.

More unfinished business needs tending to.

Could I ignore it?

Possibly.

Should I ignore it?

Yes!

But if I do, won't it just keep popping up until it's dealt with?

Just to be clear, it's been almost two years since they broke up, almost two years since I had any contact with her. Enough time, no?

So I doubt it will surprise you to know that when he comes over, Unfinished Business and I have a night out which starts with a few beers and affectionate flirting and ends up with us in bed together. We've been mates for 30 years, there's a lot of love there and maybe we should have just kept it as that, or maybe we should have just done the deed (there it is again), put 30 years of mutual attraction to bed, so to speak, and left it at that.

But oh no, not me!

Three months later I'm making the exceedingly long journey to New Zealand. I'm going for 3 weeks, and even on the (numerous) flights, I have mixed feelings about whether I'm doing the right thing.

My suitcase doesn't arrive with me – I guess that was a sign that I also shouldn't have flown all the way, I should have had a nice little holiday in Sydney, just me and my suitcase, the Harbour Bridge, the Opera House...nice and simple. But no, here I am, with only the clothes I have been travelling in for 35 hours, and it feels off. Wrong. Totally wrong.

Oh fuck. I think I have just made a huge mistake.

I'm here. I don't know anyone else (I don't think I'll be looking up my old friend, his ex), it's just me and him on the other side of the world...hmmm...as familiarity cartwheels into my mind, the feeling of being trapped tumbles out.

Oh bloody perfect.

Because, of course, it's no coincidence that Unfinished Business was part of my life when I was with The Psycho. In fact, it was him that came over that night when it all kicked off, him that came to my rescue, him (and her) that poured me the vodka to ease my shock, him (and her) that I stayed with before going back. And here I am now, trapped with him because I couldn't say no, couldn't trust my instinct and find my voice, just like I couldn't say no to going to Australia with The Psycho after he'd held a knife against my throat, just like all the other times I've wanted to say no but couldn't, just like when I was 11 and couldn't say no.

And whilst he's not a psycho, something very odd has happened to him over the past few months since we hooked up. He is being really bloody weird. To say that he is keen is a colossal understatement. He has been obsessing about what to buy in for my arrival, how we're going to spend our time, arranging this and that down to fine detail.

He's turned it into a fucking honeymoon.

He's bought new satin bedsheets, booked us a romantic couple's retreat complete with hot tub and his and hers massage.

It's all TOO MUCH!

I really don't think I'm just doing my old 'someone's being nice to me so I'm outta here' routine. There is something off about it. He is SO intense. It's like he's created such a fantasy in his head about the amazing perfect time we're going to have...it goes down like a lead balloon when I'm not bouncing up and down with the joy of it all.

I'm so jet-lagged for the first week, I persuade him to go to work while I sleep in. This was obviously not written into his fantasy script. He is as drenched in resentment as the satin sheets are drenched in sweat. When we do try to talk about it, we end up arguing. It's like he's trying SO hard to please me but it's not me he's trying to please, it's his fantasy version of me.

What the fuck has happened?

We used to have such a laugh together. We used to just click.

And when we go for a long weekend to one of the most stunning places on earth I've ever seen, all I can think is:

Christ, I wish I was here on my own!

Which is interesting because normally I would expect me to think "I wish I was here with someone else" but no, I am CRAVING my OWN company, my OWN space. It feels like a new thing starting to emerge in me, embers are being stoked and I intuitively fan the flames.

There are odd occasions when it feels OK, I notice these are when we're just hanging out as friends. As soon as we move into the realm of coupledom, wrongness seeps into my bones.

Pretty obvious what the message is, eh?

Unfinished Business spends the rest of my trip oscillating between trying to please me and sulking for continually 'getting it wrong' and being a moody angry fuck.

I spend the rest of my trip oscillating between trying to make the best of a bad situation and orchestrating moments where I can be on my own.

The sex feels totally wrong to me too. It has a whiff of incest about it. Well, I guess I'm beginning to see he has been like a brother to me. She – his ex, my ex-friend – has taken up residence in my head too. It was always her and him, not me and him, it's just not right. We crossed a line and, for me at least, it's blatantly obvious that we shouldn't have.

He, on the other hand, is likely planning our joint Christmas cards.

Then, on the last day, something very interesting happens.

My bags are packed.

Oh, the anticipatory joy of getting to that airport!

He offers to weigh my suitcase with his weighing hook thing. I leave him to it...

Him: "FOR FUCK'S SAKE!!! JESUS FUCKING CHRIST!!"

What the hell has happened?

I run into the bedroom.

My suitcase has puked out all its contents. A mountain of clothes stares up at me from the floor.

Him: "For fuck's sake! Why didn't you zip up the case first? You knew I was going to weigh it."

Me: "Alright. Calm down."

Him: "No, I won't fucking calm down. Oh I just can't do anything right, can I!"

He stomps out of the room, slamming the door behind him.

This isn't the first time he's showcased his uncontrollable anger while I've been here.

So here I am, on the other side of the world with some angry fucker, my carefully packed clothes that were ready for my escape, now in a heap on the floor.

Again.

It's almost like the universe is trying to tell me something...!

I am in such a hurry to get the hell out of there that I don't bother hanging around to put an end to it all. So after I get home, the contact continues.

Over the next few weeks, as I attempt to extricate myself, he seems to get even weirder.

Each time we message or speak, he talks about how wonderful it was when I was there, all the happy memories.

You whaaaat??? Is it me???

He also tells me he's taken up mindfulness and he wants to learn Spanish. Two things he knows I am interested in, and odd that he's never mentioned them before.

Is he still trying to please me?!!! NO! STOP!

He's also started guitar lessons. Again, nothing I've heard him mention before and he would know that a lot of my exes have played guitar and it's always been a thing for me.

OK, so maybe I need to rein my ego in a bit here, it's not ALL about ME, right?

But when he tells me the first song he's learning to play just happens to be my all-time favourite song, a fact that he then denies all knowledge of knowing, well, this is actually starting to spook me out.

For sure you fucking know that's my favourite song, we've talked about it!

If he admitted he was learning it because it was my favourite song, well, I'd still be freaked out, but because he's denying it, it makes it all the bloody weirder.

That's it.

I'm done.

Strange how unfinished business can go sometimes.

Scene Fifteen – Cycles

"Perimenopause. The Mother of All Wake-up Calls."

– Christiane Northrup

It's a thing, apparently.

Well thank Christ for that, I thought it was just me.

An incredible book, The Wisdom of Menopause, has landed in my oestrogen-depleted lap and it's a game-changer. In it, Christiane Northrup says that our perimenopausal symptoms are the body's wisdom showing us that our unresolved life issues need attending to. It's a last ditch attempt to get our attention and it's likely to throw our lives into turmoil as we endeavour to resolve our past and carve out our new future. Apparently, this time is a mirror image of our adolescence, when we are attempting to individuate from our families. At menopause we can pick up where we left off and get the job finished.

That's exactly it! That's exactly what it feels like is happening.

I'm picking up where I left off!

Is that why all these people from my past are coming back around? The chance to finish the job?

Reading this book is unlocking something that has been coded in my uterus.

She also says that normally when a woman has PMT, all of the unresolved issues around that time come to the surface each month. We wrestle with ourselves, ruminate over things that are happening in our lives, feel depressed or anxious, irritable, unsettled, angry... I've had this, to some degree or other, every month since I was 12 and it's *definitely* been heightened every time I've been in a relationship. But when a woman enters perimenopause, it's the unresolved issues of her WHOLE LIFE that come to the surface. That's a lot of shit to be dealing with every month. A veritable fistful of wrestling, ruminating, depressive anxiety-ridden angst!

No wonder all this stuff is coming up for me now, including guys from my past, giving me the chance to do things differently.

Apparently, in particular, it is the time in our lives when our periods *began* that will show up the most. It certainly feels to me that those times are *demanding* my attention right now and I know, whatever it takes, I need to free myself up to give them that time and attention. It feels like my duty to myself.

It seems that all of this is an opportunity for the healing to take place. For the unresolved issues to finally be resolved. For the grief to be felt. Whenever there is change there is loss, right? Isn't it our job then to free ourselves from our internalised struggles, so that we can now be who we are meant to be? So we can make a healthy transition into the next phase of our lives, the cycle completed.

What if we don't make time, make space, find the courage for this process to happen? Then it's just more suppression, more burying of the unresolved issues until they are so hidden they are unrecognisable, the opportunity lost, gone forever perhaps, carried forward into the next lifetime maybe.

But never mind the next lifetime! Haven't we got enough to sort out in *this* lifetime? The suppression may well transfer itself into disease in the body. *Dis-ease* in the mind, *dis-ease* in the heart, dis-ease in the soul...that can only lead to one thing sooner or later: *disease* in the body.

So I'm being given the opportunity to deal with it, not suppress it like I did in my earlier years but deal with it this time. Say No when I mean no, say Yes when I mean yes. Have the confidence. Find my voice.

It seems a woman's mid-life stage is all about saying, "ENOUGH."

It's all about no longer being able to tolerate the intolerable. It's all about finally getting creative and tapping into those resources that have previously been overshadowed by being the nurturer and carer for others. It's all about expanding and growing and shooting out all our rockets of desire that have been squashed down under the surface, and finally letting them take off. It's all about saying, "It's my turn now and if you don't like it you can fuck off."

Now I know I haven't been in a dead-end marriage for 20 years (that was never going to be me) but I have been busy being a mum, I have been stuck in the system of doing what society expects of me by working and attempting to provide a stable environment for my children. Yes, I've focused on my own needs too, making sure I still had time to do the things that were important to me, but I have certainly suppressed my desire to travel, to live a more alternative lifestyle, to be more creative, to take more risks, to break away from the system of being told how we have to live our lives.

On the other hand, I've always felt that having kids has given me a convenient excuse not to have to take those risks, given me permission to play it safe, hide behind the parental guise of "well, I would if I didn't have kids..."

But boy number one has already left home, and boy number two won't be far behind...no excuses now.

Something is brewing, the same thing that was there when I was with Unfinished Business in the most beautifully stunning place in the world, when I just wanted to be on my own. Yes, something is very slowly starting to brew for sure, it will be a while before it comes up to the boil, but I am most certainly on a low simmer.

We have so many issues about this stuff.

My whole life I've been either apologising for my hormones or denying them!

Every relationship, every man I've ever known has done the whole "Oops, time of the month" tiptoe, ooh watch out, give her a wide berth until it's all over bullshit thing.

It's SO fucked up.

No wonder many of us are so suppressed and no wonder when we approach menopause, all that suppression catches up with us. Then we're left with a choice: we can keep suppressing or we can break free.

We can embrace the fact that our intensified hormones are helping us to feel things more strongly. Or perhaps they help the defences we've been cultivating all our lives to step out of the way just long enough that we can actually FEEL OUR TRUTH.

Enough apologising!

Enough denying!

I intend to grab this incredible phase of my life by the hand and see what it has to teach me. In fact, it doesn't even feel like a choice.

I know if I don't, I'm fucked.

I can feel myself transforming. I am transmuting into the woman that I'm meant to be in the next phase of my life. It's roaring through my DNA and rather than 'conveniently sloping off quietly until it's all over' – as at least half the population might prefer – I'm OUT!

I'm perimenopausal and I'm proud!

Well, for today, at least.

Tomorrow I may well be contemplating shoving my head in the oven.

Scene Sixteen – Stories

"Dancing transforms everything, demands everything and judges no one. Those who are free dance...To dance is to use a language beyond selfishness and fear."

– Paulo Coelho

I'm sitting cross-legged on the floor at the end of a yoga class. My teacher is telling us about a new practice that she is offering. She's inviting us along on Saturday evening. I am mildly interested, I ask her more.

"Well, it's women only, it's free dancing, feminine movement, we'll all be gathered under the full moon, and it's amazing. You'll love it."

Love it? I don't think so. It sounds hideous.

My cells have repelled at more than a hint of woo woo.

Women only?

I've always been far more comfortable in a room of men than a room of women.

Feminine movement?

Dancing under the full moon?

Urghhhh! Horrendous.

It all sounds on the wrong side of 'out there' for me.

So I go along.

I don't go despite my reaction, I go because of it.

What is it about this that is so repellent to me?

I mean, she hasn't just suggested that we all strip off naked and go running through the woods, howling under the light of the moon, chanting in tongues, and sprinkling each other in stardust.

Isn't it the things we resist the most that have the most to teach us?

Well if that's the case, I'm in for a huge treat.

"Welcome to Qoya," she begins. "Qoya is movement with meaning. It is based on the simple idea that through movement, we remember. We remember, as women, that our essence is wise, wild and free."

Did someone just say FREE??

"Wise draws reference to the wisdom of yoga. Wild draws reference to the wildness of free dance. And free draws reference to the freedom of feminine movement, which simply means moving our bodies in a way that they intuitively want to move rather than in a way that we are told how to move them."

OK, this is all sounding quite fine, it's speaking my language, nothing too weird at all. And as she lights the sage and goes around the candlelit room, smudging each of us 16 women in turn, rather than running for the door...I remember...I remember that divine smell. I am back in Sacred Space, the place where I did my counselling training 20 years ago. Sacred Space was all about the sage, all about the spiritual, all about tuning into something more than just what's right in front of our faces. But it's more than just the smell of the sage, I am remembering how all this resonates with me, soothes me, gives me a sense of coming home. After 20 years of being a mum, working, trying to earn enough money, allowing different relationships to distract me from my path, I am finding my way back. A different practice, but all practices serve the same purpose: the fact that we are all just trying to find our way back home.

Throughout the evening I realise that this isn't on the wrong side of 'out there' for me. It's not out of my comfort zone at all. That's just a story I tell myself to maintain a certain image: 'Oh me, no, I'm way too cool for all that weird stuff' and 'Oh I'm much more comfortable in a room full of men' – yes, because men are attracted to me and that has fed my ego and, in a deluded way, soothed that part of me that doesn't feel good enough. And with women? Well, if I'm honest, I've always felt jealousy from them, especially if their other halves have been in that room full of men. I've always had girlfriends who have been jealous, who have tried to control or manipulate me, and who have been possessive. I've never really questioned it before, I think I just accepted that's how it was with girls, or maybe unconsciously that was also what I wanted in order to feed my ego and soothe that not good enough part of me...

If girls are jealous of me and men want to fuck me, then I must be worthy, right?!

Every experience we have, we interpret it to fit into our world view of things, and we have sought out every one of those experiences to back up our world view of things in the first place. So that has been my interpretation. And a room full of women has also always felt a tad 'unsafe' to me, kind of bitchy, like we're nice to each other on the surface but gossipy behind each other's backs. It seems, as women, we're driven to compete in a vain attempt to gain our sense of self. We're so busy judging ourselves, we can't help but judge each other in the process.

This feels different though, this – I hate to admit it – feels like pure love, and what's even stranger to admit...I feel like I belong.

The evening is a mix of huge emotions and getting in touch with all those realisations is pretty massive. I cry in the shadow contrast dance – the part where we are invited to be with and dance with the opposite of our intention, the opposite of how we want to feel, these everyday feelings that we deem as 'negative', that we are conditioned into pushing away or ignoring or distracting ourselves from, all those feelings we then suppress and push down until we are full up with them. But they are always just there under the surface and so when we actually invite them in (in a very similar way as mindfulness encourages us to 'turn towards difficulty' in a gentle and compassionate way, to sit with it, invite it in, feel it into our bodies, breathe into the edges of it, see how it might change) they're right there to be felt.

One thing is for sure: contrast is our greatest teacher. Through experiencing what we don't want, we get clearer on what we do want. But if we just keep shoving this stuff down, then we're not really connected to our experience, not really present.

Right now I don't really know why I'm crying as I let these feelings move through me to the soundtrack of something melancholy, but that's OK, I don't need to know. And there is no way you can do Qoya wrong, apparently, so that's pretty liberating too.

After that shadow contrast we 'shake' off those feelings, release them. The effects are just mind-blowing. It's the simplest thing: if we move our bodies, we change our whole homeostasis. If we want to change the way we feel, we just need to move.

The final dance comes with the invitation to, "Dance your intention. Imagine how it feels in your body when you are connected to that intention. Dance that feeling. Dance like no one is watching."

It's that kitchen dancing that usually involves a glass or two of wine and the absolute secure knowledge that no one is watching. Those are usually the only conditions in which, for me, at least, I can let myself go. But here I am, no wine, no kitchen, and although I am in a room full of other women, it still feels like no one is watching. Instead, there is a sense of community, the odd glimpse of recognition behind kind, smiling, sparkling eyes.

I don't feel judged. I don't feel compared to. I don't feel bitched about. For the first time in my life, I am starting to experience the meaning of sisterhood and I am beginning to realise how much I've needed it, even though I didn't even realise it was missing. I didn't really know it was even a thing.

Just like self-compassion – which I thought was all a bit schmaltzy and not for me, thank you! (Yes, I am aware that says a lot about me.) But through mindfulness, I (eventually) opened up to the concept of self-compassion, and then the practice of self-compassion, and I realised the absolute power of it.

Self-compassion and sisterhood are total game-changers for me.

So Qoya becomes my new favourite thing. Every Friday at 1 p.m. our tribe of women gather in a village hall for an hour and a half and we dance ourselves into existence. And each week my heart unfastens itself a little more.

All this time I thought it was men that I needed to open my heart up to, turns out it was women.

Who knew?

And that first class I went to, even when we all ran outside onto the beach at the end of the evening and stood under the bright light of the full moon and howled...I didn't bat an eyelid.

Scene Seventeen – Triad

"The curious paradox is, when I accept myself as I am, then I can change."

– Carl Rogers

I'm at a yoga festival with a friend – another one who I am beginning to realise is rather controlling, manipulating and possessive of me, and who is continually bitching about people. I can't put it all on her, for years I've been part of the bitching too, so it's not a new thing. No, the only new thing about it is me starting to feel uncomfortable with it. I think all these Buddhist teachings are starting to get to me!

We've just done a yoga class in the main tent and I'm searching the multi-coloured rubber sea of flip-flops outside. I turn to find her and see she is talking to some guy. He seems vaguely familiar. I take a few steps closer.

"And how's your mum?" she's asking him. "Is she still in Tenerife?"

Tenerife! That's it!

I recognise him from when I was there in '95. He was a friend of a friend, we all used to hang out, get drunk and stoned, he was always pissed from what I remember.

Me: "Oh God, hi. Tenerife, it's Vikki, remember?"

He looks more than a little baffled, I attempt to assist him by removing my sunglasses.

Him: "Oh yeah, I think so, but didn't you used to be blonde?"

Me: "Yep, I did. And so did you."

He laughs shyly and rubs a hand over the grey stubble which covers (most of) his head.

So here we are, the three of us.

They know each other from 25 years ago.

He and I know each other from 22 years ago.

She and I have known each other for 18 years.

Until 2 minutes ago, none of us knew that we all knew each other.

We're all just processing that piece of information as we stand here in a very obvious triangle outside a tent in a field at a yoga festival in the English June sunshine.

He tells us his mum died a few years ago and that he bought a house in Mallorca. She and I have been to Mallorca a couple of times together and are both potentially interested in it as a place to live.

My ears prick up at the mention of his house there.

She senses my ears prick up and goes into threat-alert mode.

As soon as we part ways, it's clear she doesn't like him, never has it seems, she's very derogatory about him. Bring on the bitching once again!

I, however, remember him as a really nice guy (albeit always pissed), I'm pleased to have bumped into him, it feels nice to reconnect. He seems pleased to see me too. He seems uncomfortable around her.

It's an interesting dynamic... "take your seats, ladies and gentlemen, the show is about to commence."

He and I chat a few more times at the festival over the weekend. We reminisce about Tenerife, we chat about where our lives have taken us since then. He's big into meditation, he's done several 10-day Vipassana meditation retreats – something I've been interested in doing myself. He lives in a campervan in the forest. I love that. I'm definitely drawn to his lifestyle.

We exchange numbers on the last morning.

She, in contrast, is decidedly off. She has single-handedly packed up our tent and is standing impatiently in her crisp white linen outfit, waiting to leave, car keys in hand, while I am still lying around in a field in my tie-dye elephant pants, feeling the love.

She slags him off all the way home, refers to him with the derogatory nickname she always used to have for him. It's almost like she's worried I quite like him and is doing her damnedest to put me off. It's very odd.

I'm beginning to realise she has always done this with any guy I've been with. She's tried to put me off, either by psychoanalysing the hell out of the relationship and trying to expose it for what she thought it was, or by belittling it in some way. Never has she just been delighted for me and it seems the only time that she's happy is when I'm single.

It's really just been the past few years that we've been hanging out more, going on yoga holidays together. The ending of her long-term relationship coincided with the ending of Back Garden Neighbour being in my life, and Nelly dying, so we both found ourselves with a space in our lives to fill, with a shared love of yoga and a new level to our friendship. But before that, I never really felt like she had much time for me. If I suggested a plan for us to meet up, she would be very non-committal until the last possible moment when invariably it would be a no.

I wonder why I kept trying? It's like I was trying to get her attention, get her to like me, see me, want me...hmm...now that feels familiar.

This is the first time though that I have met someone that she knows too, and it feels like all her ammunition is coming out in an attempt to keep me away from him. The more I sense she is trying to put me off him, the keener I am to see him.

She is the critical parent. I am the rebellious child. We're both psychotherapists, we know how this stuff goes.

So, like a true rebellious teenager, because I know she 'disapproves' I hold back from telling her when I've been to see him. I stop letting her in on my every move in order to protect myself, in order to protect him, I don't like the way she talks about him, I don't like her disapproval, why would I share it with her?

As a result, understandably, she feels pushed out, like I'm not confiding in her anymore. Well, I'm not. Like I'm spending more time with him than with her. Well, I am.

It's the perfect drama triangle made up of the persecutor, the victim, and the rescuer. The more disapproving she is, the more he becomes the victim to her persecutor, enabling me to rescue him. The more he grows on me and the more she feels like the jilted friend who I have left for another, she becomes the victim to my persecutor. And me confiding in him, enables him to be my rescuer.

This is how the drama triangle works. Everyone rotates and takes their turn. It keeps things even. It keeps things stuck. Until, inevitably, the shit hits the fan and the cursed toxic triangle can succumb to its own murderous death.

We're heading for that shit-hitting fan thing.

The cracks in our friendship are definitely starting to show. However, the more time I spend with him, the more I like him. I'd messaged him a week or so after the festival and it was a week or so before I got a reply. He'd been in Mallorca finishing some restorations in his house. We arranged for me to come and visit him on the campsite in the forest when he got back.

"Mine's the van with the surfboard on the roof and the motorbike at the back."

Tick. Tick. Tick!

I like the whole thing he's got going on, living in the van in the forest, close to nature. It all appeals, speaks to that part of me that's looking for something alternative. The house in Mallorca doesn't hurt either.

———————

My friend and I are meeting up for lunch.

Me: "So I spent the night with (Campervan Man) last night."

Here we go.

Her: "Really? Oh, gawd. Did you...err... did you, you know?"

Me: "Have sex? Yes, we did actually, and it was pretty nice, I must say."

She gives an exaggerated pantomime shudder from head to toe, complete with a guttural 'urghhh' sound effect. It's only a brief performance but, in that moment, I know our friendship is doomed. She knows it too.

What's interesting as well is I'm realising the dynamic between us feels just the same as it did with my friend who moved to New Zealand (Unfinished Business's ex). And come to think of it, the timing is interesting too. It wasn't long after she and I ended all contact that this friendship ramped up a notch. I think I must've had a sign around my neck:

VACANCY FOR CONTROLLING MANIPULATIVE JEALOUS FRIEND – APPLY WITHIN

She seems to be fitting the job description perfectly.

Scene Eighteen – Lineage

"Man's unconscious...contains all the patterns of life
and behaviour inherited from his ancestors, so that
every human child, prior to consciousness, is possessed of
a potential system of adapted psychic functioning."

– Carl Jung

All of this menopause stuff, completions of cycles, old relationships coming back into my life, the stirring in me to end old patterns so I can move into my next phase, the simmering boiling bubbling thing under the surface...well, it's making me think about my dad a lot.

Isn't that one of the things with the menopause anyway? The ultimate bereavement, the loss of our ability to reproduce. It's loss on a primal level and all of our other bereavements and losses, big or small, past, present or anticipated, feel amplified at this time, all feeding into this mega wheel of grief. There are definitely a couple of losses around for me: my boys leaving home and the death of my dad.

For some reason, meeting Campervan Man again is stirring things up about my relationship with my dad. I don't quite understand why, just that there is some connection there. I often wonder what my relationship with my dad would be like now. Now that I have self-awareness, now that I can see why things weren't easy between us, now that I can see the bigger picture, and therefore have a different, more adult perspective. If I'd seen that before would that have meant we'd have a good relationship? That we would be close? It's suddenly so sad that we were never given the chance to find out.

By the time I woke up, he was long since dead.

I will never know what our adult father-daughter relationship would have been like.

Now my boys leaving home...the cycle of the parent-child relationship...it frees me up to look at that part of myself that still needs to be healed before I can have a healthy relationship. Maybe it's time to tend to that now.

It's not just the menopause that's getting under my skin. Qoya places a big emphasis on our ancestral lineage, it draws on shamanic principles and encourages us to have a felt awareness of all of those who have come before us, being part of the wellspring of wisdom that is ours to tap into.

I'm feeling a gravitational pull back into my lineage.

I lost touch with the Step-Mother some years ago. She used to babysit for me sometimes when the boys were young, but for at least five years there's been no contact at all.

Something is nagging me to call her. Re-establish a connection. A connection to her is a connection to my dad. To my lineage.

The only other family my dad had here was a cousin and her two daughters. We'd seen a lot of them growing up, but again, lost contact. I wonder if she's even still alive? She'd be well into her late 80s by now. My dad died at 61, so young.

The same impulse that's telling me to call the Step-Mother is telling me to call my dad's cousin too. It's funny, these women haven't been on my radar at all, but the longer I don't act on it, the stronger the urge is getting. I have to reconnect with them. I don't know why, menopause I expect!

It all takes some detective work. I manage to trace one of my stepsisters and one of the daughters of my dad's cousin online through their work. I make contact with them both, they confirm that both the Step-Mother and the Cousin are still alive and well, and they put me in touch.

A couple of weeks later, I'm meeting up with the Step-Mother in a local coffee shop. She has a blue paper folder with her which she passes to me shortly after we sit down in the comfy leather chairs.

"There are just some things of your father's that I've put together for you, things I thought you might like."

Inside is his old equity card, a few photocopies of pictures I've seen before, but also some certificates that I haven't: his birth certificate, Omi's marriage and divorce certificates, their naturalisation papers.

Why haven't I been given these before?

I refrain from asking. It's nice to see her. In meeting up with her, I am reviving him.

I also pay a visit to the Cousin. I have a lot of fond memories of her. As children, my dad would often take us to visit her and her daughters. My sister and I were bridesmaids for one of her daughters when I was 12. I fainted at the hairdressers on the morning of the wedding when we were all getting ready. I'd also left my asthma inhaler at home and my dad made a 50-mile round trip to get it and rushed back with it so I could breathe as I walked down the aisle. I told you the whole marriage thing wasn't for me, even the anticipation of being a bridesmaid was enough to induce some kind of trauma!

The Cousin is the closest thing that my dad had to a sibling. I don't know the full story (yet) but they both escaped to England around the same time after the end of the Second World War and never returned to their native Czechoslovakia.

It's quite emotional to see her again, to be talking about my dad, to be asking her questions I didn't even know I needed the answers to. It's funny how we only get interested in our family history when we reach a certain age, by which time it's often too late to get the information we're looking for.

Or maybe that's the way it's perfectly designed.

It turns out that, a few years ago, someone from the Red Cross had contacted the Cousin and asked if she could interview her for a book about Second World War stories. She'd agreed to do it even though it unearthed the wounds she had spent a lifetime trying to forget. She'd never told her whole story to anyone, not even her daughters. Like so many refugees from that time – my dad included – they came here to begin a new life, to draw a line in the sand, to have a fresh start and leave their traumatic pasts behind them. They never talked about any of it. They never processed any of it. This is the exact opposite of all I have learnt about healing processes through my work as a psychotherapist.

I leave the Cousin's house with a copy of the book in my hand. I can't wait to get home and dive in. Because, of course, this isn't just her story. Her story is my dad's story. Her story is Omi's story. Her story is my family's story. Her story is *my* story.

It seems a lifetime of indifference to my lineage is over.

Maybe if I want to know myself better, I need to know this stuff too. Maybe that's a menopause thing as well – the need to know ourselves fully before we die.

And what do the pages of this book teach me?

That my dad's cousin was gang-raped by Russian soldiers, shortly after her fifteenth birthday, whilst she was out one evening to fetch help for her mother who had just gone into labour. Subsequently, she had to hide out in the loft of the house of some relatives in the next village until her parents could arrange, with an aunt, her safe passage to England.

Fuck!

Fifteen years old, a virgin, violently gang-raped and then separated from your parents, brothers, and new-born sister, to go into hiding before leaving for a strange country and foreign land. Her innocence ruptured. Her spirit annihilated.

She settled in England, the rest of her family eventually all moved to Germany. That single event changed the trajectory of her entire life.

And she's not alone. I read that every female member of my family on my dad's side was likely raped by Russian soldiers. Apparently, the Nazi occupation in Czechoslovakia was nothing compared to when the Russians took up residence.

A subconscious spider's web of ancestral abuse is beginning to uncradle itself from my psyche. I know I have 'carried' this.

Little do I know the can of worms I have released. Another story is about to drop into my lap. The next time I meet up with the Step-Mother, she hands me another folder, yellow this time.

Oh, here we go again, more stuff that should've been mine already!

"This is your father's story of when they left Czechoslovakia. He wrote it some years ago, a while before he died. I thought you should have it."

Too bloody right I should have it! He died 21 years ago, why am I only getting this now?

I glance inside and my heart misses a beat at the sight of his handwriting. He always wrote everything in capitals, like he was really making sure he'd be heard.

I am grateful at least that I have this now.

Here's what I already know about my dad.

He was born in 1934 in a town called Czeske Budejovice in (what was then) Czechoslovakia. He was an only child, born to a shopkeeper of Austro-Hungarian descent (my omi) and a Czech shoe salesman (my opa) 15 years her senior. Five years after my dad was born, the Nazis came along and occupied Czechoslovakia.

My grandparents' relationship was already on the rocks, he apparently was a bit of a ladies man and his job meant he travelled a lot which we assume made it easy for him to have lots of affairs. He was also a staunch Czech, extremely patriotic, and actively involved in supporting the Czech Resistance. Somewhere around 1940, Opa was caught and arrested for passing messages underground. He became a political prisoner and was locked away in the local jail in Budejovice, his fate yet to be decided. Omi filed for divorce. To protect herself and my father from any association with the resistance? Or because of his philandering? Or both? Either way, my dad was forbidden from ever talking about his father, his name was never mentioned again.

But he did recall being taken one day by an uncle to the prison fence to see his father leaning out of his cell window, waving a handkerchief, and calling out my dad's nickname, "Kajo, Kajo..."

My dad was 7 years old and that was the last time he saw his father (the same age I was when my dad moved out). I think that my opa had managed to orchestrate that sighting as a way of saying goodbye to his son as shortly after he was transported to a concentration camp, the details of which I will only find out much later.

Meanwhile, my dad's childhood carried on. Budejovice is 2 hours north of Prague and they were largely unaware of the horrors that were taking place in the capital and all over the rest of Europe. At least my dad and his cousins were, unlike their parents who would have been hearing many rumours and listening to secret news broadcasts.

My dad had a dog called Spot who he adored, a white Jack Russel with a black patch over one eye. He didn't have any siblings; I think Spot was his closest friend. He did have lots of cousins though – my omi having three sisters and two brothers. Her parents owned a farm outside of town and she and my dad were living there relatively peacefully as far as I know.

Somewhere along the line, Omi met a German officer named Hans. We don't know the exact nature of their relationship, perhaps she was being astute in befriending a high-ranking German officer who could offer them some protection. Or perhaps she knew that the worst was yet to come and that Hans could provide them with a way out. Or perhaps she was just a lonely, young, divorced Czech single mother who fell for a German soldier. Who knows? But whatever it was, I'm not sure where they would have been without Hans. In April 1945, as the Germans were losing the war, there were rumours of Russian soldiers advancing and leaving a terror of devastation in their wake. My dad's childhood on his grandparents' orchard with his beloved Spot the dog, came to an abrupt end.

He was 11 years old.

The yellow paper folder sits in my lap, its contents daringly requesting the pleasure of my company. I take a deep breath. I know this isn't going to be an easy read, but nothing can quite prepare me for what I find out.

Here's what I didn't know about my dad:

"........WE MET THE MILITARY LORRY ON THE OUTSKIRTS OF THE
TOWN, IT WAS 8 O'CLOCK, A BRIGHT SUNNY DAY AND
IRONICALLY I COULD SEE MY GRANDMOTHER'S HOUSE AND
ORCHARD WHERE I SPENT MANY HAPPY TIMES PICKING AND
EATING FRUIT. I REGARDED THIS WHOLE EPISODE AS A MERE
GOING ON HOLIDAY, I NEVER REALISED THE SERIOUSNESS OF
THE SITUATION...."

*It was an open-top lorry with several German soldiers already
aboard, in fact, mother and I were the only civilians. Hans
had used his authority to get us out of town. Soldiers kept
arriving and climbing aboard. At last, the driver started the
engine and we were off.*

*We drove for some 3 to 4 hours stopping only along the way to
discuss with the other soldiers the advancement of the Russian
front. In fact, the whole of the German army was in disarray;
German soldiers were discarding their uniforms for civilian
clothes and abandoning their vehicles by the roadside hoping
to blend in with the rest of the population. Tanks and lorries
were left scattered along the roadside.*

*We had by now crossed the Austrian border and stopped at
Unterwiessenbach. We were in the centre of this small village,
Hans jumped off the lorry and approached some people
gathered in the marketplace. Several minutes later he
returned, apparently the Russians were advancing at a fast
rate and there was no place to run. It was a case of every man
for himself.*

Mother and I got off the lorry and Hans picked up the suitcase, the only possessions we could take, and we started walking to the outskirts of the village. Hans thought we might get put up at a farm and see how the situation progressed.

We had walked about half a mile when we saw a farm up on a hill to our right. It seemed far enough from the village, so we started the long trek up. Halfway up we took a rest and looked back at the little village of Unterweissenbach nestling between the hills, this was really exciting, what an adventure, but little did I know what lay in store for us during the ensuing months.

We reached the farmhouse quite puffed and out of breath, Hans knocked on the door. It was opened by a sturdy chubby woman in her mid-forties, the husband she said was working in the fields, but we could come in and wait as she thought there was some possibility of coming to some arrangement. She gave me a glass of milk and offered Hans and mother a cup of coffee. She said if I liked I could go out into the yard and look around and explore.

It was a large square cobblestone yard surrounded with barns and stables with the customary dung heap in the middle with the typical stench of a farmyard aroma and enormous blue bottles buzzing around it. I befriended two black and white type sheepdogs, they didn't seem to mind being woken up as they slept in the shade. They soon started fighting playfully for my affections. I strolled on to the stables, they were empty as the cows were grazing out on the land. I avoided the barn and the hayloft as they would have aggravated my bout of hay-fever which I had to endure every summer.

Later that afternoon when Mr Müller, a tall skinny man with a bushy moustache, returned home, it was agreed with Hans *after some discussion that he would work with Mr Müller, out in the fields and mother would help out in the house for our bed and board, for a while anyway.*

Our room was tiny and bare, with a double bed and a cot-like small bed for me literally squeezed in the corner, no wardrobe, no chest of drawers, nothing. Well, in our situation we could not be choosy. Dinner was served on a large pine table.

The following morning mother and Hans had to get up really early; mother had to help with breakfast and Hans to go to work with Mr Müller. I got up a little later after everyone had gone.

After breakfast, I wandered out across the yard to the main entrance and looking down the path to where it joined the road below, I could see a German tank and two jeeps. They were parked in the meadow beside the road. I ran down the road expecting to see some soldiers but found I had already been beaten to it by three young lads about 2 to 3 years older than myself. They were exploring the vehicles and playing soldiers. When they spotted me approaching the lad with his head sticking out of the top of the tank shouted, "Here comes the enemy" followed by sounds of imaginary gunshots. Suddenly from behind the tank came two lads running towards me shouting, "The enemy, the enemy, kill, kill!"

I stopped dead in my tracks. One boy running towards me had a rifle with a fixed bayonet in his hands, I stood my ground and stared at them, they stopped a few feet away puffing and panting from their onslaught on the enemy. The freckle-faced ginger-haired youth put down his rifle and still panting said, "Who are you? You don't live around here." I said, "No we're visiting." "Oh," he said, "what's your name?" I said, "Karl". The

blond boy from the tank was walking towards us, he pointed to
him, "That's Peter, and this," pointing to the third boy, "is
Franzel". Then, with excitement in his voice, he started telling
me that they found this rifle in the jeep with ammunition, but
it wouldn't shoot. They were all talking at the same time,
telling me the soldiers had all run away and abandoned their
cars. I said, "I can make it shoot." There was silence. They
looked at me in disbelief. Peter said, "You can't make it shoot,
you need training to shoot rifles and you're not a soldier." I
said, "I know I'm not, but I can load it and fire it." "Go on
then," said Walter with challenge in his voice, "show us." Well,
I knew how to load a rifle because Hans had shown me, and I
had fired it several times on their rifle range. They watched my
hands.

The shots must have been heard in the village because two
elderly men came cycling up to investigate. When they saw
what we'd been up to they gave us a real good telling-off and a
lecture on how dangerous guns can be. They told us to get back
to the village, clipped Walter and Franzel around the earhole,
Peter had already started running towards the village. I said I
didn't live in the village, so they said I'd better go home
anyway.

I started walking slowly, waiting for them to get out of sight
because I knew I wanted to go back and explore the tank. I
had never been in a tank. I looked around again and they had
gone now, so I ran all the way back to the tank, climbed on top
of it and into the turret. I never imagined that there was so
little room inside, it was quite claustrophobic. Sitting in the
driver's seat I thought how difficult it must be to drive as there
wasn't a windscreen or window to look out of, just a long
narrow slot.

I climbed out again, that felt better, I didn't like it in there, it was much too close. I stepped through the barbed wire fence into the field. I was now walking away from the road towards the forest, the cows looked at me dispassionately, each in turn as I passed them. Once in the wood, I took out my pocketknife and looked for a suitable straight thin branch that would make a good spear. I much preferred being a Red Indian with bows and arrows than a soldier, somehow to me it was more exciting. I found one and started cutting it, the knife was rather blunt, and it was quite a struggle.

Suddenly I heard men's voices followed by a painful cry. My immediate reaction was to run, which I did for a few steps, then I stopped and looked back and, in real Red Indian fashion, I moved from tree to tree towards the voices.

Within a few yards, I saw them: six German soldiers in their early twenties, wearing black uniforms, and in various stages of undress. I recognised the uniforms, they were the S.S. The soldiers were changing into civilian clothes and discarding their uniforms. One blond man was stripped to the waist and was standing with his arm held in front of him, with the other hand pulling away the skin from the inside of his bicep. Another one seemed to be cutting at the skin with a knife, there was blood running down his chest, he cried out again.

I couldn't understand what was happening, they weren't doing it against his will but then we had heard stories about the cruelty of the S.S. This Red Indian suddenly became very frightened, I took off in a blind panic and did not stop running until I got back to the road.

The outcome of this episode was that, later that evening, I told mother and Hans what I had seen. Hans explained that S.S.

soldiers had the SS insignia tattooed on the inside of their biceps, so what they were trying to do was to remove these tattoos, but anyone arrested found to have scars on the inside of their arms would be considered to belong to the S.S. anyway. Therefore, this was rather a painful and futile exercise.

The rest of the week was rather boring and uneventful. Mother decided I was not to go roaming around on my own. One afternoon, Frau Müller suggested I should go with Trudi, their daughter, to the village as she wanted her to do some shopping. I mumbled something like, "I'd rather not" however Trudi was called and told, "You take Karl shopping with you and he can help you carry the bag." Sulkily, Trudi took the money, the list and the bag, and when her back was turned towards her mother, she poked her tongue out at me. Down the hill we went towards the village, she striding out two steps ahead of me swinging her shopping bag, me following behind.

We arrived at the marketplace just as some people were gathering around a horse and cart. On the cart were four dead bodies: two teenage girls and their mother and father. In this heat, the bodies had bloated like blow-up plastic dolls and their eyes stared into space through the many large flies that had gathered around their eyes, nose and lips. The smell was awful. It was a local doctor and his family, he had collaborated with the Germans, and fearing reprisals, he had taken them into the forest and injected them with morphine. They were found by some people out for a walk.

Trudi started walking towards the store so I followed and waited outside. Peter and Walter came by surprised to see me, asked what I was doing, and did I want to come with them. I *said I couldn't as I was waiting for Trudi. This was followed by typical boyish laughter – nudge-nudge, wink-wink. She came out of the shop and, without giving us a second glance, she paused only long enough to deposit the shopping bag at my feet and then continued walking. Somewhat embarrassed, I picked up the bag and followed – much to Peter's and Walter's amusement. they followed me with teasing calls and laughter someway across the marketplace.*

Later that evening, at supper time, we were all sitting around the table when two Russian soldiers burst in waving their machine guns about in an up and down motion as if they wanted us to get up and shouting orders which we didn't understand. They gathered us in the centre of the room, then one of the soldiers grabbed the older daughter by the arm and started to drag her into the hallway.

The women screamed, the men moved forward, but a burst of gunfire into the wooden floor stopped everyone in their tracks. The empty shells had fallen at my feet and I could smell the powder. I was terrified. Mother had hold of my shirt and was pulling me backwards. While this was going on, the other soldier had pulled the girl into the bedroom directly opposite. He pushed her onto the bed for everyone to see and started pulling her clothes off. But she was a sturdy well-built girl and she fought like a wild cat.

After what seemed like an eternity but in fact was only about two minutes, he realised he wasn't going to get anywhere. He stood up and took his pistol from his holster and amidst what sounded like Russian abuse, started to beat her about the face with it. Immediately, there was blood everywhere. The woman screamed again. This was followed again by gunfire. The soldier who was guarding us called out to him. He was beginning to look nervous, His comrade, after wiping his pistol on the bedcover, replaced it in its holster. He picked up his machine gun from the floor, where he had dropped it, and came into the hallway. His uniform was covered in blood, the girl lay motionless on the bed behind him. They both started walking backwards towards the front door, guns pointing at us, and suddenly they were gone.

Now the hysteria really broke loose, everybody trying to get to the room to see what could be done. A doctor arrived a little later to patch her up, her face was unrecognisable. There were comings and goings all night. I don't think anybody slept; we were all so terrified.

The following morning two Russian soldiers were found floating in the village pond. One had a blood-stained uniform and scratches on his face. They were found drinking in the store after they left us, the locals did the rest.

Needless to say, there were repercussions. The Russians took revenge on the local community and they enforced a curfew and spasmodic searches of houses. Our presence on the farm was becoming a danger to the Müllers. We discussed it with them and it was decided that we would leave as soon as possible.

In fact, the following day – which was a Sunday – brought things to a head. The Müllers, a very Christian family, usually went to church but because of their daughter's unfortunate experience, she was in bed with her injuries, and they did not want to leave her, so they decided to say prayers in her bedroom instead. No sooner had they finished when somebody burst through the front door calling for Herr Müller. It was a young man from the neighbouring farm and in between gasping and trying to catch his breath, he said the Russians had searched his farm and were on their way here. Six soldiers were already coming up the hill.

Herr Müller called out, "You must hide. In the barn – quick follow me." We ran down the stairs, across the cobbled yard and into the barn, followed by the two dogs playfully yapping at our heels. One side of the barn was stacked with dozens of bales of straw while the other side had an enormous mound of loose hay as high as a double-decker bus. Herr Müller pointed to this, "In there," he said. We dived in headfirst, burrowing like moles, followed by the dogs – they thought this was a good game. Fortunately, they heard the soldiers' voices at the gate and turned their attention towards them. Herr Müller quickly heaped piles of hay on top of us and said he'd be back when the coast was clear.

I was terrified. Mother was squeezing my hand and whispering into my ear to keep calm, everything would be alright. With my other hand, I was pinching my nose to stop myself from sneezing – with my hay-fever, I could not have been in a worse place.

We sat and waited for ages, the voices had disappeared, they must be searching the house, even the dogs had stopped barking. The voices appeared again; a woman's voice, followed by the sound of boots on the cobblestones, meant they were searching the outbuildings. Some footsteps entered the barn, I held my breath, mother's hand tightened around mine. They were talking now, moving about, it sounded like there were only two of them.

Somebody was now walking in the barn, they were joking and talking in a light-hearted manner. The voice was coming closer and he was jabbing something into the hay. The sound came nearer and nearer. I opened my eyes, staring straight ahead, expecting the inevitable, that's when I saw three prongs of the pitchfork he was using thrust inches in front of my face, and again, this time further to my left. I closed my eyes, this was it.

Just then, another bellowed command from the yard, they were being recalled. The sound of marching boots on cobblestones and then silence. Mother relaxed her grip on my hand. During my panic, I quite forgot about my uncontrollable urge to sneeze, but this feeling was now coming back. Where was Herr Müller? Mother started to speak but Hans stopped her, "Shh, not yet." At last, the barking dogs told her Herr Müller was on his way, he called out, "Alright, they've gone." We scrambled out on hands and knees, covered in blades of hay and quite exhausted from this close shave. We can be thankful that the soldiers did not do a thorough job otherwise we surely would have been found.

Herr Müller looked very worried and it went without saying that it was time we left. Hans told him that we would wait until dark then we would be on our way. He seemed relieved. As we walked back to the house, I was able to let rip with some hearty sneezes and I remember thinking that I hoped nobody would think I had been crying because of my streaming eyes.

It was midday now, which meant a lot of hours to while away until nightfall. Hans thought we had better leave the suitcase behind as it was too large and too conspicuous, we had to represent to the onlooker a German family out shopping or just for a walk depending on the situation. Mother and I could easily pass for Germans, we were both very blond and our

German, spoken mainly with an Austrian dialect, was more than adequate, and my name was now Karl instead of Karel. So Frau Müller exchanged the suitcase for an ordinary shopping bag into which we put our most necessary belongings and the rest we left behind. Mother and Hans discussed what time it would be best to leave, and it was decided about 12 o'clock, by which time – because of the curfew – even the soldiers would have settled down and we would only have to avoid the patrols. This we hoped to do by walking cross country and steering clear of the roads.

Supper time came soon enough, mother said I should have a good meal as we didn't know when we'd eat next, however, we needn't have worried as Frau Müller packed us a food parcel to last us a week. Everybody soon went to bed because of their early rising, Herr and Frau Müller offered to stay up with us but there was not much point to keep them up as well. We thanked them for their kindness, mother and Frau Müller embraced, I also got a cuddle. Hans and Herr Müller shook hands and then they went upstairs. Three hours to go. Hans said we better try to get some sleep, so I settled down in the armchair and mother and Hans on the settee. I couldn't get to sleep, my mind was full of this morning's events and the grandfather clock kept chiming, but the next thing I was aware of was mother tugging at my sleeve, "Kajo, it's time to go." All I wanted was to sleep. "Come on, we must go," she pulled me to my feet.

So there we were: one bag, one food parcel, and a map. We let ourselves out by the side door; it was a clear warm night as we walked silently and somewhat nervously down the hill into the dark.

During the next two weeks, we covered almost 300 kilometres on foot. Food was scarce and what we could get was of poor quality and very dear. The boot polish we had brought with us had gone and there were two candles left in the basket. We were still in Austria and at Sonnenburg there was a great deal of troop movement. From deep in the forests, whether we were trying to sleep or just walking, we could hear the tanks rumbling along the road. We felt safer surrounded by the Americans but when we woke one morning, we soon discovered we were in an advancing Russian zone. In panic, we walked north again, trying to cross back into the right sector. Faint from exhaustion and hunger, we finally spotted a campsite full of American troops.

The next day we waited on the outskirts of a small village, away from the main road, hoping that some form of transport would come along which was taking the turning to Eisenach. Nothing passed that Hans could safely stop. As he was familiar with the area, he told us we would have to go up into the hills to find a farm. Perhaps we could sleep in a barn for the night. We left the road and went upwards, over a hill and down towards a farmhouse we could just see in the distance. On reaching it, mother and I remained hidden, waiting while Hans went to bargain with the farmer.

That night, after eating a meal in the small farmhouse with the farmer and his very pregnant wife, we dragged ourselves up into the hayloft and I fell instantly into a deep sleep.

Around dawn, I was woken up by Hans shaking me. Mother put a finger to her lips in warning and we crawled over to the grimy window at the end of the loft. It was barely light but looking out we saw a group of men over by the pump. They *were more frightening than any I had ever seen before. They were all dressed alike, in baggy striped trousers and loose tops, their heads were shaven and looked like skulls. They were drinking from a bucket at the edge of the well, dipping their claw-like hands on the end of stick arms into the water. They had nothing on their feet. Skinny legs were showing beneath their loose trousers.*

Cautiously, three of the men approached the farmhouse door. The other two flattened themselves either side of it. One of the three banged on the door with a yard broom he had picked up. A candle flame flickered in an upstairs room then disappeared, before the glow showed through a small glass pane at the side of the door. The farmer called out, but they didn't reply. A dog chained up in the yard, disturbed by the banging, started to bark. The farmer slowly opened the door but when he moved forward, lifting his candle to see the men better, his face froze in horror. The two men either side of the door crashed down on his back, knocking him to the ground. The one with the broom whacked him with it, across the back of his head. They left him there and went into the farmhouse.

The farmer slowly pulled himself up, unsteady as he rubbed his head. One of them came outside again. He was carrying a hunting rifle which he used to prod the farmer backwards, further out into the yard. Then, pausing for a second, watching him still shuffling backwards, he slowly took aim and shot him in the chest. The farmer spun with the impact and fell facedown. We heard his wife scream. The man then walked across the yard and shot the barking dog.

As we watched, he went into the farmhouse, eventually coming out again with the rest of them, still carrying the gun.

Their arms were piled up with what they had found inside, mainly blankets, clothing, and pots and pans. The food they had scavenged was in a wicker laundry basket. They bundled everything onto a cart in the yard before two of them turned and walked towards the barn.

I closed my eyes in fear, flat on my face in the loft, as they collected the farmer's horse and led him out of our hiding place. When they had hitched the animal between the shafts, they scrambled on board and, without a backward glance, drove out of the yard. The farmer's wife came to the door, clutching her stomach as she stared across at her husband, tears streaming down her face. She waddled over to him and pulled at his nightshirt. He didn't move. She lifted her face to the sky and screamed again.

When Hans thought it was safe, we ran across the yard towards her. Mother led her away. Hans dragged the dead farmer across the yard and into the house. I noticed his blood left a trail in the dusty ground. Following him indoors, I helped mother straighten up the chaos the men had left behind.

We stayed at the farmhouse for several days. Mother attended to the farmer's wife and Hans did whatever was necessary concerning the arrangements to be made to remove the farmer's body. It was during this time he discovered that the Allies had released the inmates of a concentration camp, seven kilometres up the road from the farm. Early one evening, as we sat by the log fire listening to the wireless, a voice announced Hitler was dead. It was the 1st of May 1945.

Hans found us a small flat in Eisenach. His family's grocery business, and his wife and children, were on the other side of town. We lived there in comparative comfort for three months.

I attended a local school and mother helped support us by crocheting collars and cuffs for a nearby dressmaker.

One night I was woken by mother crying in the next room. I could hear Hans quietly talking to her. He finally left and mother, still sobbing, crept into the room and got into the bed beside me. I must have missed him, because a few days later, I asked where he was. Mother said sharply that he had decided to live with his wife. Nothing more was said on the subject and I never saw him again.

Some weeks later, I came home from school to find mother sitting at the kitchen table, reading a letter. She told me it was from Aunt Anne (her sister), who lived in England. I didn't know where England was. She then told me Aunt Anne had given her the address in Germany of family who were living in the American sector, near Rottenburg. She wrote to them and we moved into their tiny rented farmhouse with them. I went to the village school there and still spoke German. We started jumping the border, through the fields and woods. I went a couple of times on my own and returned with bacon and butter strapped to me, and money safety-pinned to my pants. Someone was paid to smuggle our furniture across the border.

Auntie Anne came and got my cousin and took her back to England in 1946 and she came back for me the following year. It was necessary for mother to establish herself in Germany and she needed to work there for some years before she could apply for a passport. So, in 1947, I left alone with Auntie Anne on the ferry for England. I travelled on her passport and I remember I was very seasick on the ferry. Mother stayed in Germany, it would be a couple of years before I would see her again."

Several things are happening to me:

I am crying. Grieving for them both. Not grieving for their deaths but grieving for their lives.

Missing pieces are falling into place – so *that's* why he was the way he was, *that's* why they had the relationship they had, *that's* why he became the kind of husband and father that he did.

Imagine yourself a 13-year-old child arriving in a country you'd never even heard of. You don't speak a word of the language, you've been separated from your mother, your father has already disappeared without a trace, and you have suffered the most unthinkable traumas.

Clearly, this was defining territory for my dad regarding the man that he would become, the husband he would become, the adult son he would become, the father he would become. No wonder he couldn't develop into a grown-up man, able to take responsibility for everything that comes with that. He was still a child, stuck in this trauma; there's no way you go through something like that at 11 years old and aren't shaped for life. He had no role model of how to be a father, the two father figures he'd had were there one minute and gone the next, never to be talked about again, like they never existed. What does that do to a young boy?

And what must it have done to their mother and son relationship? He was always complaining that Omi used to fuss over him, and they used to argue like hell. It was the only time I heard them speak Czech, when they broke out into an argument so that no one else could understand what they were saying, their secret shared language, their secret shared trauma, never talked about, never processed, just acted out throughout the rest of their lives via their turbulent relationship. Just like his relationship with my mum, just like his relationship with my step-mum, just like his relationship with his cousin (they fell out lots of times, sadly before he died they hadn't spoken for years), just like his relationship with me.

I am beginning to understand.

Understand my dad and therefore understand myself.

And I am seeing Omi in a whole different light. I always remember her as a rather obstinate woman but also a loving grandmother who seemed to live only for cooking and fussing over me and my sister. But wow! What a warrior! The risks she took and the sacrifices she made to protect her son, to keep them alive.

I never did identify with the fussy grandma that I knew, but my God, do I identify with *that* woman!

This is my female lineage. Strong, bold, independent women (my mum most definitely included in that) who have shown enormous fortitude and tenacity in the face of unimaginable circumstances. They have been raped (not my mum as far as I know), abused, oppressed, and traumatised, and they have survived.

I once had a friend who, when he found out I was half Czech, said, "Oh, that's where you get your fortitude from." I never really understood what he meant. I'm beginning to now.

Is this stuff in our DNA? Bubbling in our cells, pulsing through our veins and seeping out of our pores? Can we inherit trauma and its consequences without consciously knowing about it? I've often wondered these questions; I'm starting to know the answers.

So what else did I inherit? This eternal fear of being trapped, always needing to escape? The self-fulfilling prophecy of 'finding' myself in relationships that enables me to keep re-enacting that. So not just my own life experience at 11 years old then, with feeling trapped and needing to escape from my dad, but perhaps a whole heap of unconscious ancestral trauma too that I didn't even know about. My grandfather being in prison, my dad and Omi being on the run, escaping; a whole nation suppressed from who they really were because of being oppressed by another.

I've felt this my whole life – trapped and imprisoned, the need to keep moving, to escape, always searching for my freedom, and always feeling the need to fight, to defend myself.

Another thing that strikes me is that my dad was 11 years old when he had his life-defining experience, and I was 11 years old when I had my life-defining experience. I realise his trauma was on a whole different level to mine – they call it 'big T trauma' and 'little t trauma' now – but I've seen it time and time again with clients: the parallel process of family members of different generations going through significant life events at the exact same age.

As I sit in the garden, the sun fading, these pages of capital letters still in my hands, something is rising up in me, rising up like a phoenix from the ashes of my dead lineage...

I feel a pilgrimage coming on.

Scene Nineteen – Landmines

"Out beyond ideas of right-doing and wrong-doing,
there is a field, I'll meet you there."

– Rumi

Maybe I should have paid more heed to that word: pilgrimage. I should have really listened to what my heart was telling me about going to visit my dad's homeland. This is a trip I should make alone, or perhaps with my sister – that would also have been OK – but no one else.

Probably what I shouldn't do is go with Campervan Man.

But it seems perfect, he is keen to do a big trip in the van, I am keen to follow the route that Dad and Omi had made from the Czech Republic into Germany. The Step-Mother has even given me the original map that they used on that trip 73 years ago. Campervan Man's really into World War Two history and my dad's story, so planning a trip for 4 weeks in the summer together seems like a win-win situation.

But what about our relationship? I really can't work it out. We argue all the time. I mean, continually. Not a week goes by that we don't come up against some big issue that needs working through. But that's the thing: never in my life have I wanted to work through anything with anyone before. The first sniff of difficulty and I'm bolting. This is different. I actually want to talk about it, hear his side of things, look at things from different perspectives. That's how it's supposed to be, right? In fact, I'm riding so high on this new-found enthusiasm for working through relationship shit, that I've lost all perspective of just how much work *should have* to go into a relationship. I'm so intent on doing things differently, that I'm ignoring some pretty big warning signs about where we're heading. (Hmm...haven't I been here before?)

A few months ago, I came out of a yoga class to find five missed calls and three messages from him, worried because he didn't know where I was.

It's 7.30 on a Wednesday evening, for fuck's sake!

To make things a hundred times worse, when I got home, son number two called downstairs to me that Campervan Man had called him too to see if I was OK. I am mama bear come back to her cub to find the lair has been disturbed. A deeply-rooted, primal maternal instinct is triggered, and I flip.

If you want to go into a fucking panic with me cos you don't know where I am, even though I told you I was going to yoga straight after work, then that's one thing. But DON'T YOU DARE involve my son. DON'T YOU DARE put your paranoia and total neurosis on him. DON'T YOU DARE take him along for the ride to crazy town in your head so he can be worried about me too. DON'T YOU FUCKING DARE!

I call him.

He's all casual, "Oh, hi, yeah I did wonder where you were..." but I can hear his fear and his anger.

HIS anger?? I am incensed!

I scream at him that I should be able to go to yoga on a Wednesday evening without him raising the alarm and reporting me as a fucking missing person.

My two Achilles heels have been kicked – the idea of someone harming my boys AND feeling imprisoned.

But the following day we meet up to talk about it. He tells me some stuff about how his mum used to go off when he was a kid, and he didn't know where she was or when or if she'd be back. I listen, I become therapist, I become the good mother...again.

Oh lord, oh lord, again. Really?!

I want to see my part in it too, that part of me that can't bear someone being concerned about me, I don't know how to react, so I react with anger, I push them away.

Yes, this relationship is teaching me a thing or two about myself, that's for sure.

For him too, lots of stuff is coming to the surface about his childhood that hasn't been dealt with before, but it seems I am the perfect woman for the job. I am a mother and a therapist, I am just what he needs.

It's fucked up but I can't see it.

We walk on a field of unexploded landmines. Just waiting for the next inevitable blast. Who will trigger it? Who will be injured? We are both gradually losing limbs but seem intent on staying put and nursing each other back to health rather than running, in separate directions, for the hills.

This happens more and more so it's curious then why we decide it's a good idea to get engaged.

Yep. That's right, you heard correctly...engaged!!

I have to admit, it was me that hinted at it. Not because I

particularly wanted to get married, I think I just wanted to see what it felt like to be engaged. Not in a flippant way, I really wanted to experience it, and I thought he was someone I could experience it with. Even though, when he asks me, I am literally muted, nothing is coming out of my mouth at all...

Say it, say yes, just say yes, it's not difficult.

But it IS difficult. My voice box has locked itself away and I've swallowed the key. Try as I might, not a sound comes out. After an awkwardly long silence, I manage a wavering feeble, "yes". I put it down to nerves. I should have seen it as a sign.

When we're not dodging landmines, we have some really nice times: we go for lots of walks in the forest, we cook in his tiny kitchen, we cosy up in the van, we have trips to Mallorca – it's not a bad lifestyle.

And the really cool thing is he's got herpes too! (There's a line I never thought I'd say.)

It was revealed not long after we got together, we were on our way home from dinner in a pub. Actually, we'd had a row because he'd left me sitting on my own while he went outside for a smoke. I don't particularly like the fact that he smokes, mostly because I've stopped and I don't want that temptation there, but also because the reason I stopped was that I realised my self-care was the most important thing in the world to me, and I'm not sure if I want to be with someone who doesn't value themselves in the same way. Anyway, I'd told him I thought it was a bit rude to leave me sitting there on my own and maybe he could've just waited and had one on the way back to the car. He'd completely freaked out and said something about refusing to be manipulated by me (bit extreme?!).

So we're both duly pissed off as we are driving back in my car to his van and he hits me with, "Oh, and we can't have sex tonight, by the way."

"Oh, OK, how come?" I ask, curious.

"Because when I was out working in America, years ago, I slept with someone and caught something. Every now and then it flares up. This is one of those times."

What a pro! I am impressed! I wish I could've explained it like that. On the few occasions where I have dared to tell someone, I've got myself into a right bloody state, made a total song and dance over it, been terrified of the reaction I would get. I've locked myself in a coffin of shame about it for the past 25 years.

But this? This was a masterclass! A 'how to tell your new partner you've got an STD in one easy step'.

"Is it herpes?" I ask.

"Yes," he replies, now he's looking curious.

"Me too."

Now that, he wasn't expecting.

"Seriously?"

"Yep. Seriously."

There's nothing like bonding over an STD to get you over a row.

So here we are, a year after we met up at the yoga festival, arguing continually, stuck in some weird dynamic of detonating each other's internal bombs and taking turns to sweep up the fall-out, engaged but not really talking about a wedding, and planning a trip (which I should probably be doing on my own) for a month, during a heatwave, across Europe in his campervan.

A potential outbreak of herpes between us is the least of our worries.

What could possibly go wrong?

Scene Twenty – Scream

"If you do not know where you come from, then you
don't know where you are, and if you don't know where you are,
then you don't know where you're going, and if you don't know
where you're going, you're probably going wrong."

– Terry Pratchett

Here are all the things that go wrong:

- We have an almighty row about the sat nav on the first day.

- My travel money card with our budget for the whole trip on it doesn't work. This causes massive arguments about how I have forgotten the PIN number (I'm sure I haven't forgotten the PIN number). After several phone calls, we finally find out you can't use this type of card at petrol pumps. (I *knew* I hadn't forgotten the PIN number.)

I want to scream. But I don't.

- On day three, we breakdown on the motorway in France. We are asked by the police to show our papers and we eventually get towed to the nearest town. Unfortunately, all the mechanics are on their national annual holidays and it will be a whole week before the van can be fixed. We spend the first couple of nights camped out on the garage forecourt in 35-degree heat, but when the toilet, along with our stress levels, reaches full to overflowing, we move to a hotel in town. We are dancing between holding it together and NOT. Our budget is already blown, things are not going according to plan. A few days in I see a glimmer of opportunity to spend a couple of hours on my own (I am *DESPERATE* for some space). There is a museum in town he is interested in. He will go. I won't go. Perfect. I settle myself at a table in a street-side café to sit and write my journal. He is back in 10 minutes. The museum is closed on Tuesdays.

I want to scream. But I don't.

- Somewhere in Southern Austria, the boulder drops that I should have done this trip alone. I am seriously tempted to pack a small bag and leave. I fantasise about my escape route, away from the enemy, just as dad and Omi had done 73 years ago. I honestly know I would be fine, but it all feels a bit dramatic and I can't bear the fall-out of it with him – better to just keep making the best of it, I guess.

My saviour is reading a book called 'Rise Sister Rise' by Rebecca Campbell. Among many other words of wisdom, it offers an exercise to try. The idea is to own ALL parts of ourselves – not just the comfy stuff but the shadow side too.

Here are my responses:

The Light	The Dark:
1 – funny	1 – moody
2 – sensitive	2 – intolerant
3 – empathic	3 – judgmental
4 – creative	4 – bitchy
5 – intuitive	5 – cold
6 – sexual	6 – unkind
7 – nurturing	7 – disassociated
8 – thoughtful	8 – self-righteous
9 – authentic	9 – aggressive
10 – empowered	10 – headstrong

- I suggest we both do it and share what we've written. It could be a good bonding exercise. We sure could do with some bonding right now. But all it does is shine a floodlight on what is becoming blatantly clearer by the day: we're bringing out each other's dark sides – my aggression, his passiveness. Not the best combination.

I want to scream. But I don't.

- In Prague, it's 40 degrees and I have a hell of a headache. Unable all day to find a chemist for some paracetamol, we head out to dinner. Campervan Man asks the waiter if he has any headache tablets, he obliges and presents a single white tablet served on a saucer. I swallow it down with a glass of water. Ten minutes later all of the blood has drained out of my head and my heart is going to burst out of my chest. I am tachycardic. I somehow stagger up the stairs to the bathroom where the world falls out of my arse. Back at the table, we ask the waiter what the tablet was: ibuprofen. I never take ibuprofen, being asthmatic I've always been cautious, it seems my instinct was right. My breathing is shallow, my whole body is numb and all I want to do is go to sleep. Campervan Man is beside himself with worry. He's called an ambulance and, as we wait outside for it to arrive, I curl up on the pavement, wanting to snuggle into the gutter and sleep forever. (Of course, I look like just another Brit abroad who's pissed and gone outside to throw up.) The ambulance arrives. I am taken inside to be checked over. Campervan Man is told to wait outside. This, it seems, is beyond his capabilities. He is banging on the door, demanding to be let in, saying it's unthinkable that I am in there on my own. *Why??* He is in a total state of panic. Anyone would think he was the patient. I am calm, delirious, and furious – *why can't you just let them do their job!* The paramedics are getting really pissed off with him, especially when they open the door to tell him to just wait quietly and he shoves the video camera in their faces. *What the fuck??* I cannot believe the state he is in. I'm taken to hospital and he is allowed to come with me in the ambulance, which seems to sedate him somewhat. I am put on an anti-allergy drip and discharged a few hours later. Back at the campsite, I at least get the bed to myself while he takes the bench seat, thank God.

I'm too exhausted to want to scream.

- Two days later, like some surreal, inconceivable, beyond-bizarre twist of fate – I shit you not – I am back in an ambulance being taken to hospital. *Seriously, this cannot be happening again!* Fortunately, it's a different ambulance with different paramedics and a different hospital in a different town with a different allergic reaction. Pine nuts this time, which Campervan Man had sprinkled generously all over our salad, assuming I was OK with them despite knowing about my severe nut allergy (to be fair, pine nuts are seeds and not nuts, and to be fair, I don't think I was even having an allergic reaction to them, although I'm pretty sure I have done in the past). But whilst I was trying to stay calm, just monitor my breathing, any symptoms, observe what was happening, assess myself...he was hovering over me, EpiPen in hand, finger over the trigger, hopping up and down in a panic saying, "Shall I? Shall I? Do you need it? Do you? Do you need an ambulance? Oh my God, are you OK? What's happening? I feel so bad. Fuck. Shit. What shall I do?" *CALM THE FUCK DOWN IS WHAT YOU SHOULD DO!! I don't know if I'm OK because I can't think straight to make a clear call on it because somehow YOU'RE MAKING THIS ABOUT YOU!!* In the end, I realise I am never going to be sure if I am having a reaction under these conditions and, just so it can be over, I tell him yes. In an instant, he jabs me in the leg with the adrenalin, calls an ambulance, and I get carted off again, dazed, confused and likely not in anaphylactic shock. But at least this time I get a whole night away, they keep me in ICU for observation although I get zero sleep as all the IV fluids in me mean I fill up seven bedpans with pee overnight.

Hmm...negative vibes? Things are not going well. The universe is definitely telling me something – I am *not* in the right place at the right time, at least certainly *not* with the right person.

I am getting clearer and clearer on this feeling of needing to travel on my own. I need space. There are things I need to do for myself, and here I am feeling trapped (again) in this relationship. There is no way I can be myself in this.

- We have the row of our lives when he tells me off for sitting with my feet up on the dash in the van. He is so paranoid about men looking at me, assumes every guy just wants one thing, but he turns it all around and projects it on me. He says that I'm inviting men to look at me in that way, flashing myself apparently! He tells me I'm a flirt, an exhibitionist, and unladylike. *What the fuck?*

I want to scream. But I don't

With every kilometre we drive, I realise more that I need to SPREAD MY WINGS AND FLY. So, of course, the perfect contrast to that is him wanting to keep me in a cage, preferably with a cloth over so no one can see me. I am the child who's not allowed out. He is the overprotective, critical father. No wonder I started thinking about my dad more when I met him.

But just to add a little balance, there are good things about the trip. Like visiting my dad's hometown and feeling a strong connection there. By chance finding ourselves standing outside the exact house where the Cousin lived in the next village. Visiting Dachau concentration camp memorial where we think my opa was taken from the prison (he actually wasn't but I don't know that yet), is incredibly moving. We visit other cousins of my dad's in Germany and spend a lovely time with them all. More connections to my lineage.

So while it hasn't exactly been the pilgrimage I needed it to be (lessons learnt there) I'm glad I did it. I've learnt more about myself, what I want and what I don't want. I've learnt about our relationship, clearly, all is not well! I've learnt about my next steps in life; this whole trip I've been sitting with the question of whether to sell my house, my urge to go travelling again ALONE is calling me. I'm not sure why, but I think it's so that I have no one to fall back on but myself, everything stops with me, to know myself better, to rely on myself better, to trust myself better, to be

220

more fully in relationship with myself, no one to distract me from that, to go through the good, the bad and the ugly with me, myself and I. Other things are calling me too, I'm feeling some ideas emerging about a writing retreat and doing my Qoya teacher training.

But most of all, when we get back I realise one thing: FUCK, I'M ANGRY!!!

I'm angry with Campervan Man for trying to put out my flame. I'm angry that he's not who I thought he was, that he was so encouraging about the whole Qoya thing at first, but now he seems resentful, disrespectful, and insecure around it. I'm angry that he tried to put his victim onto me and make me feel self-conscious about being confident with my sexuality and femininity. There's nothing wrong with men looking at me, if he's not OK with it that's his problem, not mine, I'm not going to join him in his victim state so we can be afraid of the whole big bad world together. I feel like I could drown in that. I'm angry because I finally thought I'd met someone who would be strong enough to love and want me for who I am, not try to suppress or change me or be afraid of me, afraid of my independence. I'm angry because he gave me no space on the trip to be with myself and my process. Just because he would have done it differently if it had been 'his trip', it's OK that I needed to do it my way. I'm angry because it feels like I've been suppressing myself for a lifetime! I don't want to hide anymore. I'm angry because of what happened to Dad and Omi and Opa and the impact it had on them and has had on me. I'm angry that they were suppressed and couldn't live freely to express who they were and be themselves. I'm angry that they must've been angry! And they probably suppressed that too! I'm angry that dad was taken away from me too soon, before we had the chance to get closer, to understand one another, to connect.

I'm SO FUCKING ANGRY my entire body breaks out in a furious, burning, intensely itchy rash that lasts for the next 6 months.

Scene Twenty-One – Yes

"There will come a time when you can accept nothing less than the breath-taking truth of your soul, the voice of divine love within you."

– Meggan Watterson

I learnt a long time ago that the definition of a successful relationship has nothing to do with the longevity of it. No, a successful relationship is about how well we know ourselves as a result of it. Every person that comes into our lives has something to teach us and we have something to teach them. It's an exchange. And that exchange might last a moment or a lifetime. It's all about us growing individually, the relationship is the vessel that helps us to do that. Then when we're done, we're done. The trick is to recognise when we're done, when the exchange is complete. Herein lies the problem.

In our culture, we're so hung up on the success of a relationship being defined by the length of it. Until death do us part and all that crap. How can you possibly know when you exchange those vows where life will take you? How you will each change individually? How we're *supposed* to change individually? What directions that will take us in? And the person we fell in love with in 1980 might be very different (let's hope) in 20 years' time. I once heard that much more realistic, and arguably healthier, wedding vows would be, "I like you pretty much, let's see how we go." That could probably do with a tad of elaboration but it's a bit more like it. There's a sense of freedom in that, recognising our individuation.

Well, I say I 'learnt' a long time ago, but I guess I just read it, it resonated with me, and I do believe it's true, but have I really learnt it? Believing isn't the same as knowing. Believing is just a well-repeated thought habit but knowing is our unquestionable deep truth. So I guess I don't *know* it yet because I, like everyone else I know, am desperately hung up on the bullshit of not being seen to have another 'failed relationship'.

This relationship with Campervan Man has been a HUGE success if I define it by how much better I know myself as a result of it. And if I were to stay in it now, now that the evidence is there of how we are tearing each other apart, bringing out the worst in each other, rather than the best in each other (isn't that what a healthy relationship is supposed to do?), well, wouldn't staying in it be the real failure? God knows we've tried to make it work. God knows the trip has shown that we're not right for each other. We were, but the work is done, the teaching and the learning, the exchange, the healing, the reparative, call it what you like. I know, through this relationship, I have been able to open my heart up for the first time and try to let someone in. And I believe that he has been able to open up some of his old wounds that he'd never dealt with and I was able to help heal those wounds.

So the wisdom is in recognising this. All the evidence is there, the negative vibes are loud and clear saying OK YOU'RE DONE NOW, THE PARTY'S OVER, IT'S TIME TO GO HOME! To overstay our welcome would be to avoid something, right? Avoid the judgement of others for not being able to make it work, avoid our own judgement for not being able to make it work, avoid the conflict of the ending, avoid being on our own. Having someone is better than having no one, right? Isn't it considered that the worst form of child abuse is neglect? That negative strokes (attention) are better than no strokes at all? We're relational beings at the end of the day and loneliness is a killer. We're all avoiding loss, but because loss is the flip side of attachment, we can't have one without the other. But we're crap at dealing with loss in our culture, we have no conditioning for it at all and so we avoid it like the plague – anything not to experience loss. Much preferable to be stuck in an overcooked relationship that's gone toxic or stale, festering away and growing harmful bacteria.

I like to think that my 10 years of practicing meditation have taught me something about non-attachment.

OK, so NOW I *know* it. Now I *know* what I need to do.

———————

It's not just the relationship though. I know there are other endings that I need to make, culling if you like, before I can move on. If I want to line up with this huge internal shift that is happening, lots of external stuff needs to change too. Lots.

Like the friendship that I can see is no longer serving me. I guess that exchange is complete too and we're already past our sell-by date.

Like changing my yoga practice. For a few years now I've been doing Ashtanga yoga, I love how it makes my body look, I don't love how it makes my body feel. A two-hour morning Ashtanga session leaves me poleaxed on the sofa for the rest of the day, and if Qoya is teaching me one massive lesson in life, it's all about the importance of how things *feel* and NOT how they *look*. Qoya is helping me to move more into my feminine side. I feel like I have spent my whole life in my masculine energy – fight to survive! Be strong! Hold it all together! It's served me well but it's time for some softening of those edges, it's time to let go. So given that how we approach what we do on our yoga mat is a reflection of how we approach our lives, my practice needs to change. Some gentle flow, that's what I need now.

But the biggest letting go of all...I am selling my empty nest. My boys have flown off and, for better or worse, my work there is done. I realise I have a choice, or rather, I have an opportunity: I can either stay where I am, keep working, get some lodgers in to help towards the mortgage, keep living the life I'm living, keep a secure base for the boys to come back to whenever they need it...or I can sell the house and bugger off travelling with some of the money it's made!

It's the whole perimenopause thing again: this is MY time, time for ME to get back to ME, whoever the hell that is now, whoever the hell that ever was. I need to define myself for this next phase of my life, this LAST phase of my life.

Fuck!

IF NOT NOW, THEN WHEN?!

I need to explore new avenues and new ventures *as well* as finish what I started; pick up the threads of my life before I became a mother.

When I was just me.

I'm realising it's all about responsibility, or rather, letting go of responsibility. Letting go of being a mum (not entirely, of course), letting go of earning enough money to pay for the mortgage, letting go of constantly keeping a house and garden clean and tidy on my own, letting go of holding clients and all their stuff – 20 years of sitting in a room with clients, of running groups and workshops and supervising other therapists, that's A LOT OF SHIT to hold.

And letting go of the need to always be in a bloody relationship. I've been so busy looking for love or fucking men that I've forgotten to get on with my life! I've felt suffocated by every relationship that I've ever been in, right back from when I started dating at 15, and then The Psycho, Understudy, Back Garden Neighbour, Unfinished Business, and now Campervan Man, not to mention several others in between, and numerous one night stands where I was saying yes when I really meant no, still not being myself, still stifling who I really was. And the friends who have tried to control and manipulate me, I've felt like it wasn't OK to be myself with them too, that I was indirectly judged for it.

ENOUGH! Enough of the endless suppression in relationships.

I'm not saying enough of relationships, just enough of the *wrong* relationships. In fact, I'm realising that the process of opening my heart up with Campervan Man feels like I'm *ready* to let someone in. Normally when a relationship has ended, I'll put the Do Not Disturb sign up for a while. But this time, I don't need to do that, it's safe to stay open. Finally.

So every aspect of my life is changing: my home, my family, my work, my relationship, my friendships, my practices, my finances. Sure I can feel the pain of the losses but, oh boy, am I aware of the freedom.

The freedom that comes from letting go of responsibilities.

At risk of being cast onto some middle-aged cliché heap, I need to go and find myself. Yes, it's a midlife thing. But why do we have to call it a midlife crisis, for fuck's sake? Who the hell came up with that crippling expression?

I'm not having a midlife crisis, I'm having a MIDLIFE CELEBRATION.

And yes, it's scary, and yes, I'm letting go of everything that I know, and yes, there is some grieving to be done, and yes, a lot of loss to feel, and yes, I don't know what the hell is going to happen, and yes, lots of people are questioning me selling my house, and yes, it feels like I'm going against the grain, and yes, I'm taking a massive risk...but that's just it, all I can hear in all that is:

YES YES YES!!!

ACT THREE
ASCENDING

"The woman you are becoming
will cost you people, relationships,
spaces and material things.
Choose her over everything."

– Unknown

ACT THREE
Ascending

Scene One – Reclaiming

"What we don't heal in the present we can expect
to meet again in the future."

– Unknown

It is a grey and dreary afternoon, the first afternoon of 2019. I am sitting on my bedroom floor in my rented apartment near the beach where I've been living for a few months. My empty nest has been sold, my relationship ended. I have pulled out one of the boxes that live under my bed, not just any old box, I knew which box I needed, I knew just what I was looking for. Now the contents of that box lie sprawled all around me: photographs, journals, and letters from a time gone by. Twenty-three years to be precise. I know I *have* to do this, I am being drawn to unearthing these memories. I have a deep need to reconnect. Not to reconnect with anyone else, but to reconnect with Me. That Me who existed before life as a grown-up took over, before the world told me who to be. A life that, although I wouldn't change it, had taken a little piece of me, kind of swallowed up a morsel of my spirit, my essence – I need to find her again.

Is she here? Hidden amongst all these photos, these journals, these letters from ghosts of my past?

I bloody hope so.

In less than two weeks, I'll be heading to India. Five weeks in India...on my OWN. It's the trip that should have happened 23 years ago but didn't, but let's face it, lots of things maybe should have happened 23 years ago but didn't. Or 'could' have happened, as I prefer to think of it. It's like that when you've got children, guilt swoops in and crucifies you for even daring to think of a life that 'should' have been different, a life where the stars would have aligned differently, which would mean that those children would never have come to be.

But what if the stars *had* aligned differently? What if I'd made different choices? What if the girl in these photos had been allowed to continue her journey of self-discovery? What if I hadn't had to come back from that trip to watch my dad die? That trip that now covers my bedroom carpet, forever immortalised in words and pictures.

What if...?

I need to revisit that phase of my life before I can carve out the next. I am on the verge of turning 50 and, as a new decade approaches, a new life whispers in my ear, "time to change things up", "time to pick up the threads again", and you never know, perhaps along the way I can heal what hadn't been healed 23 years ago.

The black and red cover of my dog-eared journal, bulging with tickets, receipts, maps, and other mementoes, stares me right in the eye. "Go on. I dare you..." it challenges.

I am compelled.

I couldn't stop myself even if I wanted to.

I am transported back in time to beaches and jungles and temples and volcanos and sounds and jokes and laughter and whisky and shithead and friends and hammocks and bus journeys and backpacks and boat rides and bare feet...I can practically smell the freedom coming off the pages.

Ahh, The Viking, I wonder what became of him?

It feels like only yesterday that we walked around the lake in Indonesia together, talking, opening up, dancing around each other's self-consciousness. Of all the memories I have of those 3 weeks we spent together, those are the ones that have stayed with me the most.

He was special to me, we had a lovely connection.

I wonder what became of him?

I read and re-read all of his letters. They make me smile. The floodgates of my memory whoosh open...that time in my life, our adventures together, my dad dying. In one of his letters, he added a P.S. for me to put a flower on my dad's grave from him. It brings a tear to my eye again now, just as it did then.

I wonder what became of him?

I wonder if I could find out...nope, best leave it alone, let the happy memories remain, remember us as we were: two fucked-up twentysomethings who happened to meet on a minibus between Thailand and Malaysia, who happened to have an amazing connection but were too shy to do anything about it, who happened to write to each other for the next 2 years and then didn't...

I wonder what became of him?

The thing is, reading his letters again is stoking a long-forgotten flame somewhere in the attic of my mind and 3 days later I still can't stop wondering about him.

I succumb to Google.

That's him! At least I think it is, I'm not sure. Oh wow, there's an address, and a phone number...shit, that was more than I was bargaining on.

Could I?

Should I?

I do what girls do: I ask a friend. We meet for coffee and I tell her the story of 23 years gone by.

Me: "So I brought these photos of him...this was him then...and this is his Facebook photo now...do you think it's the same guy? And do you think I should try to contact him?"

Her: "Oh My God! Yes, it's *DEFINITELY* him and yes you should *DEFINITELY* get in touch."

Bizarrely, her eyes are brimming with tears and she has goosebumps all over. Here she sits before me like some kind of Cosmic Tinder and I know I need to pay attention. And I realise, on my way home, that it is 23 years to the day since I met The Viking on that minibus between Thailand and Malaysia in 1996.

A few days later, I write him a letter. I don't know what will come of it, I don't know what I need to come of it, I just know I need to do it, to quietly pick up an old thread, gently tug on it and see if it tugs back, see if this old thread has worn thin or if it has stood the test of time.

My letter:

6th January 2019

Hello (Viking)

I hope I have the right address and I hope I have the right person – otherwise, you will not know who I am! But if you are the right (Viking) then I hope you remember me from when we met travelling in Indonesia in 1996. Actually, we met in Thailand or Malaysia, but we travelled together – you and (your friend), me and Alexia.

I've recently been looking back on old photos and letters from that time and had the feeling to contact you. It's not so hard to find someone these days, Google gave me this address for you.

So if you want to reply to me then you can email:
xxxxxxxxxxxxxx

or Whatsapp: xxxxxxxxx

or if you want to write an old-fashioned letter then my address is:

xxxxxxxxx
xxxxxxxxx

U.K.

This week I am going to India for a month. I remember you used to love India. I went last year for the first time and have to go back – what an incredible place.

So (Viking), I hope that life is good for you and that you have had a wonderful 23 years!

With happy memories,

From

Vikki. (Smisek)

It's funny, since I posted the letter I'm totally relaxed about it. The intensity of thinking about him again has lessened, it's like I've done what I needed to do, now I can let it go and leave it in the hands of the universe. Trust in the process once again.

It takes 4 days for a letter to reach Sweden from the UK. It's day four. An email pops into my inbox. My heart skips a beat.

He pulled back on the thread.

In his email, he asks me if I remember our walks by the lake in the Indonesian countryside. It seems like we have picked up just where we left off.

Scene Two – Finally

"Travel far enough to meet yourself."

– David Mitchell

There's something I don't want to tell you, it's not a big deal, just a small something.

I don't want to tell you that I already went to India last year (although you will have just read it in my letter). And the reason I don't want to tell you is because it doesn't quite fit with my story of India, or rather how India fits in with my story. Finally getting to India, 23 years after first wanting to go but not going because of dad dying and falling off my path onto another one...well, finally getting there is hugely symbolic to me of finding my way back to my path.

So when I went with the 'friend' last year, it was good, but it was never the trip I wanted it or needed it to be. It was a compromise of what I really wanted. I did manage to go on a 10-day Vipassana retreat on my own to start the trip. Then she flew out and we spent a week travelling around the Ganges and then headed to Goa for a 2-week yoga retreat.

Goa? How the hell did I let that happen? Goa was about the only place in India that I didn't want to visit!

And I should have listened to myself, although we definitely did have some good times, I ended up in ICU in Goa after a run-in with a cashew nut. Proper allergic reaction this time: EpiPen, hospital, horrific experience. Again, a sign, perhaps, that I was *not* in the right place at the right time with the right person.

So I guess that trip to India feels a bit like foreplay in a relationship that isn't quite right: some of it was good and some of it not so good, and in the end you decide you'd prefer to carry on by yourself.

Even though in some ways I wish it hadn't happened because it feels like it has taken something away from the symbolism of *this* trip to India, actually in other ways it's made this trip to India all the more sacred. This is MY trip. This is the trip that was always meant to be. Just like the pilgrimage with Campervan Man that wasn't what it was meant to be, I'm doing it again – differently. I'm reclaiming my trip. And this is a pilgrimage too because this is me picking up more threads of my past, finishing what I started, in the way that I need to do it – on my own.

Except, from the minute I leave my flat and head to Heathrow, I realise that I'm not alone. It feels like two people are accompanying me...one is The Viking and the other is my dad.

I know my dad is with me because, firstly, partway through the long flight to Delhi, I start chatting to the woman sitting next to me. She tells me she is writing a book about her mum's story of what happened after the war, I, in turn, tell her about my dad's story. Here I am swapping tales for hours to a total stranger. Bringing my dad's story to life, bringing him with me halfway across the world. I only ended up sitting next to her because a guy a few rows in front wanted an aisle seat so there was some switching around going on. Out of the 400 other passengers on board, I ended up next to her.

Secondly, as I am waiting to board my connecting flight from Delhi to Gaya, two young men are standing behind me talking in a language I recognise. A glance at the passports in their hands confirms what I had suspected: Czech. OK, not particularly ground-breaking news but, honestly, there really aren't many Czech travellers in India. I am comforted, reassured. Not only is my dad with me, but I am definitely in the right place at the right time with the right person – *just me*, finally.

So maybe he is with me now to help guide me back to my path, back to myself. His way of apologising, perhaps, for having called me away from it. That would be like him. And maybe that's why The Viking is with me now too. Because who knows what might've happened between us if it hadn't been for dad dying. It was all there, the stage was set; after all, he did say in one of his letters, "You only had to give the word and I would have been there."

Would you though?

It's all very well saying it in the past tense. Anyway, it didn't happen, for different reasons and here we are again, I'm getting back on track and he's become part of that process for me.

We've already established there's no such thing as a coincidence, right? The real definition of that word being *co-incidence*, a *co-created incidence*. So I wonder what's going on for him in his life that I have become part of his process again too. He didn't have to reply to my letter after all.

Whatever the reasons, he is most definitely in my head now. We exchanged a few brief emails before I left but the last one I haven't had a reply to. I'd sent him a picture of a note I found in my journal that he and his friend had left me and Alexia when we'd all parted ways back in Indonesia. He'd written something to me in Swedish and was too shy at the time to tell me what it said. So here I am, 23 years later, sending him a picture of it and asking, "Now will you tell me what this says?" No wonder I haven't had a reply. That's probably thrown him into a right old spin. I have no idea about his 'personal circumstances', for all I know he's happily married with kids, living a contented life, and the last thing he needs is me popping up sending him visual reminders from his past.

Will you thank me for taking you back there?

Do you want to come with me on my retrospective journey?

This is something we are co-creating together, right?

Well, let's see, he hasn't replied yet and I'm about to go incommunicado for the next week and a half, that should give me some perspective. There's nothing like a 10-day silent retreat to clear your head!

Scene Three – Healing

"All of humanity's problems stem from
man's inability to sit quietly in a room alone."

– Blaze Pascale

If you've ever done a 10-day silent Vipassana course in the Goenka tradition, then you'll understand when I say:

"Wish me luck, I'm going in."

This is the Iron Man of meditation retreats.

Even though I've done one of these before, last year in India, I feel strangely nervous. Or maybe it's *because* I've done one before that I feel nervous. I know what's in store, I know how intense it is, how it asks you to dig down deep just to get through it. But honestly, what's the worst that can happen? I might feel something? Emotional or physical discomfort? Pain even? Have to sit with some difficulty? Well, none of that is gonna kill me and I know that's just all part of the process. Anyway, isn't that where the learning is?

Because this is my second course, the rules are ramped up: no food after lunch (which is at 11 a.m.) until breakfast the next day (which is at 6.30 a.m.). OK, that might be a bit much. That's over 19 hours without food, that's insane! I have some 'emergency biscuits' with me, justifying to myself that if lunch has nuts in, I won't be able to eat it and then I'll need something later. I also exempt myself from the 'no writing materials rule' on the grounds that I want to journal this experience, I might write about it one day, it's also really useful for my work as a mindfulness teacher.

Yes I need to write, and I need my biscuits, of course I am special and different.

> Day 0 – It's strangely good to be back, something comforting about the rigidity of it all.
>
> Day 1 – Sleeping when I should be awake. Awake when I should be sleeping.
>
> Day 2 – Anger rising! Why the fuck am I here?! Is it *seriously* only day 2?!
>
> Day 3 – WOW. The power of the agitated and restless mind, it really is what causes suffering.
>
> Day 4 – I've forgotten how to sleep. But I have found

something soft to sit on.

Day 5 – YAY halfway!! ONLY halfway!!

Day 6 ...

I hand in my journal and my contraband biscuits!

I actually don't want them. I'm realising that it's true, the reason they say you shouldn't is because it's a distraction from the practice. The practice is all about cultivating equanimity, meeting every experience we have without attachment or avoidance, and so if I'm journaling at the end of the day, I'm giving precedence to certain thoughts that I'm having, expanding on them, feeding them essentially. What about the gazillion other thoughts that I'm having each day? Why are they less important? Why am I choosing some thoughts over others? There's nothing equanimous about that, right?

As for the biscuits, I realise that I'm not taking any pleasure in hoofing them down my neck in the privacy of my own room, I actually feel guilty about it. Not because I'm breaking the rules but because I realise I'm doing myself a disservice by not fully committing to the course, to everything that it has to offer.

In sneakily making notes in my journal and scoffing my biscuits, I am understanding what they mean by the experience of instant karma – the law of nature. As soon as we do something unkind or (in this case) unwholesome, we are 'punished', not by some external authority figure or system but internally, by feeling bad, guilty, uncomfortable. This is exactly how it feels. Trust me, no one is more surprised by this realisation than me, and my inner rebellious child is not impressed with me one bit.

In this meditation prison you are woken up at 4 a.m., if you are fortunate enough to have fallen asleep in the first place, that is. Apparently, it's a hazard of intense practice; you spend so much time on your cushion during the day, desperately forcing yourself to stay awake, that you're actually training your mind to wake up every time it dozes off. So when you go to bed at night (9.30 p.m.), rather than being able to crash out and fall asleep after a hard day's meditation, every time you begin to drop off, wakefulness immediately gets reactivated again. It really is quite torturous.

The first sitting session begins at 4.30 a.m. On my first Vipassana I decided one morning that there was simply no way I could drag my sorry arse up and make it to the dharma hall. I needed to sleep. This just wasn't healthy in any way, shape, or form. I was jet-lagged, sleep-deprived, and I needed to rest. But I soon realised staying in bed wasn't an option. At 4.45 a.m. one of the volunteers came around and banged on my window so loudly and so continuously, screaming goodness knows what to me in Hindi until I did indeed drag my sorry arse out of bed into the dharma hall. It was only towards the end of the course that I realised she was doing this out of kindness and not cruelty, to help me get the most out of the experience. Anyway, I have no idea what she was 'screaming' at me in Hindi, it might have been the kindest words anyone has ever said.

The first meditation session lasts for an unbelievable 2 hours, most of which time is spent in a sleepy haze swathed in blankets from head to toe – there's something strangely mystical about that cocoon-huddled session, drifting in and out of conscious awareness, until after 90 minutes the assistant teacher takes his or her seat and Sri Goenka begins chanting from his grave through the loudspeakers.

After breakfast, there is a 'break' for an hour during which time you are encouraged to keep practising in the 'comfort' of your room, or in my case crawl back into bed, earplugs shoved firmly in, eye mask strapped on, willing that long-forgotten luxury of sleep to revisit me once again...

...just for 10 minutes, I'll take 10 minutes, or even 5...please.

Then begins another 8 hours of back-to-back sitting sessions, a lunch break, a tea break (as in a cup of), and an evening discourse session; an hour of the charming, charismatic, enigmatic, cheeky, and witty Sri Goenka, giving his teachings on video directly as Buddha intended (apparently). Thank God for all his magnetising characteristics is all I can say, it makes this hour an utter joy and incredibly rich learning experience. I hang on his every word. Well, in 10 days of total silence, any words are something to hang on to.

––––––––––––––

It's day six (perhaps I am about to be karmically rewarded for handing in my contraband) and I am sitting on my cushion in the dharma hall. It's one of the 'strong determination' sessions that you are introduced to on day four where you are 'firmly encouraged' not to move a minuscule muscle during the 60-minute sit. Trust me when I tell you there is no pain quite like sitting cross-legged on the floor, without moving a minuscule muscle, for 60 minutes, when you're sitting for 10 hours a day for days on end (and that's coming from someone who had two babies without any pain relief, and a brain haemorrhage).

Someone has taken a red-hot poker and has plunged it between the base of my shoulder blades (slightly to the right). They sit behind me twisting and turning and plunging that red-hot poker in further and further, deeper and deeper.

I don't move a minuscule muscle.

Not because I am being told not to, but because I have already learnt that moving only brings very momentary relief, and when the pain quickly returns there are two people with two red-hot pokers.

I understand there must be another way to be with this, this so-called suffering, and I'm up for learning it.

This too shall pass.

At some point, although fuck knows when, the glorious sound of the bell will ring, and I will be freed from the shackles of my pain...until the next time, of course.

Here I sit, just me, the red-hot poker, and my excruciating pain.

We must be over halfway through, surely??

I don't move a minuscule muscle.

Suddenly, I realise I'm not breathing.

I am so focused on *surviving* this pain that I have tensed up so *tightly* and I have actually forgotten to breathe.

And, in an instant, a deep knowing sears through me like an orgasm of truth:

"You have been doing this your whole life."

A mighty tidal wave of emotion, a familiar strangling of my

throat, a soaring vibration in my head, a pulsating around my tense lips, tears climb up into my eyes and begin to fall. They fall and fall and fall.

Still, I don't move a minuscule muscle.

A lifetime of surviving.

A lifetime of fighting.

A lifetime of keeping it all away.

I just let it happen. I let it go.

Still, I don't move a minuscule muscle.

And there, amongst the cascade of tears, the most profound realisation.

The excruciating pain...the red-hot poker plunged between the bottom of my shoulder blades (slightly to the right)...has totally and utterly gone!

Call me crazy but I think some healing might have just taken place.

I am walking slowly along the path between the dharma hall and my room, I drink in the sunshine. I'm finding it really tough being indoors for 23 hours a day when it's warm and sunny outside. From beyond the prison walls, India is calling me with her array of orchestral delights – car horns mostly, but it's an intrusive indicator that life goes on as normal out there. The contrast is stark, it is so peaceful in here, other than the chaos inside my head, although more and more I am noticing a sense of quiet. During one sit earlier I swear I actually experienced total and utter peace, wanting for nothing – just for a moment. It was blissful.

I notice the flowers outside my room. Isn't that interesting? It's taken me until day six to notice there are gorgeous, vibrant, red and purple flowers growing in the ground right outside my front door and there is beautiful primrose-yellow blossom hanging from the trees above my head. Yet I noticed the dirty bucket and shovel of the building materials outside my room on day one. Something quite sad about that really.

And in this heightened sense of external noticing, I am internally noticing more too, my process of the past couple of years is beginning to reveal itself to me. As I'd been preparing myself for the boys to leave home, I'd also been preparing myself to pick up the threads of my life before they were born, before my dad died. Campervan Man was all about that too, the trip we took to my family's homeland, he literally drove me there and I would have been more than happy if he'd just dropped me off! I felt that so strongly once we'd reached the German border, like I didn't need him anymore and I felt so suppressed because he was still there trying to control me. It's like when you're a kid and a parent gives you a lift to a party but, instead of just leaving you at the door and heading back home, they decide to come in and hang out with you and tell you what you can and can't do for the rest of the night.

The Viking is also a thread back to my life before my dad died, he was with me throughout the whole process, somehow he is part of it too and, incredibly, he is still at the end of that thread...but what we both do with it now remains to be seen.

I have such a strong sense of him being here with me now, particularly at the end of each day when I go back to my room, it's like his presence, his energy, is there waiting for me...

"How was your day?"

"Oh, you know, the usual, 10 hours of silent meditation, excruciating pain, not much to eat, random thoughts firing into my brain driving me insane, losing all perspective of time, space and reality. You?"

Something else is also beginning to emerge, a desire I have secretly had for a while now, the desire to write, a sense of my book is starting to take shape...ideas, inspiration, it's beginning to break through...hmm...it's still a formless embryo, no idea what it will germinate into yet, but the seed has been sown and I'm finally getting around to watering it.

I don't know how I ever expected it to develop without me doing that.

———

"Enjoy it," I overhear the assistant teacher telling another student during one of the question and answer sessions.

OMG yeah, enjoy it!!

I've been so intent on just surviving it, I hadn't considered that enjoying it was even an option!

I want to make the most out of the last 5 days. This is such a rare opportunity to go deep into the practice like this. This particular meditation technique apparently goes right to the root cause of the suffering mind to release it from the shackles of wanting things to be different, and it eradicates our past miseries and helps us stop creating new ones. Now, why *wouldn't* that be something to enjoy? It sounds like ultimate freedom to me. Freedom and peace, at the end of the day, are the same thing.

I would say this would be a good time to renew my commitment to being here, but I'm realising I didn't actually come in with any. Curiosity – yes – but commitment – no. I wondered what doing a second course would be like compared to the first. Well, so far it's pretty similar, which is hardly surprising seeing as I'm being just the same – steeling myself to just try to survive it, the story of my bloody life. If I want this to be different then I need to *make* it different, *I* need to be different. I can be truly grateful for the experience, all of it. Apparently, being grateful makes us happy but being happy doesn't make us grateful. Interesting, huh?

OK, so it's tough sleeping (or not) on a hard wooden frame with a blanket for a mattress, no pillow, zipped in my sleeping bag pulled up to my nose, with my hat and all my clothes on as it's so bloody cold here at night. But you know what, I've been fortunate enough to be given my own room (some things about getting older are a bonus), I have my own bathroom with a western flushing toilet (even if there was a turd in there that *definitely* wasn't mine the other day. Seriously! Western toilet it may be but a western plumbing system it is clearly not). And even though there's only ice-cold water to wash with and there are holes in my mosquito net and a 3-inch gap under the door where all the creepy crawlies and cold night air gets in, I have a roof over my head and food on the table, albeit only for breakfast and lunch, and even if I do have to eat it facing a bare wall where the plaster has gone furry – but, my God, how delicious that food tastes and the chai tea is heavenly. And it's really interesting that rather than piling my plate so high on those two meals to make up for the absence of the third, I'm finding that I'm eating plenty, really just taking what I need and no more – whilst sitting in scornful judgement of the people who are piling their plates high, of course.

In the remaining days, I learn a lot.

I learn that the harder I work at the meditation, the easier it is.

Who knew that!

The more commitment and determination I bring to each sit, the more peaceful my experience and the quicker the time goes. Not the kind of teeth-gritting, fist-clenching, jaw-scrunching determination I usually bring to things that are hard, but a gentle and compassionate – yet firm – resolve, a commitment to my well-being, a dedication to myself. That's a whole different energy.

I learn that the more my mind is restless, the more my body is restless; the more I move my restless body, the more restless it becomes; the more I entertain and indulge my restless mind, the more restless it becomes; and the more my body is restless, the more my mind is restless.

Fascinating.

It's an endless torturous loop and makes for the most agonizing and never-ending 60 minutes ever. Physical pain and emotional pain are totally interconnected, and pain is not the same as suffering. Pain is something that happens in the body, suffering is something that happens in the mind. We might not be able to remove the pain, but we can most certainly remove the suffering and that's a whole different experience.

I learn that the practice is simple, it's the mind that makes it SO difficult, and I learn that balance of the mind is EVERYTHING.

On day nine I find my posture. Once I stopped faffing around with finding the exact right cushion combination, stopped trying to look outside for help with how to sit comfortably, the wisdom of my body took over and showed me exactly how to do it. Moment by moment, day by day, inch by inch, finding my way back to a time long ago when my body was open enough to instinctively know how to sit comfortably cross-legged on the floor.

On day 10 I find the hot water tap on a wall not far from my room and realise that everyone else has been using it since we arrived!

As the silence dissolves on day 11, the buzz of conversations begin, and I am reminded how much harder I always find it to come out of the silence than I do to go into it. The sanctuary of quietude floats away, I watch it disappear, willing it to return but knowing it's time to let it go and resume a more 'normal' way of being with each other to prepare us for life beyond the tall iron gates.

It's incredible to feel how much intimacy there is with my fellow inmates. There is such a closeness to some of these women even though we haven't made eye contact or spoken a word to each other. I guess when you share anything unique and deeply challenging with fellow human beings, you are inextricably fused.

As I heave my backpack onto my shoulders, feeling a strange mix of invincibility and vulnerability as I venture out into the intensely vivid, crazily chaotic, sights, smells and sounds of India, I am aware of one thing...

It really is magical what you can learn from simply sitting with your pain.

Within two hours of leaving the centre, I am sitting under THE Bodhi tree where Buddha apparently became enlightened. Having spent the last 10 days hearing and practising the teachings of Buddha, this is pretty goddam profound.

Another very cool thing (on a completely different level) is that, having been happily reunited with my phone, I have communication from The Viking. He has replied to my email about the 23-year-old note in Swedish and he has sent me a WhatsApp message too. Given my current (and no doubt time-limited) expertise of noticing how I'm feeling, I notice I am thrilled to hear from him.

I explain my radio silence.

He emails back to ask me, "Why now? Why have you now got in touch, after 23 years?"

Why indeed...I attempt an explanation:

"I guess it's about me going through lots of changes in my life recently. I have two sons and they've both just left home, I've sold my house and quit most of my work and have lots of travel plans for this year. So travelling again made me want to look at all my old journals and letters and photos which gave me the feeling I should try to contact you, so I did, and you replied. I don't know why exactly. Maybe we'll find out. I am as surprised as you are by it."

And I am. I keep pinching myself to believe that we are back in touch with each other after TWENTY THREE fucking years. It's crazy. I notice, too, that I am fantasising about him. Am I playing a

252

dangerous game with myself? Am I expecting to bring something from the past back to life? More attempts to resurrect that which is dead?

Who knows. It feels good to be back in touch with him though, and it's helping with my Vipassana come-down. Tomorrow, I will be back on the road, next stop: Varanasi. I was there last year and something stirred in the fire-pit of my soul. I just *knew* I had to go back.

I am about to find out why.

Scene Four – Death

"When we don't allow ourselves to grieve our losses, wounds and
disappointments, we are doomed to keep reliving them.
Freedom lies in learning to embrace what happened."

– Edith Eger

I am standing inside the sacred temple where Varanasi's legendary eternal flame burns. The flame that apparently has not gone out for 3500 years or 2500 years or 5000 years (depending on who you talk to or what you read). It is the flame that has lit every pyre of every dead body that has ever been cremated in Varanasi. That's between 200 and 300 bodies per day, for however many thousand years. The drumming ceremony is about to begin, I sense I am in for one hell of a treat.

Woah woah woah!! Fucking hell!!!

A million electric particles rocket through my cells as the volume and energy in the temple vibrates off the charts.

I am standing at the back with a handful of westerners, around 20 local drummers fill the inside, and the Sadhu – dressed in nothing but beads, ash, and a loincloth – moves from his shrine in the middle to the flame just to my right. He stands on one leg from time to time, in a trance, chanting, doing his thing.

I have been transported into a holy underworld.

But then Varanasi is not of this world. There is nowhere else quite like it. It's dark, dystopian, dirty, polluted, and squalidly stinky, yet there is something utterly magical about it. And there's something else...I don't know, but I have a strong inexplicable sense that I've been here before.

Yes, I know I have, last year, but I'm not talking about that. I felt it then too, there's something really familiar about the place to me, like I've lived here before, like a past life thing, I don't know, I just knew last year when I came (not on my own) that I needed to come back again (on my own). And here I am now, standing inside the temple that last year I didn't even realise you were allowed into, and I'm only inside now because of a young, stoned dude that I was chatting to outside who escorted me in. Outside on the river bank, bodies are being burnt on the Ghats of the Ganges. Clouds of burning human ash and smoke, infused with sandalwood incense, fill the air. This could be distasteful to my western sensibilities but no, there is nothing but peace and healing floating in the air via the dust particles of death.

Ahh, Varanasi – it's SO good to be back and the reason why I needed to come back here for this next part of my journey, for this next part of my healing, is about to fully reveal itself. I think intuitively I knew I needed to come here to let go of some of the pain I have been carrying and I am about to understand a little more about the part that The Viking is playing in it all.

I am sitting in a café in the labyrinth of winding alleyways, I do my best to convey my nut allergy to the owner, order my lunch and trust that it won't kill me. I connect to the Wi-Fi and check my phone, I wonder if there will be an email from The Viking.

Yep, there is!

It's a long email, he says it took him a very long time to write it – which I believe is as much about the content as it is about the fact that English isn't his first language. He tells me two important things.

The first is a kind of confession about how he felt about me 23 years ago. That he had a massive crush on me, thought I was beautiful, funny, intelligent and his response to this was to hide away in shyness and get as drunk as possible.

Great.

The second is that he has been in a relationship for the past 15 years, she has two grown-up children, and last year he became a so-called grandfather.

Not great.

So why did you reply to my letter then? Why have you picked up this thread then? Why are you tugging on it as much as me?

And there, before my lunch has arrived, he has taken the key and let loose the aching animal that had been locked safe inside my bones.

Back in my hotel room, the tears start to fall.

It's just SO sad. To realise we had such feelings for each other but were both too fucked up to trust ourselves. Instead, we stowed those feelings away, too afraid to know what else to do. But in hiding those parts of us away from ourselves, we hid them from each other. We both felt the magnetism and we both resisted it.

A confused tidal wave of churned up YESES and NOS flood my senses. ALL the times where I said yes but meant no and said no but meant yes. Things could've been so different, we had such a special connection, and I know we still do. But maybe this is about putting it all to rest, to make an ending once and for all with my unhelpful patterns with men...and THERE IT IS...I wail like never before.

I'm letting go of something really big here. I can feel it. And it's OK that I don't quite understand it in my head, I feel it in my heart. And I know it's to do with my dad and The Viking represents all my suppressed feelings from that time...

Ahh, THERE it is again!

My heart cracks open and releases a raging waterfall of tears. I know I've just found my way there. Twenty-three years later, in this phenomenal spiritual place, with the help of The Viking, I've come home to what it is I'm really letting go of.

I am grieving...finally grieving.

I am grieving for that girl who was scared shitless but couldn't show it.

I am grieving for that girl who was finally finding her path in life when it all got taken away from her.

256

I am grieving for that girl who suppressed everything.

I am grieving for that girl and that boy who couldn't show their feelings for each other.

I am grieving for that girl who was pretending to be so cool and happy on the outside but felt so lost and alone on the inside.

I am grieving for that girl who lost her daddy way too soon.

She was already healing from the relationship with The Psycho and everything before that, then she got stuck in her unprocessed grief with her dad. She concealed *everything* and got together with Understudy and had her two incredible boys, and tried to do the best she could and worked on herself through psychotherapy, mindfulness and Qoya, trying to find her way out but *always still* feeling suppressed in all the relationships she's been in. And now her boys have grown up and that part of her life is complete, she found her way back to do what needed to be done. The cycle is complete.

I have cried a million tears in my hotel bedroom.

A lifetime of suppression now transmuted into a wet, snotty, slobbery mess on my sheets.

Some Hindus believe The Ganges flowed from heaven to purify humans. I know I have just been purified and, when these sheets are washed in the river after I've gone, my tears will flow back into the sacred arms of Ma Ganga.

Oh my God – I need to DANCE!

Instead of being exhausted by my healing process, I am exuberant! I'm not sure if this is a celebration or if there is more to shift out and shake up, I just know I have to move my body. Right here on the bed, I climb unsteadily to my feet and I turn my little speaker up LOUD. With the help of Tom Odell, any remnants of suppression that were by chance left clinging to some dark hollowed crevice of my body, mind, or soul, I make sure I get to.

What I haven't already cried out, I dance out.

When I am done, I shower and get dressed and head out for dinner.

Today is the 26th of January, it's India's Independence Day.

It feels like my Independence Day too.

That night, I have a dream. Terry Wogan is interviewing me: I'd had a number one hit single many years ago but then I'd gone off the radar as my dad had died. Terry asked me how I felt about that. I told him simply that I didn't feel anything because I'd shut off all my feelings. My sister was there to watch and my mum too. The interview was because I was preparing to make a comeback!

OH YES!!

Scene Five – Remember

"Namaste – I honour the place in you in which the entire universe dwells. I honour the place in you which is of love, of truth, of light, and of peace. When you are in that place in you, and I am in the place in me, we are one."

– Unknown

I am in Rishikesh, doing a yoga class in the school which will be my home for the next 2 weeks.

"More try!" I am told, repeatedly, by the teacher.

I am bloody trying!

Now, I am well aware of the spiritual significance of Rishikesh, of it being the yoga capital of India, of it being a place of reverence and worship and deep meaning, but I'm just not feeling it. And yes, I am well aware that that is saying far more about me than it is about Rishikesh. But it's bloody COLD here, it's raining and grey, and inside I'm feeling pretty miserable. I think the intensity of Varanasi has caught up with me and I just need to feel nurtured. Only there is nothing nurturing about the room I am staying in, the street dogs barking all night long directly outside my window keeping me awake all night, the head cold that I have complete with painful sinuses, a sore throat and a blocked nose (no fun in a 7 a.m. pranayama class, I can tell you), and now someone repeatedly telling me I'm not trying enough in this most definite advanced-level yoga class which I am most definitely not yoga-fit for.

This whole school is odd actually, it seems to be run by a bunch of guys in their twenties and I have already been told quite bluntly in one of the evening meditation sessions that, "You are 49 so I have nothing to teach you. You can teach us about life and your experiences."

Well, yeah, I'm sure I could teach you a thing or two but I'm here to learn from you because that's what I've booked and paid for!

Last night we spent 40 minutes walking around a dark room with disco lights flashing, chanting to an 'Om, Hari Krishna' backing track. I was wearing all my clothes and half my bedding to keep me warm. It really was quite surreal. And not to knock that, because I'm open to anything and I did quite enjoy it, but there's just something about this place that I'm not connecting with, and I am beginning to question whether the meditation teacher is actually a meditation teacher.

And, if I'm going to be totally honest with you, I'm also thoroughly distracted by The Viking! Since Varanasi, we have continued to message and email each other and now I can't work out whether he is a *distraction* to my process of being here or if he *is* my process of being here.

"Either way, it's happening," my sister tells me wisely when I call to talk to her about it.

Yep, it's happening alright. I am thinking about him morning, noon, and bloody night. Whenever I'm not in class, feeling every bit like the flaky westerner I'm sure they think I am, I'm chasing around town to find somewhere with Wi-Fi that's not going to cut out after 5 minutes (easier said than done in this town).

It's a total headfuck (and maybe why my head is totally blocked). On the one hand, it feels so good to have contact with him, to be back in touch after all these years, and the connection is so clearly still there (he's also sent me a couple of pics of himself and he still looks like I remember). But on the other hand, he's not available. He has a partner and do I really want to get involved in another drama triangle situation...after everything I'm learning about all my patterns and the sisterhood thing too...I feel uncomfortable and have a guilty conscience even though I don't even know her...it's him I have the connection with and so what if he has a partner...why shouldn't two old friends be able to be back in touch with each other...except that's not at all how it feels...there's more to it than that clearly...he is really being quite flirty in his messages and I am really mindful of not responding in the same way because it doesn't feel appropriate but I really want to...I feel it too...it feels really intense between us...I don't think I could just let it go now...feels like we've tipped past that point...arrrgggghhhh!!!

THIS IS **NOT** WHAT I CAME TO INDIA FOR!

Or is it?

I CAME TO BE ON MY OWN!

Or did I?

BUT NOW YET ANOTHER RELATIONSHIP FROM MY PAST! NUMBER FOUR! IS THIS ONE GOING TO END THE SAME WAY? ANOTHER ONE THAT JUST NEEDS FINISHING OFF?

Or will it be different this time?

ANYONE ELSE WAITING IN THE BLOODY WINGS??!!

Like I say, a total headfuck.

And things are about to go up another notch altogether.

I am sitting having lunch in the café along the road from the yoga school. The Viking and I have just exchanged a couple of messages, the next thing I know, his name is flashing up on my phone... he's bloody calling me!

That's right, calling me. No prior notice, no pre-arranging, no indicating that that's what he was going to do. Just bloody calling me.

I freeze.

I can't speak to him! I'm not ready for that. All this messaging and emailing is one thing but to actually hear his voice again after 23 years. No way. Not without psyching myself up first.

He rings off. I stare at my phone, back in the safety of its home screen photo. Did that really just happen? And why the fuck didn't I answer?

Back in my room, I send him a message. I've had at least 10 minutes to psyche myself up.

"Hi, I see you called? Sorry, I didn't have good Wi-Fi so couldn't answer. Do you want to try again, am back in my room now."

His name flashing on my screen again.

Deep breath.

Answer it, just bloody answer it.

Me: "Hello?"

Him: "Hi."

Oh my fucking God!

Me: "Shit. This is weird. I can't believe you just called me."

Him: "I know. I'm sorry if I shouldn't have. I just really wanted to hear your voice suddenly."

And I remember your voice. I remember the vibration of it. I remember your accent... I am 26 years old again, transported back to a lake in Indonesia.

Me: "No, it's OK, it's good to hear your voice. You sound exactly the same. This is weird, right?"

Him: "Yes, very. How are you?"

Me: "Um I'm not sure really, can't think straight right now, think I'm a bit in shock."

A bit?

Him: "Yeah me too. I don't really know what to say."

Me: "Are you at work?"

Him: "Yes, just on a break."

Me: "OK. What is it you do?"

Him: "Oh, I fix machines, engineering stuff..."

Here we are, having spent the past 10 days exchanging personally disclosing emails and flirty messages, and now we're having a question and answer session about the machine factory he works in. But I guess diving straight into "So, what the fuck is happening here between us?" is a bit much for our first conversation since 1996, in the middle of his coffee break, on a Thursday morning.

But already we're chatting easily. I remember how easy it always felt to talk to him, to be with him. There's something just easy about 'us'.

After half an hour, he needs to get back to work and I need to run around the room in a mad frenzy thinking:

What the fuck just happened?

He says he'll call again.

I can hardly wait.

———————————

On our second phone call, 2 days later, he manages to make me cry.

Him: "You're always helping others, you're always giving but you never receive it back. Stop giving out. You need to receive it back now."

This, apparently, he has deduced after reading between the lines in an email I sent. What he says lands like a fist in my heart and the tears immediately come.

How the fuck, after 23 years, does he know that's exactly what I need to hear?

Our connection is unquestionable...but...this is perfect for my old pattern of someone not being available to me. Why is he telling me I need to receive from someone else when he's not available to give to me?

Will you ever be available?

Do I want you to be?

As I cry, he tells me he wishes he was there to give me a hug, and that he wishes we could go out for dinner and have a bottle of wine (not likely in Rishikesh) and talk properly.

He also tells me that if I had sent that letter to him a few weeks earlier, it might have been different. He was ready to leave his relationship then, he'd been unhappy for some time (you don't say) but he'd gone back and recommitted to it, to try to work it out.

But timing is ALWAYS PERFECT, right? I *know* that's true.

———————

Meanwhile, as the days go by, I am feeling the vibe here less and less. It just doesn't feel like what I need right now. I'm not in the right space to appreciate it. I have already reduced my schedule twice at the school, I feel like I am slowly extracting myself. We're not a good match. I can't quite figure out if they feel disappointed in me or disrespected by me. Both, I suspect. Either way, it all feels a bit awkward. Then I wake up and suddenly realise:

I CAN DO WHAT I LIKE!

IF I DON'T WANT TO STAY HERE, THEN I DON'T HAVE TO!

It really is like a light bulb going on in my head and I can't quite believe that I haven't realised it before.

I AM FREE TO DO WHAT I LIKE!

Isn't that the whole point of this 'gap year' I'm giving myself? The whole point of having shed myself from most of my responsibilities in my life? So that I can do more of what I want and not feel trapped by doing what I don't want?

So what if I've booked and paid to stay here for 2 weeks? I'm not going to ask them for a refund, so it's my loss. But staying here when I'm not happy just because I've paid for it doesn't feel like a good enough reason for me to stay. I still have 12 days left before my flight home. I think I need to enjoy it. Oh yeah, "enjoy it", that's right!

Over the next couple of hours, a beautiful sequence of 'coincidences' flow, and I am shown where I need to go. Firstly, I receive a message from a friend from home who is also in Rishikesh, but who I haven't met up with yet as she is in some kind of yoga prison like the meditation prison I was in. She is finishing her course and plans to head south to Kerala at the end of next week, to a place called Varkala Beach.

Now, I haven't got a clue where I want to go to in India, but I do know I need a beach and I need some warm sunshine. Perhaps Kerala is a good option. But where to stay? So hard to get it right if you don't know where you're going.

I remember that an Irish girl I met on the Vipassana, and hung out with under the Bodhi Tree, was heading to Kerala, perhaps she's still there, perhaps she could give me some tips. I message her. She is at the airport literally about to board her flight home. Another 10 minutes and her phone would have been off for 12 hours. She inundates me with messages of places to stay and places to eat and places to do yoga where she has just spent the last 10 days...in Varkala Beach.

Well, that's decided then!

Within two hours of remembering I am indeed FREE to do what I like, I have booked a return flight from Delhi to Trivandrum, all perfectly timed for my flight home to the UK.

Amazing what you can sort out with a credit card, a couple of synchronicities, and some decent Wi-Fi.

Back at the yoga school, I make some excuse about a friend in Kerala needing me (49 and wise, wild and free or not, I just can't face any fallout of being honest with them) and it dawns on me that, of course...I should have known this wouldn't work out!

I remember back in the UK a few months ago when I made the booking with them, I wasn't quite sure about it from their website, but I decided to send them an enquiry to see if they had availability, telling myself I would then think about it for a while and see how it sat with me. From the minute I made contact with them, they kept messaging me, asking me to pay a deposit, it felt like they were being really pushy but instead of ignoring them and finding somewhere else, I let myself be pushed into it, even though I still wasn't sure.

I don't know why I did that. Perhaps because I just wanted it all arranged, to have my whole trip planned out – so different from when I was travelling in my twenties, we didn't know where we were going to sleep from one minute to the next then, but I guess the world has changed in the last three decades. And it was something to do with being a mum, wanting to be able to let people know my itinerary, so I didn't just disappear off the face of the earth.

Anyway, for whatever reasons, I didn't listen to my gut, I went ahead and booked it even though it felt off, so really can I be surprised that it didn't work out?

It's my last night here and, as always, my choice of where to eat dinner depends on whether or not their Wi-Fi is working. Pizza it is again then!

The Viking calls me as arranged, I tell him my plans to leave here and head south to the sunshine. Things are so intense between us and I think I need them to be different for this last part of my trip – maybe I also have a choice about whether I take this headfuck with me or not.

I want to remember the essence of this trip – to find some internal peace, to meditate every day, to do yoga every day, to be eating and sleeping well, to write, to get some space, to process the past and gain some perspective of the present and a sense of how I want my future to be. What I don't want is to be constantly obsessing over him, running around desperately looking for Wi-Fi and checking my phone every two bloody minutes.

He is struggling massively too. He tells me he feels like a bear with two heads and doesn't know whether he's coming or going. He's not sleeping or eating properly, and he can't focus at work.

We agree that a break in contact whilst I'm in Kerala is a good idea for both of us. Well, at least for a week as it's his birthday on the 7th and he admits it would be lovely to have a birthday message from me.

OK, that's a good plan. A no-contact contract. The chance to get some perspective on all this. The chance to get back to myself. I don't think it will be easy, but it feels right.

I pack my bag once again and at 6 a.m. my taxi arrives to make the 5-hour drive to Delhi airport. I say goodbye to Rishikesh, the place where people come in search of the holy and sacred practice of yoga...or, in my case, the search for Wi-Fi.

Scene Six – Sing

"Sometimes the bravest and most important thing you can do is just show up."

– Brené Brown

I am back in bare feet and I have landed in viscose heaven, stalls and stalls of brightly coloured clothing lie interspersed between coffee shops and cool hangout cafes with music playing, all fringing the Indian Ocean beachfront just a 2-minute walk from my very comfortable guest house.

Oh yes, this was SO the right move and, just in case I needed any confirmation of that, guess what? The yoga class that I am going to each morning is taught by a Czech girl.

After yoga I am spending my days moving leisurely: dividing my time between the beach, the various cafes, and sprawled flat out naked on my bed under the fan. It's hot here! I've been chatting to an English couple and having some interesting conversations but mostly I am very content just being with myself. I am also journaling like a madwoman.

As for the no contact with The Viking thing, even though I think it's good, it's also quite a distraction in itself.

Are you thinking about me?

What's going on for you?

At least when we were talking I knew the answers to those questions, now I'm just trying to be OK with the not knowing.

Where are you in your process?

Have you decided to end our contact for good?

HANG ON! Why the hell does it all have to be about **HIM**?

*What about **MY** process?*

*What about what's going on for **ME**?*

*What about what **I'M** deciding about ending our contact for good?*

*What about how much **I'M** thinking about **HIM**?!!?*

Hmm...OK...clearly I am still thinking about him way too much, but I am having lots of helpful reflections.

Like... how I've always just thrown myself into every relationship I've had. I've always been in a rush to make it happen straight away because, I am realising, I don't believe they'll wait for me. I always have to make it happen immediately, God forbid I actually slow down and see how things play out. This whole situation is making me do that, teaching me some patience, teaching me to trust that I don't need to force it, if it's right then it will happen and if it doesn't, then it wasn't right.

Anyway, he has a partner.

Like... don't we owe it to our younger selves, our 1996 selves, our messed-up, low-self-esteemed selves, who didn't have the confidence? Don't they deserve it?

Anyway, he has a partner.

Like...I don't need him to leave her for me, I don't even know what I want, I didn't consciously want this to happen when I wrote

270

that letter.

Anyway, he has a partner.

Like... I've got this whole thing going on with myself right now – changing my life, getting back to me – I wasn't planning on getting into another relationship right now.

Anyway, he has a partner.

Like... I really miss our contact, I really enjoy our chats, it's been fun and exciting, we get on so well.

Anyway, he has a partner.

Like... I must not allow the no contact to be as distracting as the contact.

Anyway, he has a partner.

Like... am I just addicted to the buzz of a new relationship? Getting attention from some guy? Can I not be happy unless I have that in my life? Is that about my dad? I've always lost myself in the fantasy of a relationship rather than the reality of it (just like poor Unfinished Business did with me, I think), does that come from childhood? I always want men to love me more and when they do I feel suffocated and want to run a mile, just like when I was a child. Is this thing with The Viking here to help me out of that pattern?

Anyway, HE HAS A BLOODY PARTNER!

Like... is it the 7th yet?

———————

I am really trying to find some balance in being present in doing my thing here, and reflecting on what's happening with The Viking, what the learning in it is for me, cos that's what relationships are about, right? But I really want to enjoy my time here too. This morning I got a ride into town to the ATM and the shops on the back of the guesthouse owner's motorbike. By the time we arrived back, mortifyingly, I had to prize the inside of my sweaty thighs away from the outside of his and extract my pineapple, which had nestled spikily between us all the way home, from his lower back. Somehow he was still grateful to me. Bless the Indian people, they are so hospitable. And I have to tell you, not once during this trip, as a woman travelling alone, have I felt vulnerable or threatened or unsafe in any way. I have received nothing but kindness and a genuine desire to please from everyone I've met. In India, visitors are considered like God and it's considered bad karma if anyone feels badly treated, so the local people are more than eager for you to have a positive experience. That's been my experience anyway, but I guess the law of attraction determines that you receive back whatever it is you are giving out. I never considered for a moment that I would feel vulnerable or threatened or unsafe during this trip.

I decide to treat myself to an Ayurvedic massage in the small family-run centre next door to my hotel. It's an interesting experience in which there is no shared language. I am instructed to wear nothing but a pair of paper knickers (I think) and trying to establish whether or not they are using a nut oil base is a virtual impossibility. I come out smelling like a freshly baked (nut-free) biscuit and resembling an oil slick that would constitute a national disaster, but I am the most relaxed and happy I've been so far on this whole trip.

Down by the beach this morning, something caught my eye. A

flyer taped to the wall announced a Singing Circle that happens each Thursday evening. I've always had a shyness around singing. I think it harks back to being asked to leave the school choir when I was 11 as I was 'out of tune'. Shocking when I think about that now. That's the kind of thing that stays with a kid for life. "Oh me? No, I can't sing." That's like saying I can't dance, or I can't draw, or I can't write. *Everyone* can do *every one* of those things. We are so creatively repressed in our culture. We are given very few positive messages of encouragement to be creative and to express our *individuality* through mediums like singing, dancing, drawing, and writing. So, for that bastard of a choir teacher who told me I had to leave when it had taken all my courage to show up in the first place let alone open my mouth – I'm going to the bloody Singing Circle!!

And I sing like never before. I sing like I don't care, because I don't. I sing like no one's watching, because I don't care if they are or not. I sing for all the people in the circle who I can see are holding back because they are too shy to be heard or because they were kicked out of choirs. I sing for all the kids who were ever told "you can't sing". I sing because it's making me feel liberated and free. I sing for my inner child who couldn't make herself heard. I sing because, at 49, I am finally finding my frigging voice!

And I sing in tune!

I feel incredible, invincible, my vibration as high as a kundalini kite. On the way back, I walk past one of the seafood restaurants. Poor swordfish. One minute happily jumping around in the ocean, the next laid out on a slab of ice with a massive bright red tomato on the end of its nose – presumably, so the poor human beings don't get stabbed by it when they walk past. It looks like something out of Comic Relief.

I'm not sure why this touches me so much, it's not the sort of thing I would even normally notice. I am allergic to fish and seafood and, just as I am allergic to dogs and would say I'm not a doggy person, I'm not a fishy person either. But something about this sorry sight feels like such a humiliating ending for the poor swordfish.

Maybe all this singing is opening something up in me.

Woohoo!! It's the 7th! Yay!

My birthday message to The Viking is sent, along with a photo of me looking suitably gorgeous standing on my veranda under a palm tree...obviously!

By the end of the day, we have exchanged 32 messages.

Zero to 32 in a day. OK, this thing has got legs!!

It seems he has been wanting to hear from me as much as I've been wanting to contact him. It's clear that the week (well, 5 days) off hasn't changed anything, except made us even keener. I am having one hell of a holiday romance – except the other person isn't actually here.

We arrange a phone call. We need to talk about what the hell is happening here.

It seems to me we have three choices. We either carry on like we are – not really an option, it's way too stressful. Or we knock it on the head altogether, say "Well, it's been bloody amazing being back in touch after 23 years, clearly we still have such a connection, I love talking to you, you love talking to me, so let's not do it anymore. Goodbye." Hmm...not my favourite option right now. Or we arrange to meet up, have the chance to talk properly, get a better sense of what this is about and where it's going – that gets my vote.

Yes, he wants to meet up too!!

But he won't.

Not while he is still in his relationship. He says he needs to figure that out first and he will only meet up with me if and when that is over.

Oh, how very noble.

Oh, how very mature.

Oh, how very sensible.

Oh, how very bloody frustrating!

Of course, I should be pleased about that, it shows he has integrity (even if he is clearly already being unfaithful) and he wants to do the right thing here, but really? Where does that leave me? Just waiting to see what he decides? (Well, yes.) But what if we meet up and it's clear that it's not going to happen between us? Isn't it better to meet up first and see how it feels before he makes any big decisions? (Well, no.) If he ends his relationship and then we meet up am I not going to feel a whole load of pressure to make something happen? Are we not both going to feel that pressure? (Well, not necessarily.) What does it say about me that I'd be happy for us to sneak off secretly for a weekend, knowing what's likely to happen? How is that OK for me? (How, indeed.)

Well, it's OK for me because it's familiar, of course. That's what I've always done, that's what both my parents seemed to do after they'd divorced. My mum has had more than one relationship with married men, in fact, her second marriage began as an affair, and my dad certainly did his fair share of sneaking around with various women. And not to entirely blame it on them because I've already set my own pattern of that in my life, but we do become a product of our upbringing...

Until we don't.

Perhaps now – thanks to The Viking clearly demonstrating more integrity than me – I have the chance to break that soul-destroying pattern.

Now, we have to remember here that he was not happy in his relationship in the first place. They've been sleeping in separate rooms, living separate lives for a while. When my letter landed in his post box, he picked it up, saw it was from England, and his heart skipped a beat. He turned the envelope over and saw it was from Bournemouth (I deliberately hadn't put my name on the back just in case) and his heart felt like it was going to explode out of his chest, apparently. Now, instead of going indoors, openly reading that letter in front of his partner, telling her it was from an old friend he met travelling years ago, showing her if she had asked to see it (I know I would), instead of that, he slipped it in his back pocket before he returned to the house, only opened it up when he was at work on his own, emailed me from a different account to the one he normally uses, left the letter at work, and never told her or anyone else about it.

I think that's all quite telling about where he was at. It's fair to say then, that their relationship was on the rocks before I came bursting back in and dropped a missile on his quiet little life in southern Sweden.

So it seems this is something he needs to sort out anyway, regardless of anything to do with me, he needs to decide if that relationship is over or not. Although who am I to tell him what he needs, right?

But is that who I am? Is that why I've come back into his life? Just to serve as a catalyst to help him out of his relationship? And is he back in my life just to help me heal from my past hurt so I can break some patterns?

Maybe that's it. Again, something to teach and something to learn. Simple.

That's the sane, aware, evolved, rational, pragmatic, adult voice in me. There is another voice in me too, crunched up in a corner of my heart – that of my scared, hurt, wounded, panicked child. And right now she's yelling at the top of her wheezing lungs:

He's not going to choose you! He's going to choose her because you're not good enough!

How can I make him choose me? I can't just sit back and wait to see what he decides. It's too painful. Waiting to see if I am good enough or not. Waiting to see if I'm not too much for him. That's it. I'm too much. I'm too emotional, too needy, too sensitive, too deep, too difficult to be with. I've scared him off. He's going to choose her because I'm TOO MUCH.

All of this process leads me to have another huge realisation: he was going to leave his relationship once before and then gone back; I wasn't part of the picture then but now I am.

BAM! It slaps me in the face: "Who? you? You're not enough to make any difference."

My deepest fear is not that I am too much, but that I am not enough.

An arrow shoots me right between the eyes and I see clearly through the wound. The fear of being too much was just there to protect me from a deeper agony: the fear of not being enough. And as I sit on my sarong here on the beach, here we go again...the tears begin to fall. More and more tears that have been stuck in my craw.

Seriously? How can there be any left? I'm on the verge of dehydration!

Of course this situation of *waiting to be chosen* that I 'find' myself in is my worst nightmare. It is the place where I shiver in an ice bath of vulnerability, where I stand on a cliff edge of fear. So of course it's the perfect place. Because it's the only place I can fully realise this, *feel* it and to be able to let go of it, step away from that cliff edge. And of course it's why I say to myself, "Oh, I don't need you to change anything about your situation because of me. I don't need you to leave her first." Not because I think it's OK to cheat but because it protects me nicely from feeling the fear of not being enough. "Actually, yeah, I do need you to sort your head out and leave her to see what this is." But because I don't think that I can expect that, because I don't think I am enough, I default back to my adaptive free-spirited cool Vik, who doesn't need anything from anyone.

I crack through another layer of the encrusted plaque of my life. I broke through the first layer on the Vipassana – letting go of my *be strong* defence. I broke through the second layer in Varanasi – grieving my dad, *grieving* my younger self. Now in Varkala, I can reach the deepest layer of all – my *I am not enough* belief. That's why I use my looks, my sexuality, my sensuality, to hook someone in, to get their attention.

Have I just done that again with The Viking?

I want to tell him all this, tell him what I've realised, explain myself to him, but – oh, there we go again – I'm afraid I'll be too much for him. That I will then put him off and I will be left feeling not good enough all over again.

Lovely self-fulfilling prophecy.

Around and around.

Over and over.

Again and again.

Does this come from childhood?

I have a flashback to memories of my dad always being late to pick us up on his weekends, of how my mum would mutter inferences under her breath about how he clearly didn't care enough. She would allow her anger with him to spill out into her interactions with me and my sister, again inferring that he didn't care about us.

I *must* have internalised those messages, taken them to heart, interpreted them to mean that I wasn't enough.

Yeah, of course I did, cos that's what children do, they internalise stuff.

But now I know more about my dad's story, now I have some insight into why he was the way he was, now I can bring my adult perspective to the table, I know that's not true. He did care. He cared a lot. He just wasn't able to grow into his adult enough to know how to be responsible in it all. I understand, too, that my mum had a tough time with her mum, she felt neglected and rejected, not wanted and not good enough, so her shit was all in that mix of how she was as a mother, how she is as a mother.

So now I can see things clearly.

Correction, now I can *feel* things clearly.

And what I *don't* need is The Viking's process to prove it to me one way or the other. I don't need to sit around and wait and see if he chooses me or chooses her, so that I can then decide if I am good enough or not. Sure, I needed his help to lead me to the awareness (that's what relationships do) but I don't need him or anyone else to fix me. I can only do that for myself. I need to know it from within. I need to remember my truth:

I AM NOT TOO MUCH AND I AM ENOUGH!!

―――――――――

My 11 days in Varkala have come to an end. This follows my 11 days travelling around India and my 11 days spent on the Vipassana course.

And they say 11 is an auspicious number. Huh! Hmm...let me think, has this been in any way an auspicious trip?? Yep! I think it's fair to say I got what I came for.

India, you have most certainly delivered! This trip has been huge for me and I feel like I am leaving a part of myself behind. I'm not sure if that's a part of me that I don't need anymore, or a part of me that I'll want to come back for another time. Either way, a piece of me belongs here in this crazy, chaotically peaceful, incredible, sacred country.

As I prepare to fly home, The Viking is left to make his decision about his life. There is nothing more I can do. There is nothing more I want to do. When I arrive back in the UK he says he will have made a decision and will email to let me know. Meanwhile, I have let it go, I've handed it over to the universe to do her thing and I am trusting in the process once again.

Scene Seven – Fifty

"Tell me, what is it you plan to do with your one wild and precious life?"

– Mary Oliver

I am home for just 4weeks before I will head off on my travels again. A lot happens in those 4 weeks...

Firstly, no sooner have I arrived home than I receive the email from The Viking. He says he and his partner have agreed to "at least give it a try". That doesn't sound particularly convincing, but still, not really what I wanted to hear. In the next sentence, he says he's been thinking about me all night – now that's more like what I wanted to hear. It's sprawled all over his email that even though he is saying that's his decision, his heart is not in it. His pain and turmoil seep through every line.

Hmm...I think he might be a tad confused.

So, because of this mixed message, I am surprisingly calm about it all. It's clear that we're not done here – whatever that means – but I accept he's just gotta do his thing, go through his process. Either way, I'm fine. Well, I'm not fine exactly. Who am I trying to kid? Yet at the same time, I am... oh dear, perhaps I'm as confused as The Viking!

My ego doesn't like it one bit, of course. The idea of him and his partner working through things, getting on with *their* connection, rather than me and him getting on with *our* connection. And my ego frequently likes to remind me that, because our connection is 23 years old, it blows their mere 15-year connection out of the water. *My* relationship with him precedes *her* relationship with him. The fact that they've spent every day together for the past 15 years and share an entire life, whilst 23 years ago he and I spent 3 weeks backpacking in Asia sharing bottles of whisky, is a minor detail that my ego prefers to overlook.

At the same time, I am very aware that I have so much going on in my life right now that doesn't actually involve The Viking. So many very good things. I've realised since I've been home that I have so much happening over the next couple of months, if this all needs more time...well actually I *need* it to all take a bit longer... or much longer... or whatever, it's all good.

I do miss talking to him though, I've really liked having him back in my life, but for once I am determined not to prioritise a relationship... It's taken me a while to realise it but there is actually more to life. Yes, really, there is!

In my reply to his email, I tell him it shouldn't be about choosing me or choosing his partner, it should be about him choosing himself. And I mean this, despite my ego, I really do. I realise what I really want is for him to be OK, whether that means he and I are together in some way or not. If I never hear from him again, well fine, I honestly just want him to be happy. Again, a first for me, I don't feel like I really have an agenda here, or at least the part of me that doesn't have an agenda is overruling the part of me that does.

Is this what they mean by unconditional love?

Two days later, he messages and asks if we can speak. He had already told me (interestingly) in his "I'm so SORRY" email that he is home alone for the weekend. He suggests a video call, another first.

Oh my God. To actually SEE him again? OK, I've seen pictures and have got used to hearing his voice again over the phone, but a video call? Surely that's taking it to another level. How can he be saying he's working on his relationship with his partner and then be suggesting a video call with me?! And is that what I want? Do I want to see him? Do I want this to go to another level when he's clearly so confused and messed up about what's going on? Well of course I bloody do!

Over the course of the weekend, we spend 7 hours on video calls.

Seven hours? Seriously – how the fuck does that happen?

It's amazing to 'see' him again. After 23 years, to see him moving, speaking, laughing...my God it's so weird, this young guy I used to know, all grown up, looking like a middle-aged man, letting me into his confused head once again, talking to me about stuff he never talks about just like before.

But why am I not ending it? Why is it OK for me to keep up our contact like this, spending all this time talking to him while his partner is away for the weekend?

Well, I am certain that if he was someone I'd just met I would definitely not be entertaining this. If I'd just met him and found out he was in a relationship I would have walked away, for sure. Trust me, that much I have learnt through my experiences.

But he's not someone I've just met. It's him. It's *us*. It's the guy I met

23 years ago who I had big feelings for. It's the guy who now tells me I was his first love but he couldn't show it. It's the guy who I climbed up an active volcano with and sat feeling the magnitude of the energy and vibration transfer into our bodies through the rocks we laid on, blown away by the experience. It's the guy who I sat next to on a minibus between Thailand and Malaysia and physically felt our energetic connection travel from his body into mine when my leg touched up against his. It's the guy who opened up his shy and shut down 23-year-old self to me when we walked around the lake in Indonesia, watching water buffaloes in the paddy fields. It's the guy who appeared right in that exact spot in that exact moment on the Koh San Road just when I was in my crisis of needing to fly home. It's the guy who I sat and wrote a letter to when my dad died, telling him all about how I was feeling. It's the guy who I had dreams about for 2 years after we met. It's the guy who pulled back on the thread when I picked up my end after nearly a quarter of a century.

That is why I don't want to just end it.

Woohoo!!! I am 50 and I feel amazing. I thought I would dread being 50 because isn't that what we're conditioned into? More years behind you than in front of you, and all that. Let's face it, we're not great at embracing the aging process, we're much better at denying it, trying to defy it, the fear of being ever closer to that foreboding thing we call death. But right now, I'm in such a great place in my life, I feel happy and healthy and it's not about death, it's about feeling *alive*.

I feel blessed to have so many great girlfriends in my life right now.

Mostly these are new friends who I've met through Qoya; we've shared a lot and gone deep together. I also feel grateful to have a mum that I can hang out and have a laugh with, despite any issues from the past that don't feel like they need unearthing now.

As for my relationship with my sister, I'm really pleased to report that we're very close. Despite our difficult early start (I cringe when I remember picking her skin out from under my fingernails after one of our many fights), we, fortunately, are able to have open and honest conversations with each other about our childhood and the impact it had on both of us. I always thought that closeness happened once we had both become parents, some common ground finally being established in our very different personalities and lifestyles, but I wonder now whether it actually happened when our dad died, that somehow this unconsciously shifted something in our dynamic. I have experienced this with clients numerous times: whenever a parent dies, something shifts in our development, regardless of our age. It's like something gets freed up or we become unstuck with some part of ourselves and can finally claim the next stage of our lives. What's interesting, of course, is that our dad dying happened slap bang in the middle of us both becoming mothers, both giving birth to sons.

I'm not sure what it's about but, ever since I became a parent, I think I've always looked forward to having a healthy adult relationship with my boys. Is it because I found the early years difficult? Like I had some fantasy about how the adult relationship with them would be easier? I don't think so. I think it's more about craving that parent-child relationship in an adult context because I never got to have it with my dad. Do I have it with my mum? Well, to a certain degree, yes – it's fine on the surface but it's not the kind of fantasy I have about the relationship I want with my boys when they're adults. I want us to be able to talk about stuff, deep stuff, under-the-surface stuff; I want us to be able to speak about the unspeakable. I want them to be able to tell me how they're feeling, hell...I want to be able to ask how they're feeling and mean it. I want to be there for them, and I want them to want me to be there for them. Right now, I guess it feels like we're finding our way there – they are 21 and 19 – it's a work in progress but isn't everything always just that anyway? Relationships are always in a state of process because we are always in a state of process.

As a parent, it's so easy to say, "but I'd be nothing without my children". Isn't that what we're supposed to say or think, particularly mothers, perhaps? But I don't think it's really true. Sure I would be a VERY different someone if it weren't for them, they have taught me so much about love and about relationship and about responsibility and about worry! But I don't think I'd be nothing, just a different something. Right now I am grateful and proud and love the fact that one of them remembers to call me on my birthday – and the other one does too, after his brother reminds him!

And guess what? As well as having a morning and evening video date, I receive flowers from The Viking. OK...that I wasn't expecting. Hoping for, of course. But expecting? Well, no, I didn't dare. On my 40th birthday, I was with Back Garden Neighbour. He bought me two pairs of socks and some underwear. The underwear was the wrong size, totally the wrong size. When he took it back to the shop to change it they didn't have any more in stock and so he exchanged it for a gift for his sister whose birthday was a few days later. So all I ended up with was two pairs of socks. Sad but true, slightly hilarious too...now!

I'm having lots of reflections...compulsory at every milestone birthday, no? And in a Qoya class I've just been to, I have just had my process in India held up to me in a giant gilded mirror.

I see that I broke through three layers of my life stages.

Firstly, I broke through my present *middle-aged adult* state of being strong. Of course, I had to penetrate that to get underneath to break through my *young adult* state of unprocessed grief. So then I could finally go deeper still into my *child* state of not being enough. Like boring into the earth until you get to the core, the protective calcification of each wound falling away as the layers got broken into, until I reached the core of my being and realised I'm OK. I don't need the protection anymore. Because when we hold on to those protective layers throughout our lives, they end up just getting in our way. We literally forget who we really are. Rather than continuing to protect us, they start to prevent us from living fully, from developing into the best versions of ourselves that we can be.

Isn't that why we're here after all?

I realise all (or at least most of) my relationship issues with men come from the fact that I didn't have the chance to resolve things with my dad before he died. Had he lived longer to a point when I knew who I was, to a point when I had enough awareness to see clearly, to a point when I had the courage to find my voice and speak my truth, well, then things could have been different. Whatever shape that process would have taken it may have resulted in us resolving things. Instead, I was left stuck with them and therefore carried them forward and acted them out in all my subsequent relationships.

But that's over now, right?

During another video call, The Viking reads me one of the letters I

287

sent him 23 years ago. Yep, that's right, he kept all my letters too, in a box safely tucked away in the attic. That's pretty amazing, eh? The fact that we have both kept each other's letters for all of those years, like somehow we knew we needed to keep them. I mean, girls keep those things all the time, I know, but guys, well, not so much.

So this particular letter he reads me is the one I wrote to him 3 months after my dad had died. Fuck! It's one thing reading back someone else's letters after so many years, it's quite another thing having your letters read back to you... "I've done the worst thing possible in my situation and met a guy...I gave up waiting for you (Viking) and realised you'd never leave sunny Sweden for me..."

*That **is** how I felt.*

I cry when he reads it. It feels so bloody sad now. The 'what could have been'.

But what about the 'what still could be'? Because the way I see it, now we're being given a second chance. We missed it first time around and, incredibly, it's coming around for us again. We're being given the chance to do it differently this time. The chance to get it right. Wow, what a gift from the universe!

Paulo Coelho talks about this in his autobiography 'Hippie', about the missed opportunity when two people meet. He says that many great love stories are lost because our souls know how huge it's going to be and we get freaked out and run away from it, then we lose the opportunity of a lifetime.

But if it's meant to be and all that...well, then *this* is what happens. We've been given this opportunity again, in this lifetime, and I think that's pretty fucking cool and not to be ignored.

What do you think Viking? Do you agree? Are you ready to take a risk? A leap of faith? Jump into the unknown with me? Are we ready now?

Apparently, he is! He says there is not much we can do about the past, but yeah, there is something we can do about the future and he says he's gonna "get his shit together", he's "beginning the process".

OK, sounds promising, but what does that actually mean?

'Beginning the process'? Where's it gonna *end?*

Anyway, let us not forget...I have my own process to stay focused on. I've started something here – my quest for freedom, my quest for indulging myself in all the things that are calling to me, my quest to be by myself, to travel alone, to live alone (I've never lived alone, ever), my quest to meet myself again and see where she and I go next.

I'm on my big Wise, Wild and Free journey for fuck's sake! Do I really want anything – anyone – getting in the way of that...again? So I guess The Viking and I both have an internal conflict going on.

Let go of control, for once in your life, girl. Allow him to just find his own way.

And then...

He calls to tell me he's left. He's packed a bag and gone to stay with his dad.

Fuck! OK! Is this happening then?

And I know it's not ALL about ME, I know he's done this for

himself, he knows he wasn't happy, and he was looking for
a way out.

*Am I just his escape route? Have we reconnected just to both set each
other free?*

But I know it's definitely about us too and with the freedom that
staying with his dad is bringing, we are able to talk even more.
Each evening he is free to speak to me and we dive in, finally being
able to do what we couldn't do 23 years ago – revealing ourselves
more and more, piece by piece, showing each other who we truly
are, baring our souls. When all you have is the medium of
conversation to develop a relationship, that conversation can take
you deep. No longer the shy messed-up twenty-somethings, we are
secure enough in ourselves now to have those conversations with
each other.

When I was in India last month, I re-read 'The Celestine Prophecy',
a book that had had a massive impact on me in my mid-twenties.
So when I saw it at the bookshop at Heathrow as I was waiting to
board my flight to Delhi, it felt fitting that I read it again, another
way of reconnecting to *that* me. Lots of things in it spoke to me
once more, in particular how we form romantic relationships and
how they are built on our patterns and subsequent projections of
our early relationships, which inevitably means they often become
unhealthy and dysfunctional in some way. James Redfield suggests
it needs to be different. He says we should only have relationships
with people who have revealed themselves totally first. This way we
can break the maternal or paternal fantasy projection; 'our version'
of them, which isn't who they really are. For this reason we must
resist love at first sight apparently.

It feels like that's what The Viking and I are doing, in all this
talking we are revealing ourselves to each other, we can understand

who the other really is – *before* we jump into bed together.

I guess it's a good idea to know who you are actually jumping into bed with. A good idea but not something I was ever taught and not something I've ever experienced, that's for sure. I knew there was a reason I didn't want to shag him in Indonesia!

So now I see him and he sees me and we both seem to like what we see, and it seems there is now nothing stopping us from arranging a meet-up.

Fuck!!! Is that really gonna happen? Are we ready to actually meet?

Well, maybe not just yet, but by the time I get back from my next trip, 6 weeks will have passed. Six weeks of him being further along in "beginning the process", 6 weeks further along in us exploring if this still feels right, now that we're both available.

We look at options of where to go. Somewhere neither of us has been before with anyone else feels important and somewhere we can co-ordinate our flights to arrive within the space of a few hours. OK, not the simplest criteria, but we have found somewhere: Budapest. For how long...2 days? Not enough...3 days? Still not enough...4? Nope...5? Yep, that should do it. One room or two? That doesn't even need a discussion.

We both book our flights for 7 weeks' time. Just one week ago, I was preparing to leave India, not knowing if I would even speak to him again. Look how much happened in that one week, who knows what the hell can happen in the next seven.

It's fair to say that things are moving at a rate of knots, they are moving in the right direction, but I don't want to give you the impression that it's all amazing and exciting...over the next week, it's clear to me that he is a mess and I'm worried about him. He's so stressed and I'm the only person that he's talking to – just like 23 years ago – and I know that's not healthy. I know it's really important to speak to someone outside of your situation to help get some perspective. And, most crucially of all, he's told no one about me. He's told no one about me sending him the letter, he's told no one about me occupying the majority of his headspace for the past 2 months, he's told no one that the reason he's left his partner is largely because I have popped back up in his life and sent his head in a spin, he's told no one that he is planning on meeting up with me, he's told no one that he's a complete and utter frenzied ball of wired, pent-up stress that is ready to implode.

I guess I should have seen it coming really.

I am out with some friends for dinner. I am feeling slightly nervous as The Viking has gone to his old house to collect some more of his things. But it's OK, we don't need to worry, I just spoke to him a few hours ago, he told me how much he can't wait to see me, how excited he is, how excited we both are. But I thought I would have had a message from him by now, letting me know how it went, letting me know he was home. It's hard to be present with my friends. I was planning on telling them about him but suddenly that doesn't feel like a good idea.

For the tenth time, I check my phone discreetly inside my bag. There! At last! But as I glance at the first line of his message, adrenalin kidnaps my senses, my heart pounds, my head freezes. I excuse myself to the toilet to read his message in full:

"FUCK. I've had a total mindfuck and everything is upside down and moving too FAST. I'm sorry. I can't talk tonight. I'll call you tomorrow. FUCK!!"

Well, FUCK indeed!! That's my girls' night out ruined.

When I get home, I message to say, "It's OK. I understand. We can speak tomorrow."

Is it OK?? Do I understand?? And if so why am I being so fucking understanding??

I hardly sleep a wink and the next morning he calls and tells me that he "wants his old life back".

Jesus, Viking! What a fucking rollercoaster you've got me on!

He's done a complete 180-degree loop the frigging loop and I'm hanging upside down, not even strapped in.

I showed you my tits on the phone, for fuck's sake!! I don't do that for everyone you know!!

How could he go from telling me he couldn't wait to see me to saying it's over in the space of a few hours? And more importantly...

Why the fuck do I want to be with someone who's still attached to someone else? Why would I do that to myself?

He's in a mess and doesn't know what he wants, but what about me?

Well, I'm gutted. I am crying. A lot. But I know I'm OK too. Again with the paradox. But you know, it's only the thinking mind that has a problem with paradox, our awareness has no problem with it at all. So both those things are true – I really am OK, and I'm really not OK.

Right here, right now, I am all in the NOT OK. I am crying my broken heart out to my dear friend who has come to listen, support and hold me. But I know I will be OK in the long run. Is that because I don't believe it's really over? Or is that because I just know deep down that, even if it is, I will be fine.

So I have my day of big, ugly, snotty-nosed, puffy-eyed crying – during which, I might add, the postman delivers an envelope from The Viking containing both a lovely letter he's written to me and a photocopy of the letter I sent him after my dad died. Talk about bloody timing – like I say, it takes 4 days for a letter to arrive from Sweden...

Never mind 4 days, things can change in 4 bloody hours it seems!

I take a picture of the envelope sitting on my carpet and send it to him. He messages back telling me to "throw it in the bin".

Why are you being such a wanker? Of course I'm not going to throw it in the bin, that's my letter in there, remember. And no, I'm not going to just erase it, so we don't have to acknowledge how fucked up this all is!

He also tells me that he "will end our contact". He's being so cold and calculated, it's like this is a version of him that I don't know; not the kind, caring, sensitive, considerate guy that I am familiar with at all. But what do I expect, I don't really know him, I guess.

But I override that because I'd probably rather not acknowledge this shitty shadow side of him, and to be honest, I don't think I know what to do with it, I'm totally shocked by how he's being and the tone of his messages now. So again, I fall back on what is familiar, I do what I do, I go into understanding, appreciating the bigger picture – "Oh, he's not really a wanker, he's just under so much pressure, anyone would crack under the strain he's been under, of course, poor guy."

So when he messages to ask if he can call me again to talk before "he will end the contact", rather than tell him to Fuck Off, I say Yes. Of course I do. I let him tell me he is still thinking about me all the time, but he's scared. I let him tell me that he's scared of all the hurt he's causing other people, that he's scared of the stress that is running riot in his body and where that might lead, that he's scared that he's so confused he doesn't know what he's doing, and underneath all that, he's scared that when we meet up in Budapest, I'll change my mind. It seems he's got some not-good-enough-shit going on too. But rather than face those fears, he's decided to run back to his old life.

Oh right, yeah, that sounds like a GREAT idea. Let me know how that works out for you!

But I'm not going to cling on. I'm not losing myself in the pain of being rejected, of being cut off, the panic and suffocation of that that I have felt in the past, drowning in the tragedy of it all. Maybe it's all perfect timing anyway, seeing my letter that I wrote to him about my dad dying and being aware that I am no longer grieving him in the same way. Reading back on that letter felt like an ending of what I'd been holding onto for 23 years with losing him...and it lands on my doorstep on the same day that The Viking is ending it with me. The link between him and my dad again emphasised, both endings tied in together nicely.

OK, Viking, do you know what? Just do what you gotta do. I have a lot of love for you and I know you have a lot of love for me. I'm heading off to Mexico tomorrow to do what I gotta do and I'm not gonna interfere with whatever you're going through. I'm not gonna get involved in your drama. I'm not gonna make your drama my drama. I'm not gonna try to influence you. I'm not gonna try to manipulate you. You go through your process and I'm gonna go through mine. Let's just see where that takes us.

I told you a lot happened in 4 weeks.

Scene Eight – Write

"Life is a daring adventure or it's nothing."

– Helen Keller

It's the middle of the night, although my body thinks it's still mid-afternoon. I have just arrived in Cancun, Mexico, and as I lay in my comfy double bed giving up on sleeping, I can't quite believe that the wall in my hotel bedroom is sporting the exact same set of mirrors that I have on my bedroom wall at home! It seems serendipity has followed me around the globe and the universe is giving me a little nudge and a wink.

Although, yesterday, as I waited in the departure lounge at Gatwick Airport, I couldn't shake the feeling that I was flying in the wrong direction. I was simultaneously obsessing about The Viking and reminding myself to let it go. The conversation we had the day before concluded that he will only be in touch if he has something different to say. I agreed that I don't want to hear from him unless that's the case and I certainly have no intention of contacting him again. Unlike my trip to India, I've not shoved him into my backpack this time.

Now is the time to focus on my writing, nothing else. This is where all the changes in my life have led me, to finally pop my creative cork. This is about ME. This is a trip that I booked before I even wrote him that goddamn letter 2 months ago. This is something that I know I have to do. I heard the call and I'm following it. A week's writing retreat which, unlike the yoga school in Rishikesh, I instantly knew was going to be a perfect fit. I've got a feeling this is going to be good.

But maybe the mirrors on the wall are more than just a nice little touch. Maybe it is a sign to let me know that things are moving fast right now in the world of serendipity. Maybe it is a sign to get my attention to what is about to happen next...

No sooner have I woken up from a few hours' jet-lagged semi-sleep, than I receive a message from The Bloody Viking!

Are you fucking kidding me?

It goes something along the lines of this...

"Good morning! I told you I wouldn't write until there was something new to say, well, I've told everyone about you, I'm back at my dad's, I've had you on my mind every minute and I really want to see you. From now on I am choosing to change my life, what happens with that we don't know but I hope you will give me the chance to meet you and find out. I hope you have a great time in Mexico!"

Are you for real this time? You've told everyone? Well, great, but about bloody time. You want to change your life? Well, great, but let's see what that means.

How do I know he isn't going to change his mind again? Has my trust in him been damaged? I guess it's not about that, my trust in the universe is never damaged, no matter the twists and turns and loop the bloody loops, I know everything happens for my greater good and because I've asked for it. I also know he's got integrity so would never deliberately mess me around. So I guess that's all I need.

S'pose I'd better reply then!

"Wow, fucking hell (Viking) maybe I should fly to the other side of the world more often if this is what happens..."

Looks like he snuck into my backpack after all.

I have arrived in paradise. No, really, this is paradise. Whatever that means to you, whatever that means to me, I think this is the picture of paradise that perhaps most of us conjure up in our mind's eye when we drift off to a faraway land with white sandy beaches, crystal turquoise waters, deep blue cloudless skies, towering palm trees, no cars, even the roads here are made of sand. Oh yeah – I think I can handle this for a while.

Eight women, eight different reasons for hearing the call, eight sets of hopes, fears and expectations, gather together in a circle of chairs on the patio area of the villa that will be our shared home for the week. Two hundred yards behind us is the beach, two yards in front of us are Dulcie and Nancy the retreat organisers. I love them already.

Let the adventure begin...

"For the next 10 minutes, write what you know to be true about yourself..."

OK...

'I am sensitive, emotional, intuitive, connected. I struggle just as everyone struggles. I have patterns that it's time to change. I love, I hurt, I bleed, I break. But I am strong beyond measure, I always survive. Sometimes that's exhausting – maybe it's one of the patterns that's reached its due date – but it's empowering to know I will always be OK. I trust wholeheartedly that the universe has my back with everything, that everything that happens to me I have asked for in some way, that I have the choice to grow and expand from everything that life offers me, so that I may humbly endeavour to be the best version of myself that I can be whilst here. When life gets tough and the pain comes through, I always remember to trust in the process. This has long been my mantra in life.'

"And now for the next 10 minutes, write what you don't know about yourself..."

OK...

'I don't know what my future looks like (yay!). I don't know what the rest of my year looks like. I don't know how long I'm here for, just like everyone else. I don't know if I'll be struck by a degenerative disease or if I'll be healthy in my body and mind. I don't know if I'll be rich, become a grandmother, get married and live happily ever after with someone. I don't know where my writing will take me – whether I'll be 'good enough'. I don't know shit about what's gonna happen with (The Viking). I don't know how long my mum will be here for. I don't know how things would have been different if my dad hadn't died when he did – before we had the chance to work through some of our stuff. I don't know what will become of my boys – of their lives, their futures, the empty roads they are yet to travel.'

"And now you are invited to read out what you have written..."

What? Really? Read it all out loud to the whole group? Well, yeah, what did you expect on a writing retreat, just keep it all to yourself?! OK, no problem, I can do this, everyone seems really nice. I can do this, I am safe, I have a voice and I'm ready to start using it.

With that, I know this week is going to dive deep. If this is just our intro session, I can only imagine where we will go next, and I'm ready, I'm so ready to go there, to explore what I can create through the written word, and to write from the heart, that's why I chose this particular retreat, I knew it was all about writing from the heart.

Is there any other way to do anything?

As the days go by and the words begin to flow, so – too – do the tears. Not just mine, I'm pleased to say, it's a thing. It seems this heart-writing is one big sob-fest of a healing process, and I don't think there is anyone from our group of eight incredible warrior women who hasn't shed a tear or cried a river or uncaged her naked soul by the end of the week. And for me, something is beginning to emerge. With my pen as my sword, I am writing my way through the shackles of suppression and it leads me to wonder:

Is this what I've needed all along? Is it really the relationships I've been in that have suppressed me? Or did I just need to write? To finally spew out all the words which have been blocking up my throat for the past 50 years.

I'm realising, too, that as far as The Viking goes, there has also been a time not to speak, not to use my voice. But this holding back comes from a place of wisdom, not fear. Very different. Like me not trying to either therapize him out of his unhappy relationship or trying to manipulate him into a relationship with me. Trust me, it took quite a lot of focus not to do that.

We spoke on a video call the other day and something in his eyes had shifted. He looked different, a vulnerable intensity holding my gaze. Something had gone, perhaps the deceit, the guilt and all the stress he'd been carrying had fallen away and he was fully there, fully present.

I really believe the rollercoaster has stopped. He found his way back and...well, I am feeling slightly smug. Not just because I'm soaking in an ego-bath of flattery, but because I was able to let go, I was able to trust. I was able to let go and parachute myself out of the rollercoaster mid-spin, to a safe landing, to step away and just see what he did with it.

I never did like rollercoasters much.

"So what changed for you?" I asked him.

"You," he answered.

OK, I'll take that. Maybe this is what happens when you let go of the idea of not being enough?

Thirty-four days to go...

Meanwhile, I'm still in paradise. Even though the writing retreat has finished, I'm moving into an apartment in town for another week. When I say 'town' I mean a 10-minute walk down the sand track into a square of graffiti-painted, relaxed Caribbean-vibe cafés and restaurants, complete with outdoor Zumba classes. Oh yes, this place is cool, very, very cool indeed. I'm no longer in the luxury beachfront villa; my apartment is basic but only a 5-minute walk from the beach. My intention is to spend the week continuing to develop some of the writing that I started on the retreat, except once again I seem to be doing a lot of chasing around town trying to find Wi-Fi. Things are crazy intense with The Viking again and I'm sure we are going to explode when we finally see each other. That is if we don't implode first. There's a danger here that we might just burn ourselves out before we even get to Budapest. But it's so hard to take it easy, and now the sneaking around has stopped, we can indulge even more. Let's face it… after 23 years there's a hell of a lot of catching up to do.

But I'd be lying to you if I didn't admit I am still getting lots of moments of fear. If I'm honest, I'm terrified he's gonna change his mind again. I've seen how quickly that can happen without a word of warning. My "you're not enough" voice keeps popping back up, resuming her seat on my shoulder and whispering menacingly in my ear (especially when I know The Viking is meeting with his ex to decide all the stuff that needs to be decided when you've shared a life with someone for 15 years). But I can spot it now. I can hear it and I can say, "Well thanks very much, I know you're trying to help in your own strange way, I know you're trying to protect me, I know you want what's best for me, but I've got this now, I'm OK, I don't need you, so thanks but no thanks." Or I might just say, "Piss off" – depending on my mood.

I need to accept this is just how it's gonna be until we can actually meet up again in person. Until we can actually have a hug. Have you ever been through so much intensity with someone and not been able to physically touch them, hug them? We are like two severed limbs yearning to be re-attached.

Twenty-eight days to go...

Anyway, enough about The Viking. I keep telling you it's not all about him! Last week on the writing retreat, after telling them all about Qoya, Dulcie and Nancy invited me to teach a class to the group. They said it sounded like their "kinda bag". This week they have a second group of eight women and have invited me to come along to run a class for them. This lights me up! This is what I want in my life – to run retreats, Qoya, mindfulness, writing, yoga, hmmm...more cultivating of the germinating seeds.

Talking of Qoya, I just have to say a couple of things. Now, I'm pretty big into autonomy (as all good psychotherapists should be), each to their own and all that, what works for one doesn't work for the next. But I really do think two things are true in life: every woman should experience Qoya and every person should do a 10-day Vipassana course. Qoya, just like mindfulness, changed my life, and – when that's the case – it's easy to get pretty passionate about sharing it. After I teach the classes at the writing retreat, I am unanimously told "Qoya is the bomb" (that's good, apparently).

It's 6 a.m. and I am leaving paradise. I'm sitting on the upstairs deck of the ferry that makes the 20-minute crossing to the mainland. On my right is the full moon, its glow lighting up the black sky and dark waters beneath me. On my left the sunrise hints, creating orange, yellow, red and pink layers in the sky. It's breathtakingly beautiful. Mother moon and father sun, the dark and the light, the yin and the yang; the joy and the sorrow, beginnings and endings, we really can't have one without the other.

As for my first writing retreat experience...well, it's not called W.O.W. (Wide Open Writing – check it out) for nothing. It's blown me wide open and I've learnt so much about writing...my relationship to it...how to move on with it...but really it all boils down to one thing...

Just fucking write!

Scene Nine – Dance

"And when we pick up her (The Wild Woman) trail,
it is typical of women to ride hard to catch up, to clear off the desk,
to clear off the relationship, to clear out one's mind, turn to a new page,
insist on a break, break the rules, stop the world, for we are
not going on without her any longer."

– Clarissa Pinkola Estes, Women Who Run with The Wolves

Who knew – there are two paradises!

A 2-hour flight and a 7-hour bus ride later and I have arrived at my home for the next 2 weeks – a pretty damn slick retreat centre on the Nicoya Peninsula in Costa Rica. The view from the room on the top floor – where I will be dancing with 60 other women for the Collective Retreat in the first week, and 10 other women for the Intensive Teacher Training in the second – is breath-taking. Set right in the jungle, with the Pacific coastline visible in the distance and a beautiful little beach just a 5-minute walk away...hmmm...just when I thought this trip couldn't get any better, any more stunning, any more special...how wrong I was.

———————

Day four and I am standing at the entrance of the labyrinth. This labyrinth is made out of 100 metres of fairy lights. The pitch dark jungle on the other side of the wall-to-wall windows fills the room, and the twinkles of the hundreds of lights are reflected in the glass, creating a kaleidoscope of lights that go on for miles and miles in every direction.

I have stepped into a magical, cosmic, twinkly, mystical world. Above the sound of the soft esoteric music playing, you could hear a pin drop. The atmosphere is palpable. I am not sure what to expect but every electric current in my body tells me I can expect something.

Now, I love a labyrinth, I have done since my counselling training days at Sacred Space, we did quite a lot of labyrinth work then and so, for me, this is another coming home to something that has fallen away in the past 20 years.

Labyrinths symbolise that all we need lies within. We just need to walk the path to get there. Of course, this 'just' is huge. Of course, if it were easy, we would all have all we wanted all the time. Of course, there are many reasons why we don't.

I am about to find out what mine are.

We sit on cushions in small groups and are invited to imagine that what our heart desires and what our soul craves lies in the centre of the labyrinth. Over the next 2 hours, 60 women will silently make the journey from the entrance of the labyrinth, into the centre, and back out again.

The journey in is all about holding the question in our hearts of what lies between us and what we truly want. Being in the centre is all about claiming what is ours, the abundance that waits for us there. The journey out is all about receiving the messages from the learning of our journey into and out of the labyrinth.

I am given a gentle nod by the Qoya teacher who sits holding space at the entrance, an indication and invitation that it is my turn. I take my first step.

Everything you desire is in the centre of the labyrinth...

Woah! Hang on! What the hell is happening? Why have my legs turned to lead? Why do I feel like I can't actually move? And why the hell do I feel so utterly overwhelmingly emotional?

Come on, just take a step. Just. Put. One. Foot. In front. Of. The. Other. How hard can it be?

Well, very hard it turns out. Every step I take feels like I am wading through thick, black, heavy treacle. A dam bursts opens and tears cascade down my face.

Everything you desire is in the centre of the labyrinth...

Why is this so hard? Why do I feel so afraid? Why should I be so scared to claim what I want? Because I don't believe that I deserve it? Because I'm afraid of losing it when I get it? Yep! There we go, that's it...here is the pain, here are the big tears...here is the falling apart as I'm trying very hard to still put one foot in front of the other.

Everything you desire is in the centre of the labyrinth...

I'm afraid I'm gonna screw it up. I'm afraid it's gonna slip out of my fingers. I guess I don't feel like I deserve it after all.

More tears, more falling apart, more treacle.

The only thing that stands between me and what I want is me and my fear. Nothing else. No one else. Just me. Just my fear.

Everything you desire is in the centre of the labyrinth...

It takes me an age – a metaphorical lifetime – to reach the centre. Along the way, I pass many other women, some dancing, some walking, some crying, some smiling, some crawling...it seems that there are many ways into the centre of our labyrinth.

Once there, I allow myself to drop to my knees, to sit for a while and cry some more. I don't even know what all of these tears are for, I simply know that I feel like I've just walked the hardest, scariest, path of my life, but I faced the fear and walked it anyway and now here I am sitting in the centre of my labyrinth.

All I have to do now is walk back out again.

But there's something very different about my journey out compared to my journey in. Yes, I'm still crying, yes, I still feel utterly emotional, but the treacle has gone. I can walk freely, I am lighter, and I feel a ridiculously enormous sense of achievement.

I realise that it's not even about what's in the centre that's important – the stuff that I want, that's just normal regular stuff, like love and success and an abundance of all that's good in life, nothing out of the ordinary there, nothing that I or anyone else shouldn't be able to receive. No, what matters is the journey in – the fears, the blocks, the obstacles we put in our way, the decades or even lifetimes of self-doubt and conditioning that we can't have what we want. "You can't always have everything you want, you know" (can't I??). My mum's voice rings in my ear. She came from that wartime generation where things were scarce and it was considered audacious to think you could have whatever you wanted whenever you wanted it, that anyone who did was spoilt in some way, and that deprivation somehow is a good thing in life. Well, yes, being able to resist the urge to splurge on material possessions whenever we want them of course is not a bad thing. But to deprive your soul of what it truly desires, resisting being the best versions of ourselves that we can be, holding ourselves back from expanding fully into our incredible wondrous selves? Well, that definitely isn't a good thing.

How did I ever think I could receive what I wanted without walking that walk? I've always been good at talking the talk, but there are no shortcuts – at the end of the day, we've just gotta walk it. The only way in is through. The only way out is in.

Sooner or later we will be given the nod to enter our own labyrinth.

Sooner or later we will know that everything we desire lies within.

The question is…will we make the journey in to claim what is already ours? Or will we forever be standing at the entrance of our own labyrinth?

———————

You may have the impression by now that Qoya is about so much more than dancing. Movement is the medium used in Qoya to travel within, to remember our essence, and I am sure as hell beginning to remember mine. It's an essence that I had started to tap into in my mid-twenties…things are starting to come back to me.

I am remembering that I LOVE all this stuff, all this ritual and ceremony. It takes me back to my rather alternative counselling training pathway at Sacred Space. It takes me back to being 26 and travelling and discovering my spirituality. And, in particular, it takes me back to remembering something that a shiatsu healer told me when I was in Indonesia. She said that one day I would work with music and dance, but not until I had balanced myself out, not before I had let go of holding on so fiercely to the need to survive. I re-read that old journal entry before I left for India. I hadn't given it a single thought in 23 years and now here it is. Well, I guess if it's part of our true essence, it will find a way of coming back up to the surface. The question is: are we awake enough to notice?

In the 2 weeks I spend at the Blue Spirit retreat centre, I take part in 23 different Qoya classes and 15 different ceremonies. I see turtles laying their eggs on the beach at night under a million stars of the Milky Way. I meet incredible Goddess women. Some of whom I know will remain friends for life. Three of those women are from my tribe at home; they fly out together for the second of the 2 weeks, for our 'intensive teacher training'.

It turns out there's a clue in the title, *intensive* it is.

Together we dance, we laugh, we cry, we share, we break, we re-build, we celebrate, we get vulnerable, we take risks, we get naked (literally – skinny-dipping under the sunset each evening – and metaphorically – baring our hearts to each other, to be witnessed, to be honoured), we remember who we really are, and who we are meant to be. Not one of us is the same person when we pack our bags to leave as we were when we unpacked them to arrive.

All of this AND I've still been talking with The Viking every day. Still processing all of my emotions around him. Still feeling the significance of our relationship in the context of everything else that I'm learning about myself right now. I know my relationship with him is part of the transformation that I'm going through, he is an integral component to some of what is taking place. And although "we don't know shit" (as he frequently tells me) about what is going to happen, I do know that I am beside myself at the prospect of meeting up with him in Budapest...or Bootyfest as it has been coined by my teacher-training tribe!

Nine days to go (in case, like me, you're counting).

It's been a life-altering heart-exploding month. I am so much clearer on what I want and don't want, and I've just learnt something huge about that thing that I keep banging on about...you know, that thing that I keep looking for and then finding and then losing and then looking for again only to find it and lose it again...that thing we call FREEDOM:

> "Freedom doesn't mean being able to do what you like.
> It means knowing who you are,
> what you are supposed to be doing on this earth
> and then simply doing it."
>
> – Natalie Goldberg

Well someone could've bloody told me that sooner!!

Scene Ten – Countdown

> "Twenty years from now you will be more disappointed by the things you didn't do than by the ones you did do. So throw off the bowlines, sail away from the safe harbour, catch the trade winds in your sails. Explore. Dream. Discover."
>
> – Mark Twain

Seven days to go.

Six days to go.

Five days to go.

Four days to go.

Three days to go.

Two days to go.

One day to go.

FUUUUCKKKK!!!!

Scene Eleven – Bootyfest

"I have one thing to say, one thing only,
I'll never say it another time, to anyone, and I ask you to remember it: In
a universe of ambiguity, this kind of certainty comes only once, and
never again, no matter how many lifetimes you live."

– Robert James Waller, The Bridges of Madison County

I stand in position. My flight arrived an hour ago, his is arriving in another hour. OK, maybe I don't need to be in position just yet. To say I am nervous is the understatement of the century.

There's not much on offer to distract myself with at Budapest airport, just a small café bar where bottled Dutch courage is only available as beer, or Lemon or Strawberry Bacardi Breezers.

I sit with my Bacardi Breezer (lemon), take out my journal, attempt to write down how I'm feeling. Every 2 minutes I look up at the screen to see if his flight has landed, nope...still 45 minutes to go. I've already squeezed myself and my tiny suitcase into a toilet cubicle to change my outfit, mostly because the temperature in Hungary is several degrees lower than England, but also to give myself something to do. The waiting is unbearable.

I've been waiting for 4 months for this, since he replied to my letter and we both realised the connection was still there, and it's been a hell of a 4 months. We've both been through so much: together, and alone. There have been twists and turns, let's face it, some of it's been bloody awful but most of it has been incredible, and it's all culminating in *this* moment. This meeting up to see what will happen, to see what *this* is, to see where it will take us.

No wonder I'm fucking nervous.

But it's even more than those 4 months. I suddenly feel every moment of waiting 23 years for this.

Twenty-three years later! Oh my fucking God. Really? Is this actually happening? In less than half an hour The Viking is going to be walking through those doors, to meet me, after not having seen each other for 23 bloody years.

I think we can safely say this is one of life's momentous occasions.

The last time I saw him was on the Koh San Road in Bangkok, when I was waiting for my flight home to be with my dying dad. I remember then how I wanted him to just scoop me up and rescue me from it all, to take my hand and jump on a bus and a boat and head back out to some cool place to carry on our adventures together, young, carefree, the world at our feet. We could have been anything we'd wanted to be back then.

But the story didn't go like that. The story went very differently. We headed in different directions and went about living our different lives. Separately.

Until now.

Twenty-three years later, we have somehow found our way back to each other.

'LANDED'

Shiiiiiiitttt!

How long does it take from when a flight lands to when the passengers come through? Ten minutes? Half an hour? HOW BLOODY LONG???

Pacing, pacing, pacing, up and down the small arrivals area, there is no way I can stand still.

Will I see him before he sees me?

I definitely want to see him first. I need a micro-moment to myself before he sees me. I need that micro-moment to listen to my heart – which is either going to give me a Fuck Yes or a Fuck No. In that micro-moment, I will know. Christ, I hope it's the first one.

Oh Jesus! What if it's a fuck no?!

I find the perfect spot, at the end of the portable railings, where I am more likely to see him before he sees me, but where I am not going to be in total hiding from him – I don't want to put either of us through the pain of him standing there, looking panicked, not being able to see me, thinking I've stood him up after all this.

Several flights have landed at around the same time and there are many passengers starting to come through. I try to deduce their nationalities using all my cultural, stereotyping, identification skills. I barely dare blink in case I miss that very moment when he first comes through the door. I mustn't miss my moment.

Where is he? Everyone but him, it seems.

My heart pounds. My legs pace. My eyes search. My mind races. Tom Odell blasts in my ears.

Breathe...

Just breathe...

And suddenly, there he is.

A moment suspended in time. Everything stops, my breath, everything inside and out is paused for a nanosecond. And then...relief dissolves into my whole being, something shifts, something falls away, I breathe again...

I have my Fuck Yes.

Thank Christ for that!

He is standing 10 metres away from me. He stops, looks around, he can't see me...

I'm here, over here, I want you to see me, but I know as soon as you do something will change forever. The anticipation of this moment, the past 4 months, the past 23 years, the fantasy of this reunion we have created, will be forever lost, gone, never to be experienced again, no matter how many times we do this, it will never be the same as this first time...

His eyes keep searching through the crowds of passengers. He spots his target and a smile appears across the whole of his face.

But for some reason, he's not moving. He's just standing there, looking at me, smiling, like he's savouring seeing me for the first time again. I guess he needs his moment too. But now we're both looking at each other it feels excruciating, I feel so self-conscious, if I thought my legs would work I could literally run and hide.

Come on!!! Just get here!!! Just bloody close this gap!!! I need my hug!!!

Slowly he begins to walk towards me, smiling the whole time.

Walk faster, pleeeease!

Then he's here, standing in front of me; I'd forgotten how tall he is.

"Hello."

"Hi."

He's dropped his bag on the floor and his arms are wrapping me up. My head rests on his chest, his heart pounds through his t-shirt onto my cheek, and my arms close around his waist.

"You're tiny," he says (I'm really not) and bends down to kiss the top of my head.

There we stand in soulful synergy, breathing each other in.

The waiting is over.

Who are you?

Do I know you?

Do I recognise your face?

Is it still you?

Is it still us?

We're lying on the bed together playing Shithead, the card game we used to play when we were travelling, the card game everyone used to play when they were travelling in the 90s. But what's really cool is the fact that we are playing with the exact same card deck. Yep, something else I've kept safely tucked away in that box under my bed all these years. They are thick with aged whisky and beer dregs and God only knows what else that's been festering away on them over the years, but they have really ramped up the nostalgia several notches. Incredibly, too, he has brought his original 1996 tie-dye fisherman pants with him, it's so funny to see him in them again (I'm the only one of us wearing toe rings these days, though). These mementos from our shared past have been preserved and carried forward into our shared present.

Am I really here, hanging out in bed with The Viking in a hotel room in Budapest in 2019?

I'm having a moment.

I keep having several moments.

So does he.

Just one day into our 5-day date and the laughs are flowing, the conversation is flowing, and the sex, the sex that we never had 23 years ago...well, that's flowing very nicely too. It feels very, very cool to be hanging out again, to be back in each other's company, to be feeling his energy once again.

It feels so easy, in between the 'moments'.

The how-the-fuck-did-this-happen-somebody-pinch-me-is-this-really-happening moments.

I need to keep looking at him to remember who he is. To remind myself that this isn't someone new in my life, this is him. But now it's like there are two of him. Two of us. There's the 1996 him and now there's the 2019 him. There's the 1996 us and now there's the 2019 us. It's a lot to get your head around.

As the days pass by I realise that the present is overtaking the past. The memories of who we were are fading and being replaced by who we are. We are creating new memories in the present that will also become us in the past.

Am I really here, hanging out with The Viking in a spa bath in Budapest in 2019?

There's a sadness to realising that those two young things who were backpacking around Asia don't really exist anymore. They only exist in our memories now. Up until a few days ago, those memories were all we had. Now we have a different reality. Now we are in relationship with *these* versions of ourselves rather than the memories of *those* versions of ourselves.

Each time I look at him it's becoming harder and harder to see his

23-year-old face – young and tanned with longish sun-streaked hair. It's been replaced by his 47-year-old face – greying beard, glasses, lines around the eyes, and much less hair. And the shyness has been replaced by a confidence. The boy is now a man. The shyness is still there though, or perhaps it's a modesty (a big Swedish thing, apparently), it's just not crippling him anymore, and I think it's fair to say I'm a lot less messed up than I used to be. So we can talk about how we feel now, that's something our younger selves could never properly do.

Am I really here, hanging out with The Viking in a café in Budapest in 2019?

"So, are we going to see each other again after this? What do you think?" I ask on day three. As if I don't already know the answer, as if I would even ask if I didn't know the answer.

"I definitely want to."

Fortunately, The Viking and I are on the exact same page. In fact, we seem to be racing through the pages together, both eager to get to the next chapter. Well, maybe after 23 years you're allowed to skip a few pages. We talk about him coming to see me, there's a national holiday weekend coming up in Sweden so he has some days off, he could fly over on the Friday, stay until the Monday...Yes, please!

No sooner have we penned in our next meet-up, we are talking about the bigger picture, the future, going travelling together again. He says he's ready to leave his job, we indulge ourselves in fantasies of where we can go, countries we both want to visit, how we can stay somewhere and make a living. We want the same things, to adventure, to travel, to live a different lifestyle...

Wow! Can this really be happening?

Well, yes, these chats are definitely happening, but one step at a time: he will come and visit me at the end of the month, after that we still "don't know shit" apparently. But what I do know for sure – as the realisation sings joyfully in my ear – is that not once during this whole date have I felt like I needed some space. That's pretty new. To be with someone and not feel the need to orchestrate a situation or just blatantly say that I need to have some 'time out' to be 'on my own'. Incredible. Because what I've realised about being with The Viking is that I still feel like I have my space even when I'm with him. It just feels easy with him, I haven't felt trapped, I haven't felt suffocated.

I can still be me while we're being us. I can be with him and still breathe.

Trust me, in 5 days of being with someone 24/7, well, it's nothing short of a biblical miracle.

———————

Twenty-three years ago I told him in a letter I was giving up on him. But to give up suggests an ending, there's something final about it, the door well and truly closed. So I guess I must have left the door slightly ajar, and 23 years later decided it was time to tentatively poke my head around it to see if anyone was there. And, yes, there he was, and this time he was ready for me, we were ready for each other. Whatever had been blocking us first time around had fallen away or been worked through via other people and events in our respective lives. The path from the slightly ajar door was clear, well, there was a bit of final clearing to be done halfway down the corridor of time. And, yes, there's still some sweeping up to do and some stepping back and integrating all the changes that have happened for both of us, but we did it. We heard the call and felt something inside, a remembering perhaps or a sense of knowing that we couldn't let it slip by again, and now here we are.

Together, we made it happen.

Wow, life is fucking incredible, how things can come back around, full circle. We're coming around again, yet meeting as if for the first time, older and wiser. We're not the people we were back then, and yet we are still the people we were back then. It's ALL now woven into the tapestry of our relationship.

I wonder where this next lap around will take us, what will happen along the way and, importantly, whether we'll be able to keep hold of the thread this time? Whether we're even meant to keep hold of the thread?

Because what really happens when you get the one that got away...?

Epilogue

One Year Later

"Our deepest fear is not that we are inadequate. Our deepest fear is that
we are powerful beyond measure. It is our light, not our darkness that
most frightens us. We ask ourselves, 'Who am I to be brilliant, gorgeous,
talented, fabulous?' Actually, who are you not to be?"

– Marianne Williamson

I am 51 years old and I am swinging in a hammock on the veranda
of the hostel that I'm staying in. I have my journal and laptop with
me, I'm writing a book you see, this book, the one that you have
almost reached the end of.

Outside it's 36 degrees centigrade but feels like 40. I'm getting too
old for this kind of heat; each day, for the past 2 months, I've been
zapped of energy, sitting on the beach just opposite the hostel is
out of the question, it's way too hot for that. Occasionally, I find
that I have dragged myself just down the road to one of the small
village's cafés, where I sit under a fan, sipping on a cold something
or other, always with my journal. But the best thing of all is taking
a dip in the perfectly cool swimming hole at the waterfall, just a
10-minute easy clamber over rocks and tree roots that have been
there since the beginning of time.

I arrived in Costa Rica in January, it's now March. I started my trip
here with another writing retreat with the W.O.W. ladies. I just had

to see if it could possibly be as good as the first one I did in Mexico last year. It was, better in fact. I'm not sure why, perhaps I was more confident in myself and as a writer, but also because they asked me to teach a Qoya session again and it went down so well...music and dance became such an integral part of the retreat for all of us. It was at the beginning of the week there that this book began to take shape. I wrote the first scene in one of our sessions and it finally felt like the pieces started to fall into place of what I wanted – or rather what I needed – to write about. The plan was always then to stay on in Costa Rica and keep writing. I've even taught a few Qoya classes in a local hotel here. Yes, it's fair to say I've settled in well and I feel so at home.

But let me rewind and fill you in on a couple of other changes in my life. Just before I came here in January, I decided to give up the flat that I had been renting for the past year and, on top of that, I decided to sell all my furniture, just leaving my bits and pieces to be packed up and taken to the attic room at my mum's. I can't tell you the liberation I felt from doing this. I thought I would be terrified, I thought I would be desperately trying to buy everything back again as soon as I'd sold it, I thought I'd feel like I'd made a huge mistake and be forever kicking myself. But no, quite the opposite; what an utter relief. There's something very containing about having everything you own in the world fit into one room. Quite counterintuitively, I found it gave me a sense of comfort and security.

Oh, and on a slightly different note, there's something else I want to let you know. Around six months ago, I had a reply back from The International Centre of Nazi Persecution (like you do!). Upon my return from visiting Dachau Memorial the year before last, I emailed their archive department to enquire about my grandfather having been a prisoner there. They replied saying there was no record of him at all, and they concluded it was highly unlikely that he was ever there as apparently the Nazis were nothing if not absolutely meticulous about their record keeping. They referred me to this International organisation, and I had all but given up ever hearing back from them. In fact, it was exactly a year to the very week since I registered my enquiry, that I got the reply from them. "Please find attached the result of our check" was all the email said. I casually opened the attachment, totally unprepared for what I was going to find. There, staring back at me from my laptop, was my grandfather's death certificate. It told me that he had died on 9th September 1942 in Auschwitz.

Auschwitz!! Fuck. I did not see that coming!

The combination of suddenly finding myself looking at the evidence of finally knowing my grandfather's fate, coupled with the fact that a little further research of the death certificate led me to conclude he had been killed as part of the medical experimentation team, and realising that he'd never even been to Dachau and that I'd made a pilgrimage to the wrong concentration camp altogether...well, it's a lot to process, I can tell you.

Then the sadness came. Grieving for this man I never met. He died 27 years before I was even born (the same age I was when my dad died) but seeing the death certificate somehow brought him to life for me. It made him real. It gave us an ending. And most significantly, I feel that I have brought an ending for my dad and Omi. They never knew what happened to him, they both died not knowing the answer. Even though I never heard them ask the question, I'm certain it was there for them both internally. So that was something I could do for them, for all of us, for my sister too. I don't totally understand it right now, but I know on some level, in finding out this information, a significant piece of my ancestral story has fallen into place. The unthinkable suffering that he must have endured, and how that got handed down consciously and unconsciously through the generations, through my lineage…maybe now the healing can take place.

Anyway, I digressed, but it felt important to share that with you here. Everything is linked after all.

So, back to Costa Rica. When I arrived here I booked a week on the writing retreat but didn't know where I would go after that and didn't know when I would return home. It feels like when I sold my house I took the first step, but it was too scary to put the second foot where the first one had gone and leave behind my secure base. So I spent 15 months straddled with my legs akimbo, one foot in my new life, one foot in my old. Well, sooner or later we all need to close our legs, it's a strain if nothing else. So once I had a feel for the territory that I had stepped into, and once my boys had experienced another year and a bit of independence, I felt safe enough and strong enough to take that second step, to go against the grain of everything we're conditioned into and go nomadic.

> *"I've come to believe in something, the physics of the quest. The rule is: if you're brave enough to leave behind everything familiar and comforting and set out on a truth-seeking journey – either internally or externally – and you are truly willing to regard everything that happens to you on the journey as a clue, and if you accept everyone you meet along the way as a teacher, and if you are prepared most of all to face and forgive some very difficult realities about yourself, then the truth will not be withheld from you. I can't help but believe it, given my experience."*
>
> *– Eat, Pray, Love (the movie)*

Oh me too, me bloody too!

Every word of that lands and I'm so grateful that I found my way to this place in myself. Absolutely everyone I'm meeting is teaching me something, the synchronicities are jumping out at me every corner I turn, and I am certainly facing things about myself and accepting them, which feels like the same thing as forgiving to me.

As for my 'plans' all I know right now is I'm signed up to the same annual Qoya retreat that I went to last year which is happening in a few weeks' time, a few hours up the coast from here. Then in June, I have a trip to Peru arranged. Other than writing, which is my main focus, I'm leaving myself open to go with the flow of what happens in between.

Little did I know.

Little did any of us know what was coming.

Something seems to be going on in the rest of the world. I'm getting lots of messages from home talking about some virus that is sweeping the globe and the newsfeed on my phone is painting a picture of some major event.

Global pandemic? What does that even mean?

There seems to be a lot of freaking out going on beyond this palm-fringed land, and I feel like I am in a parallel universe – honestly, it's 'Pura Vida!' business as usual here.

Until it isn't.

I am at the local market with an American lady I've met. Last week, this market, albeit a tiny place, had its usual buzz and chilled-out vibe going on. But 7 days later, there is a distinct turn in the air, even the usual clear blue sky has been replaced with dark ominous clouds. The conversations at the stalls have changed from friendly chatting over some handmade jewellery or the abundance of fresh fruit and veg, to talk of local businesses needing to close and people getting home (wherever home is) as quickly as possible as countries all around the world begin to shut their borders at a rate of knots. There is a subtle but definite sense of dread and doom.

Closing borders? What does that even mean?

I know it's game over here when I see the police come to put 'no entry' tape across the access points of the beach.

'Paradise is closed until further notice.'

What the hell should I do? Seriously, aren't I just better off staying here? Surely it will all blow over soon? (As global pandemics do, right?!) I mean, I could make this the ultimate retreat, just get my head down and write. It sounds pretty hideous at home right now, why would I want to go back there? I'm not overly keen on England at the best of times, do I really want to be there at the worst of times? Anyway, can I even get a flight? It looks like it could take me up to 35 hours to get home and three changes – that's four airports, four planes, four sets of passengers, and they all transit via the U.S. where I am apparently not allowed! Nope, I'll stay. I'm sure it's all a big exaggeration anyway, a storm in a teacup, a big old song and dance over nothing. On the other hand, what about my boys? They're both asthmatic (that's not good, apparently) and so am I – if I get ill, do I want to be here or there? What about my mum? She's 84, so high risk too. What if it's true what they're saying about if you don't get home now, it could be months, many, many months before airports will re-open? What if I stay here and live to regret it? Or not live to regret it? And if I do go home, where the hell will I live anyway?

Self-quarantine? What does that even mean?

This is my deafening internal dialogue on a loop, for 10 days. Meanwhile, the COVID clock ticks and the line to the British embassy remains continually engaged.

But much like having your legs akimbo, sitting on the fence for too long also becomes bloody uncomfortable. It's not really a place you can function and, sooner or later, you need to fall off it one way or the other. My sister is visiting Bournemouth for the weekend and will be at my mum's this morning, I decide to call a family conference, this decision feels too big to make on my own.

What the fuck? We've never had a family conference in our lives! We're not a family conference kind of family. How does it even work?

Surprisingly, it seems to work quite well. Within minutes it's quite clear that both my mum and my sister think I should come back. But the really surprising thing is that it seems like my mum actually wants me to come home to her.

Now, why would that be in any way surprising, right? Wouldn't any mother want her daughter back with her safe and sound in the midst of a global pandemic (whatever that means), why would it even be a question?

But for me, it's been a huge question since all of this 'what the hell should I do' came about. Actually, if I'm honest, it's a question that has never left me for the past 40 years. A question that has now made me feel uncomfortable, uneasy, sad, vulnerable and like an 11-year-old child all over again. Does my mum really want me? I mean, I know she wants me, but does she want me enough? Trust me, I've entertained every other possibility so as not to even test the answer to that question, including exploring other options of where I could stay if I did go home. But the thing with a global pandemic (apparently) is that there's no one else I really can stay with. No one is going to welcome me with open arms into the comfort and safety of their own home, given that I will have just flown halfway across the world, exposed to this deadly virus to get there.* So it really does feel like I have nowhere else to go. I am dependant on my mum to welcome me into her bosom, thus proving how much she wants me, something I've really never wanted to fall back on.

But here it is. It took a global pandemic to make it happen but the aid to the wound always needs to be as great as the wound itself. Otherwise, it's like sticking a corn plaster over a 10-inch laceration.

So I am on my way home. I have managed to get a direct flight, the last one until 'further notice' and it only cost me the price of one of my kidneys.

How much, British Airways?? You are taking the piss, surely? Shame on you.

More than a little trepidation accompanies me along with a good supply of hand gel, plastic gloves, and a face buff which my lovely landlady has sent me on my way with. I take a small domestic aircraft to San Jose where I need to spend the night in an airport hotel, then catch my 10 and a half hour flight back to London. I feel like I am in a real-life, sci-fi disaster movie, where the hero (heroine!) is taking their life in their hands to get back to their loved ones.

---

*I will come to see these events quite differently over the months that follow.

Goodbye, Costa Rica. Hello, strange new world.

––––––––––––––

"We must be willing to get rid of the life we've planned,
so as to have the life that is waiting for us."

– Joseph Campbell

I am sitting in the back seat of my sister's car, she's in the front, driving. Apparently, it's safer that way, we can keep our distance. In the perfect re-enactment of me being a child sitting in the back, both of us wearing 'masks', she has picked me up from Gatwick and is driving me back home. Just as exactly 40 years ago I held her responsible for the reason I had to leave that home in the first place, she now delivers me back, back into the arms of our mother – except, of course, there will be no hugging, no big emotional display; all the more perfect and manageable, perhaps.

Despite my jet-lagged-still-in-shock-what-the-fuck-is-happening-to-the-world state, I am vividly aware of the symbolism of it all.

But it's really when I'm up in my childhood bedroom later on, my sister already departed, that it really hits me. As I begin to unpack my stuff, resigned to the fact that I may be here for some time, I set about making my space as comfortable as possible. I unpack some books and realise with a smile that the last time I lived in this room 'Enid Blyton' was on the bookshelf, now it's the 'Wisdom of Menopause'. Talk about the female cycle from adolescence to midlife...you couldn't make it up.

Then what I'm actually doing slaps me in the face: I'm reclaiming my room. The room I had to leave unwillingly four decades ago. I had to leave my room and I had to leave my mum, I was taken away – displaced, if you like – and now I'm back. OK, I know I came back when I was 15 and stayed for a few years, but that felt different, I didn't have any awareness then of how I'd been 'taken away' and certainly didn't get in touch with any feelings about it. But now I have found my way home, and as I hear my mum pottering around downstairs, I realise this is the scene entitled: *This is how things should have been.*

Another startling insight is that I will now be finishing writing my memoir back in the place where it all began. The last scene will be written in the same room where the first scene took place. I have exactly come full circle. I have come back to finish what needs to be finished. This is the reparative, the gestalt, the healing. I mean, this is a psychotherapist's bloody wet dream!

You may have a feel from this book that there have been different stages in my life, just as there are for all of us. A significant turning point in my life was when I had my brain haemorrhage. This was when I really got my call to *fall awake*, to change my life, to break my patterns and do things differently. Literally my Wake Up Call. Well, half of this book was written in Costa Rica and half of it was written back in my childhood bedroom. And the point in the book that marks what was written there and what was written here? Yep, you guessed it...my brain haemorrhage. That was the last scene I wrote in Costa Rica, the rest I wrote here. Gotta love that magical parallel process.

So I have returned, just like every heroine. Of course, we don't necessarily have to return to our childhood bedrooms to have a sense of coming full circle, coming back to where the separation began, it's more of an internal process, of coming back to a part of ourselves. But the point is we don't come empty-handed, we come armed with our learning, our wisdom, our story of all that we have experienced along the way. We return changed. I wonder how my learning, my wisdom, my story will continue to unfold now that I am back? And I wonder how, in telling my story, sharing it, having found the voice that I didn't have the last time I slept in this little bed, well I wonder how that will become part of it all...

I guess I will find out.

What's that? I haven't mentioned The Viking?

Ahh, well, that's a whole other story...

"Above all, be the heroine
of your life, not the victim."
– Nora Ephron

Music

Like many of us, music played a huge part in my early life. From growing up hearing my dad crooning his way through a mega-mix of country and western songs in various hotels and bars (actually he was pretty good), to making up a dance routine with a friend to 'Save Your Kisses for Me' by Brotherhood of Man, using our hairbrushes as mics and her sofa as a stage. From crying myself to sleep to 'I've Never Been to Me' (on loop) by Charlene every night, aged 11, to religiously taping the Top 40 every Sunday night (pressing pause every time the DJ spoke) through my teenage years, and moving onto to dancing around my handbag to Soul II Soul on various dance floors in various nightclubs with various friends in various states of disrepair.

Several years later, many a day or night, I would be twirling around under the mirror disco ball hanging from the palm tree in Nelly's garden, letting my hair down to a Donna Summer number or the like. There would then come a time shortly after when I would be strangely comforted by Paloma Faith's vocals to 'New York' hauntingly drifting in and out of my semi-conscious state through my earplugs in the dark small hours, as I lay in the high-intensity ward in the hospital, not knowing whether I would make it through the night.

Then more recently, one of the things about Qoya that I am most grateful for, is how it has brought music back into my life on a whole new level, really appreciating just how evocative music can be to us, how it can transport us back in time in a few simple opening bars, or just make us feel so deeply. And when we add movement to the music...well, the results can be anything from exuberant joyful fun to profoundly transforming.

I have chosen a track for each scene of this book. Songs that I was either avidly listening to at the time, or that represent something to me about that period of my life. Here is my soundtrack:

INTRO – "Moon River" by Audrey Hepburn

ACT ONE
Scene 1 – "I've Never Been to Me" by Charlene
Scene 2 – "Take Me Home, Country Roads" by John Denver
Scene 3 – "Save Your Kisses for Me" by Brotherhood of Man
Scene 4 – "Rhinestone Cowboy" by Glen Campbell
Scene 5 – "Eagle" by Abba
Scene 6 – "Itchycoo Park" by Small Faces
Scene 7 – "Harvest for the World" by The Isley Brothers
Scene 8 – "Ghost in My House" by R. Dean Taylor
Scene 9 – "Don't You Want Me" by The Human League
Scene 10 – "Everybody Wants to Rule the World" by Tears for Fears
Scene 11 – "Do You Really Want to Hurt Me?" by Culture Club
Scene 12 – "Tainted Love" by Soft Cell
Scene 13 – "Sweet Love" by Anita Baker
Scene 14 – "Bridge Over Troubled Water" by Simon and Garfunkel
Scene 15 – "It Doesn't Have to Be This Way" by The Blow Monkeys
Scene 16 – "Fast Car" by Tracy Chapman
Scene 17 – "Teardrops" by Womack and Womack
Scene 18 – "Back to Life" by Soul II Soul
Scene 19 – "Ain't Nobody" by Rufus and Chaka Khan
Scene 20 – "You Do Something to Me" by Paul Weller

Scene 21 – "Don't Dream It's Over" by Crowded House

Scene 22 – "Common People" by Pulp

Scene 23 – "Marta's Song" by Deep Forest

Scene 24 – "One Slip" by Pink Floyd / "Streets of London" by Ralph McTell

ACT TWO

Scene 1 – "An Everlasting Love" by Andy Gibb

Scene 2 – "The Blower's Daughter" by Damien Rice

Scene 3 – "Yeha Noha (Wishes of Happiness and Prosperity)" by Sacred Spirit

Scene 4 – "Last Night" by The Strokes

Scene 5 – "Babylon" by David Gray

Scene 6 – "Fisherman's Blues" by The Waterboys

Scene 7 – "And If I Fall" by The Charlatans

Scene 8 – "California Waiting" by Kings of Leon

Scene 9 – "Back to Black" by Amy Winehouse

Scene 10 – "New York" by Paloma Faith

Scene 11 – "Go or Go Ahead" by Rufus Wainwright

Scene 12 – "McArthur Park" by Donna Summer

Scene 13 – "Soul Love" by David Bowie

Scene 14 – "Love's in Need of Love Today" by Stevie Wonder

Scene 15 – "Coming Around Again" by Carly Simon

Scene 16 – "Hero" by Family of the Year

Scene 17 – "Thinking of a Place" by The War on Drugs

Scene 18 – "Sunrise (Always Comes Around)" by Unkle

Scene 19 – "Me and Tennessee" by Tim McGraw and Gwyneth Paltrow

Scene 20 – "Going Back to My Roots" by Odyssey

Scene 21 – "Adventure of a Lifetime" by Sarah Menescal

ACT THREE

Scene 1 – "The Church of What's Happening Now" by Sia

Scene 2 – "Ventura Highway" by America

Scene 3 – "Ong Namo" by Snatam Kaur

Scene 4 – "Here I Am" by Tom Odell

Scene 5 – "Wait for Now/Leave the World" by The Cinematic Orchestra

Scene 6 – "Oh Baby" by LCD Soundsystem

Scene 7 – "Girl on Fire" by Alicia Keys

Scene 8 – "Unwritten" by Natasha Bedingfield

Scene 9 – "Movement" by Hozier

Scene 10 – "Tomorrow Never Came" by Lana Del Rey and Sean Ono Lennon

Scene 11 – "Somehow" by Tom Odell

EPILOGUE – "Yo No Se Manana" by Luis Enrique

To listen and download the full Soundtrack on Spotify please follow the link: **https://tinyurl.com/e9jtmw22**

Alternatively, you can access the playlist, and make contact with me, from my website:

www.victoriasmisek.com

Acknowledgements

In the couple of years leading up to me writing this, there are some books I read which directly inspired and influenced me:

'Autobiography of an Orgasm' by Betsy Bakenblanker Murphy

'Rise Sister Rise' and 'Light is the New Black' by Rebecca Campbell

'Qoya – A Compass for Navigating an Embodied Life That is Wise, Wild and Free' by Rochelle Schieck

'Clothes Clothes Clothes, Music Music Music, Boys Boys Boys' and 'To Throw Away Unopened' by Viv Albertine

'The Choice' by Edith Eger

'Reveal – A Sacred Manual for Getting Spiritually Naked' by Meggan Watterson

'Eat, Pray, Love' and 'Big Magic' by Elizabeth Gilbert

'The Wisdom of Menopause' by Christiane Northrup

Thanks to you incredible Goddesses, Warrioresses, and Shield-Maidens for your work.

Rebecca Campbell's words on writing became my mantra throughout this process:

   - Write for yourself

- Write what you would want to read

- Write to heal

- Because when you heal, others heal too.

To Deanna for those early 'roomy writing' pieces. For shaking hands over the breakfast table on that retreat in Isla Holbox where we struck a deal to keep writing and sharing together. Thank you for the co-created safe space which provided an invaluable opportunity to practice the art of writing.

To Robin Gaines, for your guidance, insightful comments and for helping me to reframe the whole ordeal of 'rewrites'.

To Buddy Wakefield – spoken word artist and all-round power slam of enthusiasm and genius – for helping me to see that clichés are so cliché and that my anger is my superpower.

To Dulcie and Nancy from Wide Open Writing. Every now and then a teacher comes along and lights you up from the inside out. If you're really lucky they'll come in a pair and you'll be doubly inspired. Thank you for what you do and for teaching me about writing from the heart.

To Nicola from The Unbound Press, for having the vision to 'support women to tell their transformative stories'. I love what you stand for and thank you for the permission to be beautifully unbound!

And to my soul sisters, Karen and Sarah. I love you both dearly and I honestly don't think I would have got this finished if it hadn't been for your ongoing, unwavering, enthusiastic, endless support, encouragement and love. Here's to doing it all again!

Lightning Source UK Ltd.
Milton Keynes UK
UKHW022320160621
385627UK00007B/202